Seaside Square

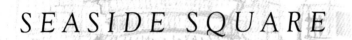

# SEASIDE SQUARE

Robert Edwards

Dominic Evergreen

Burble

*For John Sladden and Karen Grace*

Published by Burble
12 Marine Square, Brighton, Sussex, BN2 1DL

ISBN  978 0 9525909 89

Book design by Dominic Evergreen and Robert Edwards

Printed by One Digital, Brighton, Sussex

Printed on recycled paper

burblebooks@btinternet.com
www.burblebooks.co.uk

dominic_evergreen@hotmail.com
www.dominic-evergreen.co.uk

*A CIP catalogue record for this book is available from the British Library*

# Contents

**Robert Edwards** has published four collections of poetry on themes predominantly of landscape and architecture, and a prose autobiography:

*Attitudes to Sussex (second ed. 2006)  978 0 9525909 2 1*
*Brighton Burble (1999)  978 09525909 5 6*
*Bridge Bluster (2002)  978 0 9525909 1 3*
*Beech Blurt (2004)  978 0 9525909 6 4*

*Verse Vendor – Diaries of a Part-Time Sussex Pedlar (2008)*
*978 0 9525909 7 2*

**Dominic Evergreen** has exhibited his landscape oil paintings and prints in several successful exhibitions. He has also participated in exhibitions in galleries and  artist open house schemes as a member of the Sussex Arts Collective. His linocut prints appear in:
*Light and Dark (2007)  978 -0 9555013 0 2*

# Preamble

In the first year of their marriage, 1948, my parents rented a flat in the square. My mother had grown up in this part of the town, and my father was not the first member of his family to live in the area. In the 1970's and 80's they lived at the other end of the seafront. Visiting them from outside the county, I would invariably walk along this part of the front. From the pavement, by the railings, I would glance across at the square as I passed. I was intrigued by it, but a little in awe of it and I seldom if ever examined it closely.

Many years ago, in a ruminative and confiding conversation, a friend said to me that if she could give me anything in the world it would have to be a room with a view. Years later, on the first occasion of my walking into this first floor flat, it was this window, more than anything else, that enchanted and conquered me.

In my second year here, for twelve months I kept an irregular journal of what I saw from the window. The result was too long for an article and too short for a book. Ten years later I did it again, from summer to summer instead of winter to winter – and, ten years later, from January to December once again.

Shortly after its completion the original one-year journal was shown to a friend who complained he found it altogether too austere. Extended since by the addition of the two subsequent journals, then severely reduced by rampant deletion, it is now undoubtedly more austere than ever.

Just as the third journal was embarked upon, a chance conversation with artist Dominic led quite suddenly to this project in which visual material might in some way be woven with the verbal, thereby producing a volume that should be at least twice as satisfying. Few attempts would be, or indeed were, made by either of us to refer in the respective art and writing to particular scenes in the other's work.

When, recently, shown the finished written work and asked if he found it perhaps – well – dull, the artist replied by diplomatically contrasting its almost zen-like character to the quirkiness of the writer's previous work. It was agreed that for the benefit of readers prone to the ill effects of monotony, it should be supplemented with some contribution of a more personal nature. Hence this preamble.

In fact, the unedited journals contain numerous references to a number of secretly nicknamed residents. The omission in the book of most of these vignettes is motivated by a mixture of respect for privacy and fear of offence and reprisal. There is, however, a literary reason for leaving them out. They reflect something of the intimacy of the square for its community, something that was difficult to convey in the near rhapsodic style in which the play of light and air current are relentlessly expressed.

There were self-imposed rules in the writing. Only the view and the audible sounds were to provide the content, except when they were very directly affected by scenes or events elsewhere, most commonly the presence of the unseen sun. Occasionally certain changes or developments since the previous period had to be pointed out.

'The gardener' has not been the same person throughout. There were three main gardeners, one during each period. There have been very few others during the whole time.

In some respects, the garden bears a resemblance to a bagatelle board.

Apart from garden beds and plants, and the people, their cars and clothes, little seems to have changed in the outlook – apart from the paint colour of the front doors. With a passion of absurd and enduring intensity, my greatest wish for the square is that each of the doors might be painted a different pastel shade – blue, yellow, green, pink, grey, lilac, coffee, orange, and so on. All sorts of questions and issues are raised by this idea in respect of historical authenticity, ownership, choice, judgment and personal taste. Meanwhile my abiding belief is that such an arrangement would suit the exuberance of the architecture and its light cream elevations, and would be a cool and refreshing sight in the summer and provide a cheerful and soothing effect in the winter.

RE

I had mentioned that I was collaborating on a book with a writer friend of mine. The response to my somewhat misplaced bravado was inevitable. "So what's the book about?" Looking out of a window did not seem much of an answer. I attempted to paint a picture of a sea view with a garden but the stark truth remained and there was no getting away from it, the book was about looking out of a window. It sounded about as interesting as watching paint dry – nevertheless by that time I had watched several paintings dry and more were to follow.

Our collaboration: two views of the same view, neither describing nor illustrating the other. We just hoped they would not look out of place together.

The first drawings of the square were quite bold sketches using a thick marker pen that was partially used up giving a range of wet to  dry inkiness. Watercolours followed, fairly loose in style. My 'grappling' - Robert's word - with the view, demanded a variety of approaches. The square, an appropriate shape for the theme, suited two oil paintings and a coloured drawing; the watercolours are landscape and the charcoal drawings are portrait. I resisted the temptation to add colour to the drawing of 'The Pale Blue Door' (opposite). There are also pen and pencil studies of the ironwork on the balcony. Later some ink sketches of life in the square were added. Discussions as to the presentation of the landscape colour plates in the book were frequent, the dilemma being should these occur smaller to suit being 'the right way up' for the format of the book or would it be better to print them larger but necessitate turning the book around to view them? Eventually a decision was made.

In the language of portraiture, the 'three quarters view' from the window created something of a dual portrait: one sitter with familiar features - houses, doors, balconies and windows; the other less familiar, the mysterious moody figure in the background. The sea, glimpsed through the gap between buildings is the real personality the viewer is drawn towards, but the grace and charm of the buildings in the foreground catch the eye; a beautiful child playing with toys whilst the mother, deep and more beautiful looks on.

The waves and rhythms of the sea influence the front. Here is an architecture bedecked with balconies, their ironwork embellished with flowing patterns. Over there, the flow of traffic along the coast road and on the promenade, another tide, as the sea of humanity is drawn to the front with its ebb and flow of workers, runners and watchers. The seaside square quietly set a little further back. Its rounded garden suggests a circle within the square, the sense of geometry completed by the distant arc of the horizon.

Those living on the coast, have found themselves in a place of change. Like dusk or dawn, the coast is a border, a transition between land and sea, an edge between two elements. In the square there are other edges too. As in a painting, one colour set off by another, each house in the square exhibits subtle differences from its neighbour. One house has a particular type of balcony ironwork, the next has a style of canopy that its neighbour has not. Even the balconies themselves are set at different heights. Here in the seaside square, edges define idiosyncrasy. Each house has its own place, giving the square a lively sense of democracy.

Sea and garden merge, like an inlet with water flowing in between rocks. The bushes in and around the garden like waves rolling in from the sea ... Yet between the garden and the sea and almost hidden by a long hedge lies the coast road, its roar remaining a constant reminder of where and when we are.

I have a sea view of my own now. It is another three quarters view with a clear, if sideways, angle to the sea. The move, a seed germinated by my involvement with *Seaside Square* had drawn me towards another large bay window - a good space for an easel.

DE

# Seaside Square

## Introduction

The square was laid out in the 1820's. A hedged garden occupies the centre. The buildings form three straight sides of a quad, the fourth dimension being the open front overlooking the sea to the south. The three built sides are each a continuous terrace of housing, and join at the north corners. In the side terraces the nine houses on either side are of four floors, plus deep basements and in a few cases shallow attics. The terrace of seven properties along the top, facing the sea, has five storeys plus basements. The majority of facades, in smooth stucco, are painted a cool white cream. The upper elevations of six of the houses on the west side are of unpainted golden ochre brick. Two of the houses near the north-east corner were covered in a rough brown-grey rendering, the north terrace house having since been painted cream. There is a balcony or veranda at the first floor of every house. Most of the north terrace verandas, jutting from the pale cream facades and supported by deep architraves, are encased in full-length conservatory windows, forming a continuous flat front under one long narrow raked roof. Supporting the serial architrave are pairs of thick simple tapered columns flanking steps to the recessed front doors. The balconies, mostly open air, of the side terrace houses are railed in decorative ironwork, and overhung with bonnet style canopies of various designs.

The square slopes down in a gentle gradient perpendicular to a wide coast road, on a reinforced cliff that drops about sixty feet to a parallel beachside road. The beach cannot be seen from most of the properties. Around the square a U-shaped road brings traffic in an anti-clockwise direction. At both front corners of the square, the architecture, though of the same period, differs in scale and detail from that inside the square. The kerb around the square is of lengthy and broad low slabs of cream-grey stone given surface grip by close diagonal grooves sprinkled with small shingle. Tiny patches and strips of flat green moss appear at corners and edges of the slabs. The main paving stones are of various shades of grey.

At the foot of the square, parallel with the coast road, a slender segment of grass, enclosed along the south by a straight tall hedge and along the north by a curved low fence – later a railing – is separated from the square by a crescent road.

The view is from a first floor window in the north-west corner of the square.

*1989*

# 1989

Behind fine, quickly drifting materials of grey cloud, the morning sun is pale and distinct. It could be mistaken for the moon.

Two tall gulls land on tall white chimney tops and stand facing the same way, briefly statuesque, on the square's highest building, in the south-east corner. A young starling crawls around the top of the street lamp about eight feet from, and level with, the immediate balcony.

At noon, the sky generally clears to a hesitant shade of blue, the sun lights the sea, and through a brilliant rhombus of floating light a lone white sailing boat proceeds in a straight line from left to right. Soon the vast area of light diminishes to a little crescent close to the shore.

*Thursday 5 January*

The sky looks cold and hard – pale blues glimpsed between expanses of light metallic grey with occasional crumples of white fluff. The sea, too, looks hard-set, grey green blue. After two nights of rainfall the square looks clean and everything is sharply clear. The diamond-framed lamplights burn with particular force.

In the evening the rain is more insistent. The sea is very loud. A young man runs round the square in the middle of the road to a basement, with two young alsatian dogs, one at each side held on tight leashes, keeping pace with him, slithering down the steps.

*Monday 9 January*

In the late evening the lights of a boat, two or three white and one red, appear from the west, about half a mile out to sea, heading east. When the boat is half way across the chunk of sea, it turns right and sets off towards France, continuing straight for several minutes, one bright light alone, like a star, against the night blackness of the calm water. The light shines until eventually disappearing behind the building, recently repainted in lemon cream, on the left at the foot of the square.

*Wednesday 11 January*

Fresh from recent rain, the green grass and hedge and the brown flower-beds are distinct – the only two colours there.

*Saturday 21 January*

A sunny morning. The sea looks deep and powerful, and for a time blazes like a furnace.

Two young men drop the hoods of their sports cars – a tomato red ten-year-old Triumph and a sage green fourteen-year-old MG – and drive away, like two birds taking flight close to the ground.

Standing in the road in the middle of the bend, a man in a straw hat, a long jacket, jeans and battered leather shoes, stares up at a flat for sale; then turns and gazes at the sea.

The afternoon sun's reflection in the windows of the west-facing houses creates a series of pale brass-coloured shapes, angular and sharp. The garden is also divided diagonally into light and shadow. When the sun falls, and the sky in the south turns to grey, the brass tint alters to copper.

*Tuesday 7 February*

The surfaces – the road, the grass, the railings and some chessboard-chequered doorsteps – are fresh and crisp. The windows of the cars are covered with mist. In a cloudless sky twelve or more stars glisten. Many others are visible.

*Saturday 11 February*

In a round flower-bed near the top of the garden, three rust-coloured bell-shaped flowers have bloomed. A dark tortoiseshell cat – its coat gleaming in the sun like malt and treacle – emerges from the west side.

A brisk woman in a dark green tartan outfit and swinging a black executive case briefly speaks to a big dusty workman outside a house receiving protracted repairs. All winter a row of cement bags or suchlike have leaned against the railings. Elsewhere someone at the top of a wooden ladder is repainting a black balcony.

## Sunday 19 February

After fierce night winds, with the sea extremely loud, dozens of daffodils twitch, quiver and sway in the semi-shelter of the hedge and in the exposed beds in the middle of the garden.

## Monday 20 February

4pm    The sea is a sheet of severe steel blue, darkening towards a clearly defined horizon. The sky resembles a fan of alternating feathers, white, soft grey and sweet pale blue. In the houses, here and there a golden window corresponds to the lights of the coast road street lamps. Against the sea, the pale turquoise railings blend quietly.

## Tuesday 21 February

A profusion of small yellow and red striped tulips appears.

*Wednesday 22 February*

A twelve-year-old sometimes climbs out of a basement with a skateboard which he puts down on the pavement and scoots to the other corner; then he slowly free-wheels down the east side pavement to the seafront.

The sea has been rough and foamy for three days. White crests, far from quickly dissolving, form entire expanses, carried like deep-pile rugs and carpets over the tidal area.

*Thursday 23 February*

Not much sound from the gulls. Then suddenly, somewhere unseen, there is an exultant squawk and a jazz-like ensemble of reedy cries and calls.

At dusk, the gardener stoops over an implement in the small separate crescent of grass at the foot of the square, sheltered by a black sou'wester and black serge coat from a sharp wind, bitter particles of rain and the aggressive sound of the sea swirling below.

*Friday 24 February*

A powerful wind blows everything in the garden about. The hedge perpetually shakes, and the daffodils swing over almost to the ground.

*Sunday 26 February*

In the middle of the afternoon a pale thin young woman with short black hair calls at a house in the north terrace. Receiving no answer at the door, she drops her shoulder bag on the pavement and kneels on one of the six grey stone steps of the porch. Bent low, resting an elbow two steps higher, she writes out a note. Her long soft black coat falls over the steps, her grey scarf flutters, and her hair is feathery in the fast winds.

*Monday 6 March*

8.30am    The air is warm. The dark blue municipal dust lorry moves very slowly round the corner curves of the square. Its engine throbs loudly. Four or five dustmen weave among each other, lifting the rubbish from the pavement and hurling it into the hatch of the cart. Most are in sleeveless T-shirts. Someone walks along the front in shorts.

*Tuesday 7 March*

The air is cold, and is filled with a variety of fervent birdsong, into which the gulls tear, howling sounds of appeal. A male and a female starling walk on the grass. They fly into hiding below the layer of stone supporting the rustiest veranda, and after a minute reappear to fly over the square, swerving to the left to go up over the highest chimneys of the east terrace. As usual, several pigeons flap about on the fourth storey ledges in the north-east corner.

*Saturday 11 March*

11am   The sea shimmers in a hazy silver sunlight. The first group of white boats sail close to the land. A few minutes later, a second group appear further out to sea and more dispersed.

After the winter closedown, amusements on the lower promenade are re-opening. None is visible from the square, with one exception: the two or three highest seats of the ferris wheel. Of the twelve bucket seats that come, anti-clockwise, into view above and behind the railing of the upper promenade, one only is occupied for the present spin. Two people thus appear in the air, their backs to the sea, facing across the coast road to the square.

6pm   Dusk falls with a crimson sunset reflected as rose pink in the west-facing windows. A small white motorboat turns a repeated small circle close to the shore. Its little green light is disclosed at a certain point in the circling.

*Tuesday 14 March*

3pm   The seafront railings have been repainted. Three workmen clear and clean the gutter on that side of the road and rake and hoe the narrow strip of vegetation between the kerb and pavement. The wind is very strong and their heavy clothes flap. Sheets of newspaper escape from their wooden rubbish cart and fly about above the road.

*Friday 17 March*

Hailstorms have brought the ferris wheel to a halt.

Meanwhile, a new apparition has risen, situated alongside the top of the wheel. What it represents is unclear. A wiry structure shaped like the peak of an obelisk, it involves a lot of flashing coloured electric light bulbs. It appears through the space between the two main branches of the tree.

Although many are still standing, the yellow and white daffodils have suffered from this week's violent weather.

*Tuesday 21 March*

The ferris wheel seats are stationary and the obelisk lights are switched off. At mid-morning, fine soft flaky sleet falls, landing soundlessly, forming wet shapes on the road, pavement and balcony floor. Among the daffodils other plants have flowered: stock, primula, marigolds.

The wind current briefly whirls in this corner of the square, batting the drops of sleet. When they hit the window they form minute ornamentation, glassier than the glass, in the design of lilies, parachutes and wine glasses – remaining so for some minutes.

At noon, in a firm drizzle, the gardener, in his hat, digs up two areas of turf at the foot of the garden, removing with a spade the slices into a wheelbarrow.

*Wednesday 22 March*

Midnight. The full moon is in the south. The sky is clear. The whole of the visible expanse of water trembles in a dim, cold luminosity. The light extends to the horizon, a base below the studded dark blue.

*Monday 27 March*

6pm    The sky and the sea blur in a pale blue haze close to the coast. Along the front, people saunter in spring and summer clothes.

When the wheel stops, the occupants of the top seat look down and around. After the time it takes for the seat at the ground to be vacated and reoccupied, the top one moves forward and down, and another pair of riders arrive at the circle summit.

The round structure beside the wheel is in fact a decorative ball on the top of a helter-skelter. Its lights, green, red, white and yellow, flash until 11pm.

*Monday 29 March*

Late in the evening, wafting in from the west-south-west on a light breeze, coiling waves of mist veil the seafront, so that the amusement lights flare like flames at the heart of a mass of smoke. The fog in the square thickens.

*Sunday 2 April*

As the daffodils wilt, the tulips flourish, red, pink and yellow – some in formal clusters, others anarchic among the stock and primula, and some wild and idiosyncratic in the shadow of the hedge with occasional bluebells and blue irises.

4pm    High in a deep blue sky, the gulls glide languidly, frequently resting almost motionless, dreamlike.

**West**  *Charcoal drawing*

*Tuesday 4 April*

Snow in the afternoon does not settle.

*Wednesday 5 April*

Again the snow turns to rain, heavily dripping, in which the garden is surveyed from a young sycamore and a forsythia by a shiny blackbird and a robin.

*Saturday 8 April*

6.30pm    The sun is blindingly reflected in a third floor window of the east row of houses, whose pale paint is rich with sunlight. The shadow of an unseen bird follows an undulating flight along the terrace facade. As it passes out of sight, a second bird casts a similar shadow in the same way.

*Thursday 20 April*

7.30am    A thin sunbeam falls across the grass. Inner beds are crowded with maroon, red, pink, orange and yellow.

*Thursday 27 April*

A cold, hard rain falls very vertically. Only the merest unsteadiness in the balcony plants registers what movement there is in the air. In the garden the yellow tulips look forlorn and huddled.

*Friday 28 April*

7pm    In bright evening daylight the tulips wave in a tangy breeze, the petals broadening heavily on the stems. A few random feathers of cloud lie in the blue sky. The sea is blue, and the incoming tidal current looks determined and latitudinal, moving east.

Seven boats very slowly race from left to right, against the current. Their milk white hulls and greyer sails match the colour of the herring gulls.

A woman in a long grey dress and a black shawl stops for five minutes, facing the sea from the turquoise railing; then continues walking away to the left.

*Sunday 30 April*

Four small red-sailed boats pursue four of the familiar white.

The lower buds on the sycamore tree are beginning to open, pear-coloured.

3pm   A mild afternoon. Every seat on the wheel is taken.

*Monday 1 May*

Outside a house on the north terrace, four young people are intensely engaged in thoroughly cleaning their mountain bikes. The paraphernalia is extensive and includes a lot of long thin implements and multifarious waterworks. One of the men has a hairstyle consisting of one cubic inch of tuft at the centre above his brow.

### Wednesday 3 May

Above the square the sky is perfectly blue. The shoreline has been hugged by mist all day, and the sea is totally invisible, while the seafront railings are completely clear and bright.

### Thursday 4 May

6pm   Bright weather. One of the houses has balconies at all three upper floors. On the highest, people sunbathe in swimming costumes. Many of the windows and doors around the square are wide open.

### Sunday 7 May

3pm   A few birds coast and hover – dark and mellifluent – probably jackdaws.

5pm   The traffic going into the town centre is practically at a standstill. Interspersed with the ordinary vehicles are vintage buses, coaches, vans and fire engines. In the garden, twenty-five people are spread in groups on chairs, blankets and clothes.

7.30pm   When the tide retreats, the wind drops, and the water is flat. The blue of the water is striped with paleness while the sky is an even paler blue.

Subsequently as the eastern sky develops layers of lilac shadow, the western sky glows in a light of pale flame. The heavy traffic has gone. Everyone departs from the garden. The street lamps come on.

*Monday 8 May*

6.30pm   A warm evening. Up on the roof of a house on the east side, behind a railing of delicate black iron, a man is seated, reading.

*Tuesday 9 May*

8am   When the sun appears, over the north-east corner, it is fiercely bright. The watery blackness of the window panes along the shaded east side are featured with sinuous reflections of the sunlit west side buildings opposite.

*Thursday 11 May*

At 7.30am, the gardener is mowing the grass with great urgency. He withdraws fast when caught in a sudden heavy downpour of rain.

*Tuesday 16 May*

Materials for the construction of a shed have been assembled close to the hedge in the north-west corner of the garden. A jumble of wooden planks that look like floor boards rest just above the height of the hedge. The gardener's face and hands are coated in something that looks like soot.

*Sunday 21 May*

Every day for a week, people have sunbathed in the garden. The sky has been hazy and the air heavy; the wind, warm. The rose geraniums are out, hanging in the north-west balcony. On an east side balcony, a white-haired woman is seated on an amber box under a bright coloured sunshade, sewing. Her right hand reaches high each time she pulls the thread from the material on her lap.

*Monday 22 May*

In continuing thick warm south-easterly air the gardener works all morning, digging up and shifting on the wheelbarrow all the wilting primula and the wallflowers and the withered tulips, leaving the inner beds generally plain with dry dirt. For a few hours, a water jet revolves in consecutive areas of the grass.

In the early evening a water-skier is drawn across the hazy sea at a moderate speed by a light blue powerboat.

The air is alternately still and blowy. Now and then a bee, or a crane fly, passing by the window, encounters a gust and zigzags or ricochets off course.

*Tuesday 23 May*

The horizon is again lost in haze. Breezeless, and with the tide in, the sea is so flat in certain places it resembles a frozen lake. A sailing boat is motionless, parked. The sail sticks up like a white feather quill, thin and slightly curved.

Overleaf:  **Balcony Window**   *Oil on canvas*

**Green Bagatelle**   *Watercolour*

**Chair on Balcony**  *Watercolour*

**Dusk**  *Coloured drawing*

A young child plays cat and mouse with the hose water, while the gardener plants fresh green bushes, and small plants in bloom.

The sail is let down and the boat drifts indolently with a bare mast. Three water-skiers travel steadily from east to west.

At 9.15, in the dusk, when the sea becomes indistinguishable from the sky, a boat – perhaps the same one – dawdles past. It is decked with three glimmering lights: green at the front and at the top of the mast, and uncoloured at half mast.

Dimly lit by the sparkling lamps, the garden looks entirely dark green. The gardener ambles out of his flat, into the garden and turns off the hose, its grasshopper rattle silenced.

*Wednesday 24 May*

8.30am    Two modern young men are seated in the hot sunshine on the balcony of a west-side house, their feet up on the railing.

11pm    On the east side, two women, neighbours, hold a conversation on their adjacent balconies, one balcony two feet higher than the other.

*Thursday 25 May*

Half the men still wear shorts and little else. Then the temperature drops rapidly, and by 9pm none of the balcony windows is open to the fierce wind, and no one is wearing shorts. By midnight the wind can be heard tearing through the vegetation and hauling the shingle on the beach.

*Friday 26 May*

2pm    The sea is darkish and faintly green, but the sun is bright and the sunbathers lie on the grass. Two young women have made their lunch arrangements on the pavement outside a north-side house. With them is a baby girl in a white hat seated under a white parasol. Both women, in shorts and white vests, are on roller skates, on which they practise unsteadily in the road.

*Saturday 27 May*

In the middle of the central flowerbed stands a pale grey cherubic ornament, four to five feet tall, the figure holding above its head a circular bowl, into which this morning the gardener places plants.

*Sunday 28 May*

In the evening a thin man from the west side goes into the garden to fetch his black and white cat. She refuses to be caught. After three or four swoops on her, he shrugs his shoulders and eyebrows, and leaves her.

*Monday 29 May*

In the morning the thin man walks down the west-side pavement. His cat follows him obliquely, trotting, in the road, close to the cars parked by the hedge. Fifteen minutes later he goes into the garden and successfully scoops her up and carries her home.

A water-skier's boat does an about-turn, inscribing a narrow bend and two parallel trickles of silver foam darkening into crusts of deep blue.

*Wednesday 31 May*

Considerably colder. Very few windows are opened. Shorts and bikinis have given place to jackets, even overcoats. Out on a sombre sea, twenty-three sailing boats twist and lean, plus one small pink and white windsurf sail. The boats, white, look like vestiges of snow on a grey slate roof. The sky is like a slab of marble, the soft-edged clouds of white and grey impressed on a background of cold blue.

*Saturday 3 June*

At noon, dark clouds pass across the white sky, changing the sea, as though green ink had been poured into it.

*Sunday 4 June*

Altocumulus clouds waft across the blue sky, casting stripes, checks, ovals and triangles on the sea – compositions of two alternating discrete colours: pale green and dark blue.

Alone on the water, a few miles out, a long, low, white tanker moves east.

Sparrows and starlings run, jump, compete and quarrel on the grass, rapidly pecking at something.

Monday 5 June

In the two circular beds at the top of the garden, dozens of different roses sway in the wind, which carries a powerful smell of the sea.

Tuesday 6 June

11pm   The days are cool, the nights cold. The road is patched with water. Beneath a sky of cloud, the light is dull. The grand seafront street lamp lantern is hidden from view by the garden tree, while its light is caught in full by the clean turquoise hipped roof of the oriental seat shelter.

Friday 9 June

The flowers are radiant. The two circles of earth contain roses – dark red, white, salmon pink and cream. Calendula marigolds proliferate in the upper central tapering plots, intermingled with geraniums – scarlet, white and mauve-pink. The hedge border shrubs include diverse yellow ragwort, mallow, azalea and buddleia, along with dense, broad, low bunches of mauve daisies. In among these are sharp-toned fuchsia, clusters of white stock and wallflower, a few poppies, and rust-coloured lilies with leathery leaves.

Saturday 10 June

Throughout the afternoon a sale is held at the top end of the garden. Behind the half-dozen tables whose cloths flap in the breeze, and the three dozen people who mill around eating, drinking and smoking, on the permanent wooden bench seat an elderly person from the north terrace sits, receiving frequent attentions. She is small and rounded and as usual is wearing a green hat and green coat.

*Wednesday 14 June*

Two boats work their way east and west, passing each other quite close to the shore. Of a practical appearance, they are not the same size, but have much in common including a sizeable cabin and a deep, heavy hull. A flock of gulls surrounds the bigger boat. Flapping restlessly, nothing could look more like white bunting suspended between and trailing the masts.

*Thursday 15 June*

The hot weather has returned. The hunched old lady walks down the pavement, a big ochre beret on her small round head, for once no coat but a fawn cardigan, all buttons done up. She watches her step, suspicious of pavement cracks and occasional litter or dog droppings.

*Friday 16 June*

7.45pm   A couple walk along the front, pushing a maroon pram. The woman's hair is long and loose, as is her grey dress. The man wears a white shirt and trousers and a black and white straw hat.

*Sunday 18 June*

1pm   A woman in rolled up culottes and a rolled down blouse sits on the pavement with her back to the railings. A young man arrives on a bicycle and finds no reply at a door. He discusses the address with the woman. His bicycle is yellow; his shoes are black and yellow; his skin-tight costume is yellow from the waist to the knee; above, the yellow is broken by a diagonal band over the chest, of rainbow colours; his helmet is yellow and white.

Elsewhere, four young children fence inexpertly with sticks.

5pm   In addition to some of the garden's more frequent sunbathers, two men lounge on either side of a woman in a white bikini. All three have very dark tans. The men's shorts are respectively black, and black and red. At their feet, laid on the grass are two bicycles, respectively black, and black and red.

*Monday 19 June*

Once in the day, and once late at night, in the somnolent warmth, a barking cry of a trio of gulls shocks.

*Tuesday 20 June*

A paradox of the sun's brilliance: the light so blazing and the heat so intense, the blooms in the flower-beds appear to melt and, far from seeming dry with thirst, to be on the point of dripping, liquid, on the parched earth.

*Friday 23 June*

8am    Attached to the north wall of the detached lemon-cream building in the south-east corner of the square is a rusty iron spiral fire escape, running from the fourth floor to the ground. It is only seen from the entrance to the gap between the building and the terrace. However, when the sun is high enough to project on the wall, a shadow of the fire escape appears – a stack of angled and curved patterns.

*Tuesday 27 June*

At dawn, the long awaited rain arrives, announced at 5am in a sound of clattering on the roofs and windows, along with the surging of the sea and the wind in the trees.

The morning is clear and bright and the garden and sea have a fresh clarity. Five white cars are parked consecutively around the north curve. They too look very bright.

At 1pm huge banks of dark grey cloud move in from the west, bringing thunder storms, making the sea manic and pungent, then moving on, leaving sunshine, more showers, and a vast complexity of sky, grey, white and blue.

*Wednesday 28 June*

The air is cool and the breeze is wild. The sky is a shuffling multiplicity of pale stone shades. The sea is rough, and green.

**Sea Garden**  *Charcoal drawing*

*Tuesday 4 July*

The sun is hot, the sky is completely blue, and the sea is brilliant. The wind is muscular and blustery.

*Wednesday 5 July*

6pm   The air now is calm, warm and humid, the sky is pale and the sea is a hazy pale grey. Everything in the garden is still. A few swifts darkly hurtle and dance in the pale light above the buildings.

9pm   The wind has got up again. The street lamps light up first at the inland end of the square, under the lingering brighter cloud. The sea is dark green; the horizon furry; the sky over the sea steel grey while overhead a light indigo. The painted stucco loses its clarity, cloaked in humidity so thick that the walls take on a mucky cappuccino look.

The wheel turns, carrying one couple.

The wind drops. The wheel stops. The horizon dissolves, and the rain begins to fall. Scents travel on a capricious wind.

*Thursday 6 July*

At midnight, remote flares of lightning and rumbles of thunder occur. They continue for an hour before reaching the immediate area. Then for an hour, they continually fill the square with light and surround it with sound. The rainfall is brief but pounding.

*Sunday 9 July*

Friday's prolonged rain has revived the garden geraniums and marigolds. They stand out like oranges and lemons.

*Monday 10 July*

1pm   Three pale butterflies move among the few little trees in the hedge and among the roses in the centre beds.

6pm   Three nursery age children play football in the road.

8pm   For five minutes two women in denims dance energetically on the only second floor balcony, by an open window, in exaggerated gyration.

*Tuesday 11 July*

The lady in the green hat and green coat goes out at midday, carrying the green shopping bag. Returning shortly afterwards she stops to pause for breath before climbing the steps to her front door. The bag looks heavy.

After lunch, a new lawn mower is taken out of an old car by the gardener and a neighbour, and into the new shed.

After tea, another neighbour mows the grass, pushing the machine to and fro beginning alongside the hedge at the foot of the garden. Under a cloudless blue sky, he wears only a pair of dark blue shorts.

A light north-westerly wind touches the tips of the trees and bushes.

*Tuesday 18 July*

1am    The sea is lit by the full moon. The moon lends the square a special clarity.

*Friday 21 July*

All day the air is very warm, and increasingly humid. The sky and the sea turn from blue to pale grey. The evening is hot.

A group of nine tall young people walk enervatedly along the front, all wearing small shorts, and with full packs strapped to their backs. The wheel turns, empty.

An hour later, the air as warm as before and even thicker, sixteen elderly people pour out from the four-columned entrance of the lemon-cream building, all in formal evening dress, and walk east of the square along the front. The tanned man on the second floor balcony wears his crimson long shorts with a black top and white trainers, and leans back on the open window ledge – his right leg angled high, the foot up on the railing – watching the people below.

From a pale sky, large drops of rain lightly fall for a few minutes. Suddenly, fourteen people, some of them shrieking, are turned on the near-silhouette of the wheel. Soon the rain ceases, the horizon is misted and four people are revolved on the wheel.

*Saturday 22 July*

The gardener tours the flowers with a watering can.

After a fiercely hot morning, the sky turns light grey and by 6pm the sea is like a pond of very pale blue mud, or jelly.

10pm     Patches of smoky black thunder-cloud shift about under a dark blue sky overhead. Abrupt dry squalls leap into the square bringing smells of the sea and sending up scents from the garden. In the distance over the sea, a wide screen of yellow and grey gives out flashes, preceding rapid blue streaks above the coast near here, followed by rumblings and short showers of tentative rain, releasing fresh smells of the stale ground and the parched greenery. The rain soon moves on, and the air is calmer but scarcely any clearer.

*Monday 24 July*

1pm     The gardener is clipping the hedge at a furious rate. Dry, and appearing tired, the hedge is green but hints at yellow, brown and blue. The gardener gathers the clippings in armfuls, puts them in the wheelbarrow and adds to the mounting heaps of twigs and leaves by the west gate.

*Tuesday 25 July*

The first scaffolding to go up since the winter has been erected in front of a house in the south-west corner.

*Saturday 29 July*

A Japanese man comes out from a black door, goes into the garden and sits on a seat. Looking through the gap in the hedge to the sea, he smokes a cigarette, then goes back in.

*Sunday 30 July*

Evidently there has been overnight rain. The sky is a cool grey muddled with soft white fluff.

An elderly man with a military moustache and bearing treads past the shallow puddles in the road. He wears a stern outfit in smart finished natural fabrics, sand and cocoa coloured, and strong leather shoes. From his hand dangles a small transistor radio.

At midday the movement of the clouds accelerates: the clouds expand and darken and pass at a fair pace. A wind blows through the garden.

The early twilight sky has a porcelain character, painted in tones of pale blue, grey and white – delicate formations in countless shapes and contours, seen through clear fresh air as rain clouds hover from the north, quickening the diminution of immediate light.

Birds let out plain and weary sounding screeches.

*Monday 31 July*

9am   The sun is baking hot and blinding. The sea is rather dark.

The dust lorry is a new one, painted in the present council's turquoise gloss based on the longstanding seafront scheme.

6pm   A sharp drop in the temperature. Along the balconies all the windows are shut. Two cats, both bolt upright, scan their territorial scenes, one from a doorstep, one from the precariously slender arm of a garden bench.

*Tuesday 1 August*

8.30am   A woman, silhouetted in the bright light and clear air, walks along the front. Her headscarf is driven back by the wind. She supports herself with a stick in the right hand and by the horizontal wooden top rail to her left.

*Wednesday 2 August*

2pm   Every day lately, a dark, leaden-looking, medium-sized dredger-like vessel has passed to and fro, not far from the shore, accompanied by a small tug type of boat.

7.30pm   Far away a gull whistles, while, out here, the white boats crawl by.

*Thursday 3 August*

A grey-haired man from a grey-brown house pushes a pram round the square. The pram contains weekly free newspapers which he delivers in bundles dumped outside the front doors. Later he takes his dog out – a grey spitz-like female.

*Friday 4 August*

5pm   Four young children play, disorganised on the shaded grass.

7pm   The sky and the sea are perfectly blue, spelling out the grey wooden handrail and richly painted framework of the promenade railing.

10pm    Between the stars over the sea, the lights of an aeroplane blink, south-eastwards.


*Saturday 5 August*

9.20am    The air is bright and hot. Within five minutes a mist, the first since May, has engulfed the neighbourhood, and the sea has disappeared in a pale damp screen.

Almost immediately, the mist starts to break up and depart. After an hour, it has gone, the air is very bright and very hot, and diverse and scattered boats are revealed in the shimmering light blue water.

Midnight. The black and white cat climbs out on to the curved lead canopy over the bow window of her first floor. She miaows assertively, before being distracted momentarily by the loud dance music and singing coming from an open-windowed flat in the diagonally opposite quarter. Then she notices a couple of people walking towards her own corner, and she launches into an unremitting monologue straight at them. They fear she is in trouble. When the facts are put to them they stare up at her in disbelief. She continues for some time until finally their alarmed regard gives way to laughter and they retire into a house.


*Monday 7 August*

7pm    Two women stand at the railing on the promenade, looking across the sea. One is dressed in a pink sari, the other in a yellow one. Six young children sit along the bench on the pavement behind them.

*Thursday 10 August*

Rain fell through the night. Cars make splashes in the puddles. The day is overcast. At dusk, the cloud breaks, and in front of a sunset, a woman in a loose black shirt and a full white skirt pushes a bicycle along the seafront pavement.

*Friday 11 August*

10pm   The sound of the sea is loud. The buddleia bend and turn in the wind.

*Saturday 12 August*

2pm   The sea rolls heavily beneath a blue and white sky, shifting through parallel gradations from dark blue at the horizon to pale green at the front, ruffled with whitecaps and, close to shore, muddied by sand and seaweed. A cargo vessel goes by, a mile or two out.

The clouds pass away. The garden, enlivened by the midweek rain, and animated by the wind, is populated by six women. Four are on the four respective benches; two are in full-length armless deckchairs.

*Sunday 13 August*

4pm   The grey-haired head of a woman appears at a rusty veranda window. She leans forward so that her head, shoulders and an arm are in the open air. She waves with a folded cloth in her hand, to a car leaving the square.

*Monday 21 August*

10.30am   A tall woman in a short yellow dress walks along the front, taking long brisk strides, her right hand swinging through nearly 180 degrees. Her hair is plentiful. She stops and turns for a moment, steadying her hair in the warm breeze with the palm of her hand, looking along the road. The sun is very strong and the colouring of people is burned and blurred with glare, as is that of the ironwork paint, the motorboats and the birds.

*Monday 28 August*

The sun beats down from a virtually clear blue sky. Five cabbage white butterflies are busy in the garden. They visit the balconies. A scrawny thrush hops along the pavement, tapping at some of the rubbish covering with a long ineffectual beak.

*Saturday 2 September*

6pm   Two tall men in dark blue jerseys and straw boaters walk round the road, extremely slowly, halting after every few steps, turning, looking up at the buildings, pointing, talking, and peering into the garden over the gates and through the hedge.

In the garden, the grass is hardly green. The dahlias, geraniums and roses wearily live on.

*Sunday 3 September*

7.30pm   A high sunset of pink and purple cloaks the east.

8.30pm   The late sunset becomes a striped pattern of cobblestone grey and infinitely pale green.

10.30pm   An athlete lopes along the promenade.

*Thursday 7 September*

6.30am   Dew has formed on car windows and on tiled doorsteps. The sea is invisible, screened by a pale shroud lit but unbroken by the sun.

10am   Under a full sun of bright pale light, in warm air, the gardener ferries buckets and cans of water from the pump by the west gate to the wilderness at the south end.

*Saturday 9 September*

For a moment in the morning, the sun appears, white and defined and diminutive, above the shifting layers of fine wet cloud. Before long, drizzle falls.

*Monday 11 September*

Few and far between, the pale green sprays of pampas grass shake in the light breeze, close to the hedge. Saturday's rain has restored a little colour to the grass. The gardener has dug new rose beds in the crescent.

6.30pm  Below the grey sky, in the mild air, an elderly man, bespectacled, in a dark grey suit, sits on a bench in the garden, reading a newspaper.

8pm  The man has left, and a woman in a jacket and trousers, white sandals and a headscarf sits on the bench, coaxing a black cat from the rose bed to go to her and play with something on the grass. Eventually, near darkness envelops them.

*Tuesday 12 September*

8am  A dark fog hides the sea.

All day the air is warm and humid; the sky is dark and close.

The cloudbursts, at 10 and 11 at night, blast the clammy atmosphere. Light from the windows and the lamps is reflected in the water on the road, and the pale stucco glistens, even more so the architrave of the north terrace.

*Wednesday 13 September*

10am  The sun hangs in a heavy grey sky, heaviest over the indiscernible sea. There is no wind or rain. The garden has a puffed and flushed look, yet undernourished, tantalised.

In the afternoon, a thunderstorm rages.

11pm  The cloud finally breaks up and a gentle cool breeze blows. The sky is like a crumpled quilt of dark and pale blue. The moon is hidden but its light touches the sea at the horizon – a ribbon of pale silver on the dark blue water.

*Thursday 14 September*

8am   Before the sun's emergence over the east of the square, its light glitters on the black iron railing on one of the roofs.

6pm   Layer after layer of grey cloud speeds to the north-west over a fizzy sea dark grey furthest away then white and green and finally beige closest to land.

The marigolds, orange and yellow, begin to take on a slightly bitter tone. The square is empty of birds and cats, and the few people to be seen hurry, damp, through doorways. The evening is wet and blustery. The sea crashes and constantly roars. Busy traffic swishes on the shining coast road.

*Friday 29 September*

6am   At dawn the stars directly above and to the south scintillate in a dark sky. As the light advances the blue pales and the black sea appears grey. The east terrace, overall, looks like a soft cotton blanket. Minutes pass without the sound or sight of a vehicle on the main road. Soon the garden can be seen, emerald green, framed by the six lights of the old diamond street lamps. At 6.20 one person walks out of the square. At 6.40 one walks into it.

*Saturday 30 September*

11.30am   Easterly lenticular cloud passes without interrupting the bright sun. To the left the sea is a blaze of burning silver – undulating masses of light moving from east to west. To the right the sea undulates, but grey and hard-set. The wheel turns, empty.

*Sunday 1 October*

1pm   From the north-east corner comes the sound of a dozen or more voices, old people, young people and children, singing "Happy Birthday".

*Friday 6 October*

4pm    A cool wind blows, and the first seasonal sighting occurs of serge jackets and heavy woollen jumpers. An adult in denim with a shoulder bag on the back, roller skates briskly along the seafront pavement, followed seconds later by a straggle of about ten young learning disabled people.

*Monday 9 October*

5.30pm    In clear sunlight, backed by a velvet sky of blue, white, grey and gold, and through fresh air of quiet north-westerly motion, the sea is a uniform cool, hard, pale blue.

The ruling long-haired marmalade cat prowls about the grass which is daily greener as dry weather alternates with rain.

*Sunday 15 October*

In the middle of the day in bright sun, a lot of sail boats were out. At half past five the sea is deserted. The light is sensitive. The air is mild. The east side terrace is like a block of vanilla ice cream, while the window panes, reflecting the retiring sun and a sky of distinct, soft, dappled pastels, are like glasses of white wine. The gulls glide and flap, silent.

*Tuesday 24 October*

A red admiral flits from balcony to balcony. At one end of a balcony on the west terrace, a black mannequin has been stood. Clothed in a short thin maroon blouse and a three-quarter length thin navy blue skirt, the figure stares, through blue-framed spectacles, out to sea.

In the garden the last bright flowers are the shrivelled calendula marigolds, and the fuchsias, bent almost flat by the weekend's pelting rain and storm winds.

*Saturday 28 October*

The green of the grass is dark and bright. A handful of roses endures in each of the beds: two salmon-pink, a couple of cream, some dark red and, poised and firm, one yellow. The sycamore's leaves are more green than brown but they are curled and depleted – the sea can be seen through them. The sea is rough, and loud, and the smell of it is strong. South-westerly clouds move fast, infrequently chucking rainfalls.

All the seats have been removed from the wheel, which is whipped round by the increasingly powerful wind. Shortly before midday, three people stand at the railing, watching the sea. Their open jackets fly out behind them and boomerang on their heads. As an immense accumulation of rain-cloud arrives, the trio dash to get into a parked car. A second or two later the rain hits the square. A gull gives out a sound like panic.

Within fifteen minutes the cloud's rear edges trap the sunlight so that white beams flare down on to the sea then move across the sky like wind-borne searchlights. Streaks of dazzling silver trail through the clay-coloured charging water.

*Monday 30 October*

Midnight. Fragmented in the tree's reduced leafage, the light of the seafront lanterns resembles that of a chandelier.

*Thursday 2 November*

The leaves on the tree are thinning fast. Through them, the flow of white-crested waves can be followed. The form of the tree is that of the branches and twigs, no longer the overall outline of foliage.

A small lorry tips out a neat angled heap of dark fine dry manure on to the road by the west gate. The gardener pours it over the lower flower-beds. Its dark brown, sharply delineated by recent spadework on the beds, is vivid against the grass which has received a lot of rain lately and is getting quite long.

*Sunday 5 November*

11am   The air is crisp and cold. Under the sun, the sea is a blinding sheet of gold.

Like walking blots of dark oil, silhouetted promenaders in a steady trickle peer down at the lower esplanade and into the path of the staggered flotilla of the racing white sail boats, almost vanishing as they enter the centre glare of the water.

The seats, intact but untaken, turn on the wheel.

A megaphone from the beachside drive is loud but the language is inaudible.

*Thursday 9 November*

Midnight. The rain is shot about the square by a violent wind, lashing the windows, walls, cars, and the few people out in it. The sea resounds, tumultuous.

*Friday 10 November*

Surfaces are smeared and streaked with salt-thickened spray.

*Saturday 11 November*

Noon. In the sun and wind, below a mild, hazy blue sky, the sea sways, like fields of platinum corn.

*Monday 13 November*

3pm   Close to the land, fog clouds the sea and, pierced by the sun, glows, yellow, like a chilled parted melon, obscuring a tiny white boat, tucked in the veils like a frosted pip.

*Thursday 16 November*

9am   The sun streams in from the south-east with fresher air and white clouds. Five students assemble around one of the seats, eating breakfast. Cries come from a tangle of gulls.

*Sunday 19 November*

In the distance over the sea, three gulls, flinty and muscular, flap and swerve.

*Saturday 2 December*

The ferris wheel has been removed.

For seven days the temperature has been close to zero, sometimes falling below, twice leaving a hard morning frost. Pressure has remained high and the air has been mostly windless. Patches of fog have often seized the square.

The hedge has been clipped, flat-topped and flat-sided. The clippings lie on the ground in light, loose gatherings. Smart, sharp, small green shrubs nestle in the earth near the hedge.

*Monday 4 December*

In cold, bright air, a tall man from the north terrace, in blue denim, collects up the clippings and places them in sacks.

*Wednesday 6 December*

1pm    The pressure falls, the temperature rises, the sun shines, and the air is warmer. Two young workmen, one bare-armed in a T-shirt, dig a big hole in the east-side road. In the north-west corner the silky black and white cat lies on the pavement in the mild air, getting up to talk loudly and at some length to every passer-by.

*Saturday 9 December*

In the late afternoon, at the horizon, a mountainous range
of billowing cloud, white, cream and pink, stands.

*Monday 11 December*

The morning's clouds are lilac, high, clear-edged. The
afternoon's are grey, low and murky. The man who wore a T-
shirt on Wednesday is now in a jacket of serge.

A lone rose bloom, yellow, lives on.

5pm   Suddenly a cold brisk wind arrives.

11pm   The patter and shine of a sparse, cold, fast rainfall
brings a number of figures and faces to their windows.

*Wednesday 13 December*

All morning in a milder temperature, rain comes constantly,
frequently in heavy downpours. The sky is leaden, and the
sea is green. Lights are left on in some of the houses.

All evening the sea is mightily loud, and late in the evening
the rain returns.

*Thursday 14 December*

8pm   Heavy rain is flung around the square by the wind.

*Friday 15 December*

Drops of rain roll from the street lamp lid and from the lead canopy rim over the balcony, like glass beads.

*Saturday 16 December*

11am    The rose wobbles, pale and torn. The rain persists, while a gale arrives.

After midnight, the rain has passed, leaving a dark blue sky, bright moon and stars – and succeeded by a terrific wind. The sound of the sea is wild.

*Sunday 17 December*

Throughout the early hours the sea roars under storm force winds. By dawn the first fast clouds have arrived. By 11 o'clock the sky is full of rain-clouds and soon the square is battered with showers. The sea is a mass of foam. An elderly man walks down the east side. He fumbles with his umbrella; while it works he holds it ahead of him like a shield; it is uncontrollable, and he lets it down and uses it as a stick. With his other hand he holds down the trilby on his head. At the foot of the square the wind races round from the front. He is pulled up and pushed a yard to his right, and then to his left. He grabs the railings and clambers round the corner out of sight.

By the time it is dark, the wind has dropped to less than fifty miles an hour, and the rain has stopped.

*Monday 18 December*

Looking like a screwed up piece of brown paper, the garden rose has withered.

The sea appears, through the light windswept drizzle, like a Russian cake: first a layer of pale coffee, then a band of aquamarine, and finally at the horizon a ribbon of bilberry.

*Tuesday 19 December*

Hours of teeming rain. The gardener, in dark serge and the sou'wester, attends to the plants in the inner beds.

*Wednesday 20 December*

8pm   The rain, much of it torrential, has scarcely paused for forty-eight hours.

Midnight. The wind kicks the rain in every direction. The noise of the sea is enormous.

*Saturday 23 December*

A dark morning of drizzle. A crowd of gulls converges close to the square and keeps up a prolonged vocal melee.

The high white waves ride and roll. The annual cobweb on the street lamp brim defies another torrent of rain. The mannequin keeps watch over the sea, blouse and skirt retaining faded colour.

After a while the sea turns brightly silver under a soft blue sky and wafting pastel cloudlets.

The old man walks out, down to the front, meeting the gale with measured footsteps.

*Sunday 24 December*

2am   Festive tree lights, red, yellow and white, glow all night in the ground floor bow window of an east-side house.

The daylight is dim, the sky pale with intermingling broad patches of grey, white and cream.

A formidable gale shakes the hedge, and the tidal area is covered in froth.

*Monday 25 December*

A dull, dry, mild day. The wind is quiet, and the sea is calm.

*Tuesday 26 December*

11am   14 degrees C

Blue sky and bright sunshine. Cirrus and lenticular cloud. The sea is a sheet of dazzling light. In the garden, the grey-haired bespectacled man smokes his pipe. The marmalade cat sits on the sun-roof of a car. A gull, close but unseen, lets out an informative cry.

Overleaf:   **Open Window**   *Oil on canvas*

**Sea and Empty Chair**   *Coloured drawing*

**Indoor Outdoor**  *Watercolour*

**Picnic**  *Watercolour*

*1999 - 2000*

# 1999-2000

*Saturday 3 July*

Altocumulus clouds cross, west-south-westerly, extremely fast. A cool gloomy morning precedes a warm breezy afternoon. The hydrangeas, light and dark pink, pelargoniums and the roses, particularly twenty white in the lower bed, are bright, strong and animated. The grass, for a long time increasingly dry until some recent rain, begins to look a little greener. It is dotted with daisies, dandelions, clover and groundsel.

*Monday 5 July*

A smell of cut grass. The grass is pale and dry. The sea and the sky are a hazy pale blue, the sea languid in the warm, still air. Along the wide seafront tarmac pavement, by the pale turquoise railings, two women in black T-shirts and black trousers walk with a high pram, followed by two men. A woman passes in the other direction, confidently striding in a black short-sleeved short-skirted dress on high thick heels.

Some young gulls croak and circle low above the square. On the roofs of the east side, the slender orange-brown chimney tops, in rows of four, upheld by unpainted stucco bases, are stark against the soft blue sky. Beneath, along the third floor facades, between the white wooden window frames, shadows of the west side chimneys are cast on the pale cream paint.

9pm     The sea is flat, lightest blue, practically white. Occasionally an inaudible speedboat creates a length of ripple that gradually approaches the shore. The hazy sky above the horizon contains a lilac colour.

*Thursday 8 July*

5.30pm   Under a cloudless sky, the air is very warm. The sea is a bright dark blue, and lively; the horizon a clear line. In the garden, the outer branches of the sycamore wave in the breeze. The gardener, stripped to the waist, waters the roses with a large green can while a sprinkler shoots a sprayed jet of water up, down and around the grass.

*Sunday 11 July*

Yesterday evening and today a lot of small children ran and shrieked in the garden. All day today couples and groups and several lone sunbathers lay there.   A trio held an evening picnic under the tree, then played with a frisbee.

9.30pm   25°   Now only one couple, an elderly husband and wife, are there, on the wooden bench seat backed into the hedge – and a cat, dark with a light chest, leaping after insects, clapping its outstretched paws.

*Friday 16 July*

The gardener hoses the roses while the grass is sprinkled. An elderly resident is seated, summer clothes flowing to her feet.

*Sunday 18 July*

Six or seven groups of residents and guests bathe in the hot afternoon sunshine.

7.30pm   A woman in a dark blue and gold sari waits for a toddler in pale blue dungarees to tire. She picks him up and holds him, walking slowly on the warm, dry, shaded grass, talking quietly to him. Her long hair almost reaches her legs.

8.15pm   Beyond the seafront railings, a temporary bungee jump contraption operates into the evening – riders flung about in the sky, watched by about twenty people spaced along the sunlit railings.

9pm   Motorboats and water-skiers withdraw from the pale, flat sea, except one little boat motionless in the distance.

*Tuesday 20 July*

4am   Suddenly a heavy rainfall beats down, lasting an hour, washing the hedges, shrubs and grass.

*Sunday 25 July*

No rain since the 20th. Three or four days of 26° heat. Sultry. A slight breeze. The sunbathers lie on mats or towels on the short, dry, pale grass – individuals, couples, families, groups. On the sea, sailing boats drift, sails unhoisted.

*Monday 26 July*

The breeze is from the east, cool in the bright warm sunshine, and the light is much clearer. A crane dismantles the bungee apparatus. At 11pm the moon casts a pale blue shimmer on the dark water.

*Friday 30 July*

27°    The grass is predominantly straw-coloured. The gardener puts the sprinkler out and pours water in a full jet over the grass.

*Sunday 1 August*

5pm    30°    The light from the bright hot sun is hazy over the flat sea. A large sailing boat has halted in the centre of the sea. After a quarter of an hour the pale grey sails disappear and the hull and masts drift slowly off to the west.

A small workmanlike pleasure boat carries passengers by, close to the shore. A few people lie, reading, on the grass.

*Tuesday 3 August*

7.30am    In the middle of the night a light rainfall started, developing into a quiet shower so steady and continual that all exposed surfaces have been soaked. The garden is immediately greener and the mauve buddleia have appeared.

6pm    24°    Hot sunshine assaults the east side houses. A newly painted house glows.

*Wednesday 4 August*

6.30pm    The sky is a thick pale grey; the air warm, muggy, with a mild, uneven breeze. A band of dark grey cloud develops over the horizon, multi-curved, pointing upwards.

7.30pm    A taut white sail, a perfect triangle, speeds from west to east as a flash of lightning occurs over the sea. Spots of rain fall as thunder rumbles.  Four hours of rain ensue, very vertical, by 9 o'clock quite heavy – golden needles around the black replica Georgian street lanterns. The grass becomes greener, the dry straw colour less dominant.

*Sunday 8 August*

5am    Heavy rain bounces on the balcony and streams down the road. Through its loud sounds, a few birds can be heard.

6pm    Hundreds of starlings float silently like a long serpentine scarf across the square, low over the buildings, east to west.

*Wednesday 11 August*

11am    Eclipse of the sun.    22°    A clear, fresh quality of air, very light breeze and clear light – blue sky with a soft fine patch of grey-white cloud here and there and a bank of soft, very pale cloud along the clear horizon. A few people sit or stand in the garden. The sea's blue turns to a steel grey. The sun is reflected in dazzling small points of white light on each of the cars in this north-west corner. The hedge glints, darkening. Shadows of the balcony railings and the potted conifers are pronounced on the balcony floor. The temperature drops a little. Some gulls get excited above the square. The lights of the coastguard helicopter, as it routinely passes, shine brightly. For a minute, twilight. A sail boat slips across. The sky and the sea rapidly become bluer again, and the grass greener.

*Tuesday 17 August*

6pm   19°   The shrubs and flowers gyrate in a loud blustery wind. The grey-green southerly sea is choppy – vigorous glossy waves with little foam. Periodically rain arrives in swirls. There is no movement in the hedge, cut recently slender and low: eight feet at the tallest and six at the lowest.

*Wednesday 18 August*

7pm   21°   Gulls whistle and hector.

*Saturday 21 August*

10.30am   24° in sun, 16° in shade   The large sprinkler whirrs and softly chugs as the spray shoots and twirls over assorted, mostly dark red, roses in the circular beds. Two new smaller sprinklers in the lower garden produce plumes of spray that wave in the rolling breeze. Sky and sea are blue.

*Friday 27 August*

6pm   23°   In a bright, hazy, humid atmosphere, a large vessel has halted a few hundred yards out to sea and gently rocks on the calm, breezy water. It is twelve times the length of the white sailing boat that passes it. The hull is black, with white, brick-like horizontal rectangular marks. Above are three tall white masts, the closest to the bow crossed high with four thick white horizontal features, each thinner and shorter than that below. The mast closest to the stern seems to support a diagonal pole holding a flag beyond the stern.

The haze and humidity gradually lift. From somewhere unseen comes the whistling clamour of a crowd of starlings.

*Wednesday 1 September*

8.15pm    21°    The sweet fruit-like glow on the east-side houses disappears as the reflected crimson sunset descends. A green light heads a fast motorboat, close to shore.

*Friday 3 September*

2pm    27°    The sea gleams, dark blue, glossy, spangled in sunlight, the waves clear, concave, swift and foamless.

*Saturday 4 September*

9am   Hot sun beats down on the west side buildings. In the garden the dense and sturdy sedum heads have begun to turn from pale green to rhubarb pink. They form a fat and rounded windbreak guarding the upper rose beds alongside the low curves of euonymus.

*Wednesday 8 September*

11am    23°    The sea is an expanse of multifarious brilliant silver pulsations, the waves muscular, fast and smooth in a fair breeze. The pampas brushes wave. In the lid of the centre statue, the crimson pelargoniums from this distance appear quite strong and rich.

**North East** *Charcoal drawing*

*Tuesday 14 September*

7pm   16°   Since 28° of humid heat at the weekend, a cool, strong wind has delivered several firm showers. Apart from the pelargoniums and the red roses the colour is muted, depressed. The cream pampas swing in the wind.

*Sunday 19 September*

8.30am   16°   Under a layered heap, like cushions, of dark grey cloud, the sea divides into sections: pale yellow-green at the front, mainly turquoise, and a strip of dark blue at the sharply clear horizon. The dark green leaves on the sycamore rustle and shake as a southerly gale arrives. In the east border, the mallow is less mauve and more pale and blue. The red roses in the top beds and the white roses in the bottom bed remain. The crimson pelargoniums, reduced, nevertheless retain the overall mounded shape on the statue.

*Friday 1 October*

After ten days' heavy rain, the grass is a deep, rich, radiant green.

11am   19°   All morning, mountainous light grey ranges of cloud move from west to east – vast papery vessels based at the horizon. The sea is fast and wavy, and carries intermittent dazzling and dynamic silver reflections when the sun is bright and clear of the passing white clouds.

The young postman hurries round the square, in and out of basements, with the second post. At the front, two colleagues join him and they walk fast and freely, all in shorts.

*Sunday 10 October*

10.30am    18°    Woolly blue-grey cloud unravels through marble formations letting sunlight on twenty sailing boats inclining west close together across the sleek pale grey sea.

In the garden the roses have revived, almost all varieties in bloom. The crimson pelargoniums have settled into an almost cardboard crusty texture.

*Saturday 16 October*

11am   The gardener's wife has long fair hair. They wheel the baby down the grass and out through the west side gate.

*Saturday 23 October*

In the late evening, an immense coalescence of rounded rain cloud, grey, white-edged, moves north-east.

*Sunday 24 October*

9am   A violent channel gale attacks the coast, overlaid with racing grey creating a pale light. White foam floats forward on the massive waves. The buddleia, forsythia, pampas are flung and bent; the whole hedge staggers. At times the rain is horizontal. Sycamore leaves fly off the tree to the corners of the square. A clutch of pelargonium remnants lingers.

*Sunday 31 October*

7.30am   14°   The sky is a very pale blue. The light is bright and open. Over the east-side houses, especially half way along, an indistinct arch of brighter golden-white glows. Along the horizon a vast bank of crisp white cumulus travels west. The sun gradually flares above the buildings. The crests of waves are first to reflect the blaze. Dozens of roses are still in bloom in the top three beds.

*Saturday 6 November*

10.30am   Altocumulus clouds move from north-west to south-east. The sea swings, brilliant platinum in the sun. The sycamore leaves are thin, sparse and dull. The soil is dark brown against the bright soft green grass.

*Tuesday 9 November*

7am   10°   In the light blue sky, behind the buildings in the north-east corner, a thin, otherwise white cloud is pink. South-east the clouds are pebbled grey. Soon the south sky is full of a shade of pink-lilac-grey. In the garden the only sweet colour is in the still crimson pelargonium in the statue pot. A little mauve remains in the tired mallow. A black and white cat examines grass close to the hedge and sneezes.

*Saturday 13 November*

11am   10°   The sun on the sea dazzles, gold turning silver as each small white cloud from the north-east intervenes.

Two sailing boats cross to the east against a strong easterly current, their white sails black silhouettes in the sun on the laminar water. The grass in the garden is high and thick, a multitude of soft clean mounds. The gardener stands in the centre bed, removing the pelargoniums, to replace them with green wallflower plants.

*Monday 15 November*

3pm    Under a clear blue sky some gulls drift and swing, dipping over the square for a moment, calling out incidentally and unhurriedly.

*Saturday 27 November*

9am    Blindingly, the pale gold sun bursts over the lower east houses, its rays caught by the moist light green conifers on the balcony. In a short-sleeved shirt, the gardener wheels barrow-loads of dark manure to the rose beds and shovels quantities across the soil with a large spade. Practically all the leaves have left the sycamore's branches.

Standing at a ground floor window, a resident white spitz rests its front paws on the window sill to watch out.

4pm    The south sky is pink, blue, mauve, white and grey.

*Sunday 12 December*

10am    12°    Above the seafront and the silver-green westerly-driven sea, the gulls, three or four at a time, hover and arc.

*Thursday 16 December*

7.15am   In blue-toned darkness two sailing boats drive east on a calm sea, perceptible only by a few bright white lights.

*Saturday 18 December*

Midnight   All evening, rain, sleet or snow has fallen, the latest being large flakes of watery snow arriving in a lightly spiralling diagonal descent. The balcony floor is partly covered in a thick sleet. The windscreens, bonnets and roofs of the cars are coated in watery snow lit by the replica street lanterns, and the grass in the garden, less brightly lit, is pale.

*Sunday 19 December*

10.30am   Under a cloudless sky the frozen snow stays on the cars, grass and soil until the sun reaches it. The skeletal sycamore is motionless.

*Monday 20 December*

8am   2°   Following a fire at 4am in one of the east houses, the first floor is gutted, empty and dark. The window frames are buckled and the middle of the facade of the building is charred and smoke-stained. Three hours after the flames ended, a smell of burning continues to waft around the square. A pile of jagged wood and metal rests on the balcony.

6pm    A torch light moves, darting and circling, in the darkness of the burnt first floor.

*Friday 24 December*

2pm   12°   The four full-length window frames of the burnt flat are boarded in wood of different shades and texture.

In the strong blustery wind and heavy drizzle, an elderly woman resident, jacket billowing, forces open her car door, pulls hard to close it and drives off. The white spitz trots beside its owner as he strides to the seafront.

A long, thin, tiered train of starlings – thousands – flutter and weave swiftly west, low over the centre of the square.

Throughout the afternoon and evening the wind and rain strengthen. By 9pm squalls coil and flare continually under the high white oval lamp on the near side of the front road.

*Saturday 25 December*

9am   The waves roll, wider and lower than yesterday's. The pale turquoise railings are quietly vivid against the pale olive sea. Over the square, herring gulls glide and circle and occasionally call out. One persistently and rapidly treads the thick grass to produce worms.

*Tuesday 28 December*

10am   6°   A gull walks on the grass. In the sycamore, some starlings waddle briefly on lower branches, while a blackbird is perched very high on an inner twig. From one roof to another, a group of jackdaws fly – glossy, black, fluent, undulating, silent.

*Friday 31 December 1999*

7pm    Many of the windows whose curtains tend to be drawn in the evenings are tonight open, and sets of festive lighting sparkle from ten households on various floors along the east side.    Sounds of fireworks burst from the town centre. Within an hour, drizzle falls.

*Sunday 2 January 2000*

11.30am    10°    Sail boats nod steadily east on a bright silver sea. The garden grass is deep and spongy.

*Wednesday 12 January*

8.30pm    8°    Spacious and stately, soft white clouds glide, uncommonly from the south, precisely to the north.

*Friday 14 January*

10am  7°  The gardener removes a smart supermarket shopping trolley from the garden rubbish receptacle. The herring gull repetitively treads the deep turf. The white spitz is walked.

3pm  A broadly blue sky, faded by thin high drapes of white, descends, ice blue white, over the horizon. The sea, a very pale blue-grey, flat but for its tremoring, is deserted by boats. Gulls shout. In the north-west corner of the garden, shadow encroaches on the bright green bumpy grass.

A cyclist, dressed in a grey suit, clipped above the ankle, dashes up the road on his racing bike, dismounting at speed.

*Saturday 15 January*

10am  7°  In the very light drizzle, an unaccompanied child wanders in the garden with a miniature maroon umbrella. A blond woman appears and, cigarette in hand, accompanies the child across the grass to converse with the gardener.

3pm  A tall, fair-haired man stands quietly and placidly while his sons direct remote control toy vehicles trundling across the bumpy turf.

*Sunday 23 January*

4.30pm  4°  Clouds come from the north. Arriving over the sea, they shift from heather red to dark blue-grey – long, rounded, discrete objects in a very pale blue background over a very pale blue-grey sea.

*Tuesday 25 January*

8am  2°  The car windscreens are frosted. Crusts of frost mottle the deep tufty grass. The sea is completely calm, silky, very pale bright blue, glowing. The faint hazy horizon underlies a pale pink base of sky.

Noon  A blinding wide triangle of sun, yellow-silver, points to the south. In the middle of the garden a herring gull waddles in one place, infrequently stooping to peck. The sun passes out of sight. The shimmering silver, and silhouettes of two people's heads and shoulders, are framed by the wooden surrounds and metal hipped roof of the oriental seafront pavement seat. The gull walks patiently to the north-east corner of the garden where it settles into a treading posture.

*Friday 28 January*

10pm  8°  The temperature rises, a light gale blows, the incoming tide is loud, and the balcony conifers shake.

*Sunday 30 January*

9am  10°  A variety of small birds, individuals, many of them singing, dart and flit from tree to hedge and from building to building. Silent, forty black-headed gulls glide, tilting hesitantly from side to side, in a mild west wind, interweaving, some turning horizontal curves or circles – all travelling over the square from east to west. When out of sight they let off a brief general wailing. From time to time a few reappear throughout the morning.

*Tuesday 1 February*

1pm   A herring gull stands on the sunroof of the long silver-grey Mercedes. After a minute it walks about, sliding momentarily on the rear window, then stands on the boot.

2pm   A herring gull stands in the grass close to the centre bed, wiggling in search of worms. A second gull lands near, but within seconds a third gull swoops and guides the second away towards the sea.

3pm   Two gulls, no more than a few inches apart, stand by the centre bed. One wiggles with increasing vigour, while the other's action is subtler. The latter then steadily turns a half-circle on the spot, peering upward, not at the ground.

3.30pm   The sea is rather rough – pale sandy brown, foaming and droning. In the heavily clouded light, the street lamp half way down the east side comes on, a pale orange flamed tone in the black-framed lantern. An hour later, the other lamps light up.

*Wednesday 2 February*

4.30pm   For ten or fifteen minutes, the starlings pass over the square – in groups, crowds and multitudes – shifting pace, direction, formation, but, with whatever hesitation or marginal diversion, all heading west.

*Thursday 3 February*

8.15am   In cool, clear, dull light on a calm pale sea, not far from the shore, a small boat rocks along from the east, and turns back. Its hull is low, and red. The prow and stern-post are high. There may be a small dark cabin at the back.

*Sunday 6 February*

8am   10°   Fog conceals the sea. High in the thin top branches of the sycamore, a bird, probably a blackbird, perches in effect vertically, frequently moving its head and shoulders. Gulls call, tilt and turn above the seafront cliff. At half past nine the usual couple descend and wander in the abundant grass, a few yards apart, gobbling the findings snatched from the soil by their bills.

*Wednesday 16 February*

1pm   8°   A large white and red helicopter travels loudly and slowly, low over the sea, close to the land. Ten minutes later it passes in the opposite direction, equally low and close.

6.30pm   4°   The helicopter comes by, indistinct in the darkness, higher than before, directing a spotlight along the shore diagonally from over the sea, its main light sparkling in clear blue-black sky, green light constant, red light flashing.

*Saturday 26 February*

8am   At the horizon, the contrast between the silver sea and the panel of golden cream sky is extremely stark. Outer features of the south-east corner building are sharp against the sky: the curls of a Corinthian pilaster capital; the vertical bars of the first floor's continuous balcony railing.

*Sunday 27 February*

5pm   Thirty herring gulls hover, dip and dart high above the square. Their call is harsh and plaintive. After disappearing, they are heard again, above the sound of the sea's rush and the soft volumes of intermittent wind.

*Monday 28 February*

Some flowers have appeared in the garden: daffodils, primula and little yellow and red tulips.

*Tuesday 29 February*

7am   A stormy morning. The balcony conifers shiver, twitch and shake, sprayed with rain in the loud fifty-mile-an-hour winds. In a sage green basin hat and fluorescent yellow uniform anorak, an elderly road sweeper takes a broom from the narrow metallic cart before continuing round the road.

*Wednesday 1 March*

8am   3°   A tanker, two or three  miles out, monochrome, crawling west, is visible between the sycamore's bare shoots.

*Thursday 2 March*

5.30pm   The grass has been cut, flat and slippery, a grid streaked with loose blades.

*Friday 3 March*

Lots of tightly packed daffodils have bloomed in the thin rectangular bed between the circular beds at the top end.

*Friday 10 March*

11am   Mist recedes and drizzle is brief. Twenty black-headed gulls intermingle in curved flight above the north terrace. They whistle, and make a thin, high-pitched barking sound.

*Sunday 12 March*

10am   15°   On a west side balcony the owner rummages through plant boxes and re-fills  them with dark compost from an enormous white plastic decorative pot.

*Thursday 16 March*

8am   6°   On the same balcony, cartons of purple and yellow pansies are attached to the top rail. In the garden the forsythia, tucked in the hedge by the west gate, has flowered.

*Saturday 18 March*

10pm   In the cold clear air the lamps in the square are bright flame; the tall seafront lamps are bright violet white.

*Friday 24 March*

5pm  14°  The gardener puts clippings and weeds from the borders into the wheelbarrow.

*Tuesday 28 March*

During the afternoon a handywoman repaints the low black crescent railing along the lower garden.

*Saturday 1 April*

10am    The elderly man, with a rusty bicycle, delivers newspapers and talks to all the cats.

*Tuesday 4 April*

After loads of recent rain the grass and hedges are bright green. The hedge along the lower garden has been cut today and is narrow and hard-edged compared with the soft bushy breadth and height (eight to ten feet) of the hedge round the main garden. A few crows and gulls, croaking, cross each other's paths in fast flight.

Scaffold and painters have gone from the house affected by fire, the front elevation renewed except for the first floor bay windows whose frames now contain neat pale boards.

8pm  1°  The effect of the interior lighting in three balcony windows recalls three different shades of brandy or whisky, golden orange, orange-yellow and golden yellow.

**East – Meeting**  *Charcoal drawing*

*Wednesday 5 April*

1pm    The grass is cut by the farmer. He pushes the motor mower slowly through the overgrown grass creating lateral ridges of cuttings.

*Friday 7 April*

6pm    14°    Under blue sky the west buildings are lit by bright warm sunlight. In the shade at the top end the gardener works in the beds and borders. The daffodils wilt and shrink. Two flowering currant bushes have blossomed with a profusion of little mild red-pink flowers. Scarlet tulips have opened. The gulls fly slowly, and flap in silence.

*Saturday 8 April*

11am    Motorboats occasionally pass.; one pulls a water skier.

*Sunday 9 April*

In crisp afternoon sunshine, jackdaws undulate smoothly.

*Tuesday 11 April*

The grass has been cut and raked and, after a day of rain, has softened in texture to that of crushed velvet. The main hedge is voluminous. A mile or so out, a long dark red tanker slowly moves from west to east.

*Wednesday 4 April*

The boards are removed from the balcony window. The grass, trimmed and cambered, now looks like a lawn. The mellow flight of the gulls is very high.

8pm  3°  Big hailstones bounce loudly on the balcony.

*Thursday 13 April*

8.30am    In white overalls three painters on wooden step-ladders work on the replacement windows and the canopy.

*Sunday 16 April*

The gulls are occupied all morning with a pale piece of very hard rind. The male bangs its beak on it; the male and female experiment by holding each end in their mouths and pulling away from each other. The object proves indestructible and indivisible. One of the cats creeps up towards them, and they jump and flap, then with wings outstretched leap towards the cat, which turns and retreats.

*Wednesday 19 April*

In the centre bed about a hundred red and yellow tulips bloom, clustered over a mass of upright green leaves.

*Monday 24 April*

Bluebells emerge among the tulips.

*Tuesday 25 April*

Tiny yellow-green leaves have broken out on the sycamore.

*Friday 28 April*

7pm  9°  The hedge, cut, is now neat, vertical and angular.

*Friday 5 May*

1.30pm  19°  The air is windy, warm and rather thick. Stripped to the waist, the farmer mows the grass. A man and woman in singlets and shorts lounge on the ground near the lilac whose white flowers have begun to appear.

*Saturday 6 May*

11am  20°  The gardener saws a shrub down to a clump. His daughter toddles in the grass, yards from her pushchair. Throughout the sycamore's crown, pale leaves have opened.

A large bee hovers around the neighbouring balcony plants, and suddenly travels away, rising through the square at thirty miles an hour, disappearing over the east roofline.

A long-haired man wearing simply calf-length trousers lies on the grass, propped on his elbows, head facing down studiously over a book. Later, a long tabby takes his place.

*Sunday 7 May*

3pm   21°   Under a muddled sky of hazy grey, white and blue, four people picnic on a rug, while further down a man and woman in shirts, shorts and bare feet sit, drink, smoke and converse. On an east balcony, a couple in a sleeveless shirt and pink top, both in shorts, are seated on chairs.

In the evening the sea is flat and, in the heavy warm air, practically indistinguishable from the pale grey sky.

*Monday 8 May*

10am   In the big round beds, the stems of the roses have risen to about twelve inches and are growing red-gold-green leaves. The sycamore leaves fill out fast.

*Thursday 18 May*

18°   Fresh north-westerly wind blows light, high clouds, mostly white, crossing the bright sun and causing the colours on the sea to change continually – blue, grey and jade, smooth and undulating with linear frills of white foam.

The sycamore leaves are densely layered and large. The thickly leaved lilac branches shake in the wind, waving the pointed oblong white flowers.

*Wednesday 24 May*

6pm   15°   Rain has fallen almost every day for a week. In the north-east corner of the main garden, and visible in the lower garden, magenta foxgloves tower. Blue iris flags appear among the small green border shrubs near the east gate.

*Friday 26 May*

14°   Between 8.30 and 9am, for about twenty minutes, a spacious and unregimented crowd of white sailing boats pass from west to east, a few hundred yards from shore, on a high tide – more than a hundred boats, in a loose procession, in dull clear light, on a moderate swell, in a moderate wind.

Some roses have bloomed in the upper beds.

9.30pm   In the centre of the view of the sea and southern sky, a huge band of soft pale turquoise blue sky appears between the dark grey above and below.

*Saturday 27 May*

10am   Across a blue sky, quick white clouds, progressively darkening, throw articles of black shadow, like cloth, on the smooth high jade-green white-topped waves.

Overleaf: **Seaside Square**   *Coloured drawing*

**Balconies and Canopies**   *Watercolour with body*

**Dark Green Day**  *Watercolour*

**Looking Left**  *Watercolour*

*Sunday 28 May*

As fifty or sixty mile an hour gales are preceded and succeeded by heavy rain, the daytime temperature drops below 10°.

*Tuesday 30 May*

8pm   A mile or two out to sea, mildly lit by a weak sunset of silver, a grey and white tanker steadily slides to the east.

*Saturday 3 June*

10am   19°   The statue bowl has been emptied. Below, one bright pink rose and two yellow stand still in the light breeze.

*Monday 5 June*

10.30am   14°   The sound of an engine comes from the lower garden. A bright yellow four-wheeled scooter is driven from a central black seat by the farmer, trailing a wheeled black plastic cuttings receptacle. Later, walking with a machine stick, he trims the main garden's borders and beds. Then he drives the scooter all over the grass, pausing regularly to empty the case.

5pm   The gardener hoses water into bushes by the hedge. A man from the south-east corner picks herbs. A young brown-skinned woman in a brown pullover and black trousers, a sandwich in one hand and a mug in the other, wanders down the garden and slowly returns to the top gate.

*Tuesday 6 June*

9.30am  A woman rides a big old black bicycle with a large front wicker pannier round the road to her west-side home.

2pm  The elderly woman, in a short navy blue coat and dark trousers walks down through the garden to the white-flowered olearia bush at the centre of the south hedge, and returns to the north terrace, looking up to speak to an elderly woman on the balcony of a neighbouring house.

6pm    13°  The gardener, accompanied by a slim brown tabby cat, puts pale busy lizzies in the north-east corner.

The statue bowl is filled with earth in which this year's pelargonium geraniums stand sturdily – at present one pale lilac bloom above a base of green leaves.

9pm  The sky above the pale grey sea is made up of streaks of light blue, pink, light mauve and white. The paint on the east-side houses has a warm glow in the low sun's reflection. In half an hour the pink sheen turns to a yellow butter tint.

*Wednesday 7 June*

6pm    19°  The sprinkler shoots a spray across the grass towards the west gate. In the bright sunlit garden, the elderly women sit talking, one on the bench and one on a foldable chair. On a seat at the south end a young woman sits reading a book. The sea is bright, glass-like dark blue, and the sky is pale blue. At 6.30 the garden is deserted and a fluffy black cat sniffs the grass.

*Thursday 8 June*

5pm    22°    In warm, humid sunshine a young man sunbathes near the east gate, while another young man lounges, reading a newspaper, in the north-east corner.

*Friday 9 June*

8.30am    21°    A fishing boat passes not far from the shore, trailed by a fluttering of gulls.

7.30pm    16°    After rain, in the thin bed between the circular ones, two roses have bloomed, big, brilliant, pink.

*Wednesday 14 June*

5.30pm    During a third consecutive day of low cloud, mist and damp, cold wind, the gardener, in olive green wellington boots, hoses the grass. The lilac pelargonium petals have increased, and several lemon yellow roses have appeared in the bed below. Tucked in the east border of green hedging and bushes, a clump of stiff-stalked red-pink carnations shiver in the cool wind. On the grey-green sea, rolling south-westerly, visible most of the way to the misted horizon, white crests, disparate, isolated, rise and somersault and disappear quickly.

*Friday 16 June*

5pm    20°    In the garden a wild-mannered white child demonstrates to three boisterous black boys  opportunities to cause maximum commotion with his plastic machine gun. He walks in the flower-beds. The three brothers' mother arrives and removes all four of them.

7.30pm   18°   Two happy heavyweight women from the west side arrive in a black sports car with the hood down, take their bags in and then sit alone on a garden bench, reading, with a tall tin of crisps.

*Saturday 17 June*

23°   Surrounded by blue sea and sky, a regatta takes place, the races involving boats with bright light-coloured billowing sails, little bumper boats and capsulated white yachts. In the garden twenty people sunbathe. Three generations of a family gather. In a separate group, a supper for six is hosted.

*Monday 19 June*

1pm   24°   The sea is unexpectedly lost in a screen of white mist which drifts into the lower garden where the farmer is working on the flower-beds.

9pm   Gulls create a dissonance of spirals and cascades of screeching like flutes and whistles.

*Wednesday 21 June*

6pm   20°   Gradually, rolls, folds, planks and flags of grey and white cloud break up in the late afternoon, and now the sky is blue above, while the cloud is woven with blue to the south over the sea. The horizon is almost clear, and most of the sea is a vivid, satin, dark green turquoise marked with bright white parallel bars of crested foam drifting and spilling in the audible breeze.

The strong sun grips the east facades: they look like blocks of dairy ice cream. The windows withdraw, very black, and the black cast iron railings and balcony and veranda supports are repeated in sharp black vertical shadows on the brilliant cream walls.

The garden is in shade. The statue's lilac pelargoniums are quietly conspicuous against the green grass.

Along the tarmac seafront pavement a large-framed square-shouldered man, hunched forward, in beige shorts and a white shirt hanging loose, rollerblades.

2009

# 2009

*Wednesday 31 December 2008*

Midnight   0° C   The air is very still, the sky clouded, but local visibility is clear. The black replica Georgian street lanterns in the square emit pale orange light. In windows, festive tree lights glitter: traditional white in one; red, green and gold in another; contemporary blue in a third. Various elements of similar lighting can be glimpsed along the frontage of the north terrace.

At midnight, whizzing, crackles and bangs break out. Beyond the south-east corner building, plumes and showers of white, gold, green and red explode. In many of the windows of the east-side houses, reflections of displays from the westward seafront flash and flare.

Some small groups and pairs of assorted people huddle and hover at the seafront railings. From the north-east corner of the square a trio in black run down to the railings.

*Thursday 1 January 2009*

1pm   3°   Under the pale grey sky, the sea, almost entirely flat, is pale blue-green-grey. In the garden some thin or lightweight plants tremble in an easterly breeze. The sole flower to be seen is a white rose in the narrow crescent of earth towards the foot of the main garden.

3.15pm   A very thin elderly tabby with neat white markings and flirtatious eyes hurries along the pavement. She suddenly stops and begins to practise her croaking howl, a prolonged and resonant address appealing for indulgence. Then her head switches to left and to right and she sets off in her stiff, quick walk.

*Saturday 3 January*

11.30am   3°   The sea ripples in a strict east-south-easterly current under a cloudless light blue sky. Platinum white, the sun fills the south sky and floods the central area of sea in dazzling reflection.

*Saturday 10 January*

9am   1°   During the night the temperature dropped to -5 or lower. The sea and sky are shrouded in a pale grey haze. A thick frost covers cars parked around the top of the square, half of which are silver-grey. The sea is exceptionally calm.

*Monday 12 January*

2pm   7°   After several weeks of high pressure and northerly and easterly air, the ocean wind and rain return. The rain strengthens, and the white foam spreads on the sea's twisting rolls of grey-green-brown. The roar of the sea is loud.

*Sunday 18 January*

11am   7°   The sun shines, bright white, on the sea whose great foamless waves race from the west, jostling like animals.

*Sunday 1 February*

2.30pm   2°   The sea changes from grey-blue to a pale cream-green, and then a steelier green, the finely serrated straight ripples more faint in fading light. Small snowflakes fly by and fly down. In the corner of the square they zigzag or somersault, like winged insects. In the garden the resident pair of herring gulls dig into the grass.

7.15pm   Suddenly, thick snowflakes fall, faster, sometimes flying horizontally  round the lamppost.

8.45pm   The grass is covered in whiteness, and on the road in the square the snow is an inch deep. Occasionally a yellow gritter lorry goes along the main road. A huddle of young people from a house on the east side throw snowballs at short range and shriek.

10.15pm   Illuminated from the seafront lamppost lanterns, the pitched roof of the pale turquoise wooden seat shelter is coated in snow.

*Monday 2 February*

9am   1°   Almost everything is caked or dusted in snow – the grass, plants, hedge, the first floor railings and canopies. The street lamp stems are lined with white, as is the scaffold at two houses. On the coast road the sparse traffic passes at half the usual speed. Two women stand at the north gate, cartons of delicatessen coffee in their gloved hands, while their shih tsu scampers around the garden as fast as her legs will go, long pale grey hair flopping and bouncing.

Some of the snow melts, then under the domestic railings the drips freeze to form icicles. In the late morning some herring gulls arrive, one or two landing on roofs and chimneys before flapping and curving away. A lone black-headed gull flies in from the sea, turns in the square and returns to the sea.

In the afternoon a fishing-boat, or similar, floats past close to the shore at a slow pace. It soon reappears in the reverse direction, then halts for a short time before turning to continue in the former direction. A busy man in a luminous orange jacket appears more than once to lean over the side of the boat with some sort of equipment.

By the evening, most ice and some snow has melted.

*Sunday 8 February*

4° During the afternoon, the blue sky whitens, while the crisp silver-white puffs banked on the horizon subside below a development of chevrons and cushions of soft grey and swathes of white patchwork. As the sky goes grey and dark, the sea, a strong-toned turquoise, turns a vivid dark blue with a slender band of pale silver-grey along the horizon.

*Friday 19 February*

8am  7°  The entire outlook is filled with mist. The only colour is from the orange of the street lamp in the square, and one fanlight over the front door of a house.

3pm  The sea remains completely screened in mist. Gulls fly silently from and to the sea, disappearing into the mist. Suddenly there is a flurry and calling around the roofs of the square, some of the gulls settling on the north terrace roof.

*Sunday 1 March*

6pm   9°   A sunset is reflected in most of the window panes on the east houses as cranberry red.

*Sunday 8 March*

11am   8°   In the lively bright silver-grey sea, far apart, sailing boats lean and lurch and dip.

5pm   7°   A woman dressed in black jersey, trousers and shoes hurries from a house, through the black steel-barred garden gate to cut some leaves from the herb bushes.

*Saturday 14 March*

11am   14°   Part of a row of daffodils can be glimpsed along a narrow upper bed in the garden – rich yellow and orange.

*Sunday 22 March*

3.30pm   14°   In a long scarlet jacket and black trousers, her hair tied in a low bun, a young woman makes her way, very slowly, across the grass, leaning on a walking stick. Seated on a bench, facing the sea, she flicks through a notebook.

*Friday 27 March*

6pm    12°   The grey sky grows darker to the south, darkest over the horizon. The sea is lead grey in the far distance, green in the middle distance, and sandy green closer to home with lengthy lines, uneven and broken, of white foam.

On, or in, the water close to shore, two diminutive dark figures, upright on surfboards, ride the dip and swell of waves, east and west. From their outstretched hands they steer huge kites – flat banana shapes, one plain red, one yellow and black.

*Saturday 28 March*

5.30pm    9°   A hailstorm draws a white curtain across the square, and creates an apparent complexion of black flecks or dots on the dark green-grey sea.

After the hail, the sea, quiet and slow, meets the north wind in lengthy perpendicular striations of thin surface ruffling.

The great lid of grey cloud moves away to the south-east, leaving a blue-white sky overhead and pursued above the horizon by complicated formations of white, grey, dark blue and light turquoise blue.   Then the southern sky turns to cream, the sea silver-cream, and windows in the corner house a bright orange flame.

By 6.30 the same southern sky is dominated by patches of washed pink and ragged smoky mauve.

*Saturday 4 April*

2.30pm    11°    A wren flits on to the balcony railing and darts to the nearby veranda railing. Continually switching its head left and right and up and down, it frequently jumps on the spot to face a different direction. Its tiny dark eyes are bright. It leaves the railing and for a moment flutters like a butterfly close to the French window, before returning briefly to the railing and then flying quickly up to the top of the scaffold at a house on the east side. It twitches about, then flies over the top of the buildings and out of sight.

*Sunday 26 April*

4pm    17°    In the beds at the top of the garden, a palm tree and a cone-candled candelabra pine, both dark blue-green, have risen above the height of the brilliant yellow-green euonymus hedge, as has a bush, softly and densely plumed, by the west gate. A child clatters to and fro around the pavement on a slender aluminium scooter.

*Tuesday 28 April*

1.30pm        15°        The sea is a brilliant turquoise blue. The horizon is sharply lined at the base of the light blue sky.

8pm        12°        In the pale matt light a municipal road-sweeper pushes a two-wheeled barrow along the seafront pavement.

*Monday 4 May*

11am   14°   A second child scooterist accompanies the first.

*Friday 22 May*

9am   18°   Sixty sailing boats, mostly white, pass from east to west, some close to shore. The light is fairly bright, a brisk westerly wind prevails and the sea is smoothly animated.

6pm   17°   On the front of the south-east corner building, eight levels of scaffold platform timber have been erected. Along the east side, the clean pale cream of a row of six houses glows brightly in the unseen sun.

*Thursday 28 May*

7pm   Additional small areas of scaffolding, perched on the facade's parapet at the top, surround the two front stacks of tall cream chimneys.

*Saturday 30 May*

2pm   22°   Sunbathers – two trios and a quartet, generally aged probably in their thirties – lounge and drink and talk. The neat elderly woman from the corner, in a white cotton cap, walks down the pavement to the front, supported under the arm by a relative.

*Sunday 31 May*

5pm   24°   The blue sea is busy. Some speedboats create white ridges of wash. In the garden a man from the west side sunbathes in pale khaki-coloured shorts.

*Monday 1 June*

2pm   25°   Five men climb orange ladders to the eighth level of scaffolding. After some discussion, three descend to the lowest levels.

Two slim young women walk round the road, one pale-skinned in a white knee-length frock and one dark-skinned in a similar black frock, both wearing black-framed sunglasses, each in a different coloured lightweight trilby hat and each holding on a long leash a wire-haired fox terrier. They pass under the scaffolding into the building.

Later, all five men are at the eighth level, scraping and treating the windows' woodwork.

For several days the breeze has been north-easterly and has increased in warmth. This afternoon it has strengthened: the green foliage of shrubs erratically swirls while the sycamore's thick tall crown pulsates.

Briefly the trilbies occupy the south-west corner, sunbathing on black deckchairs.

7pm   22°   Seated on the second highest of the main scaffolding platforms, out beyond the corner of the corner building, with a view of every direction except the north-east, a man and woman from the fourth floor sunbathe on chairs.

**North West**   *Charcoal drawing*

The pastel blue door of the adjacent house is, over time, being bleached by the sun. Calm in its arched and stepped recess, it possesses a quiet radiance against the green hedge.

*Thursday 4 June*

10pm   14°   The moon, nearly full, has moved during the evening to the west and is above the sycamore. Below the tree's mass of leaves, visible through the angle in the divided trunk, waves of moonlight are white on the dark blue sea.

*Wednesday 10 June*

8.40pm   15°   A great rainbow reaches from the blue-grey sea, up through the sky, well clear of the corner building, high above the east-side houses, descending to the mid-terrace roof of the north side.

Two crimson roses have appeared above some low bushes in an upper bed. In a lower bed a white rose has bloomed.

*Sunday 14 June*

Noon   24°   The hedge has been trimmed into a neat shape. Along the flat top, the profuse cuttings glitter.

*Thursday 2 July*

8pm   26°   The sky is veiled in hazy pale grey marbled cloud.

After five days of daytime temperatures above twenty-five degrees and night times of twenty degrees, with no rain, the grass is mottled in fawn. The leaf cuttings, lying strewn in patches on the bright green hedge, have turned a bronze and copper brown. The faded pale blue door glows unobtrusively in the intensely humid air.

*Monday 13 July*

3pm   23°   The scaffolding on the corner building has been removed to reveal a salted butter cream coating.

*Wednesday 15 July*

9pm   19°   Fifty or sixty gulls glide and hover, from east to west, some calling out. Most continue on their way, but some tilt and turn north. For a minute none is to be seen, then a few, far apart, curve or circle, wings in a shivering motion, above the roofs. Under a very pale blue sky, draped with soft southerly mushroom-coloured clouds, a handful of the gulls linger, swooping and sliding, high over the square. Eventually a few descend, and from time to time one or two land on disparate chimney tops. After a short while, in the rapidly fading light, forty or fifty reappear, gradually and spaciously, stately in a constantly shifting formation.

*Thursday 16 July*

8.30pm   21°   The sea is a flat plate of uniform pale green, like thick frosted glass. From the horizon to the top of the sky is an equally uniform plate of opaque deep blue-grey.

The nearest street lantern slowly lights up, taking about thirty seconds to develop from faint white to pale violet to pinkish cream to bright orange. A deep rumbling introduces thunder. Then it trundles through the sky reminiscent of a heavy vehicle on an uneven surface. Someone walks along the front with a high umbrella. Crackling explosions occur, and, keeping some distance in the west, flashes of lightning. Rain falls, lightly but audibly. The gulls vanish. The sea turns dark green-grey; the sky, pale green-grey. The rain stops. Someone cycles along the front pavement.

By 9.30, in the half-darkness, the sky has broken into dark shapes moving from the south-south-west. One unseen gull quacks. Lightning flares, once, over the south-east sea. Two adjacent white lights gently undulate, half way out to sea.

After ten o'clock, a few times every minute, for about twenty minutes, mild momentary lightning flickers, with very little sound of thunder. Then after a brief spell of pounding rain, the air, until now quite still, suddenly rushes loudly round the square. The gust is as brief as the shower.

*Saturday 18 July*

1pm   21°   A strong blustery south-westerly wind swipes the garden plants. The sea is a glossy pale green, fast flowing, choppy, silvery in the streaks and openings lit by the sun's breaks between clouds. A small white sail above a little black figure slides across the near sea from the west. Turning away towards the south it bobs, wobbles, jumps and jerks, then turns to sail smoothly at a high speed against the current.

On the balcony of the building with the grey-brown rendering, pot plants of masses of tiny flowers pour over the edge, a mixture of soft white, blue and magenta flecks.

*Friday 24 July*

6.30pm    21°    In the lower garden, a group of at least ten new flowers, huge, spherical, purple-blue, sway on tall bare stalks in the strong southerly wind and bright sunshine. To the right, towards the west corner of the crescent garden, just visible, is a thin little apple sapling, tied to a wooden post. In the main garden, the grass is bright green.

*Sunday 26 July*

7.30pm    20°    Beyond the big round blue agapanthus flowers, the hedge between the lower garden and the main road pavement is trim and straight, like a furry green wall.

*Saturday 15 August*

3pm    22°    Under a sky of white folds, in a choppy green south-westerly sea, a regatta takes place. Not far out, white sailing boats tilt to and fro, navigating around yellow buoys. Further out, a line of sails, brightly coloured and billowing, push east, followed by some curiously coloured angular sails.

4pm    A small dark sort of sentinel boat removes a buoy.

9.30pm    Firework displays, half a mile west, over the sea, are reflected in third and fourth floor windows – kaleidoscopic and liquid effects of green, blue, mauve, red, pink, gold, white and, finally and briefly, orange.

*Sunday 23 August*

2.45pm   27°   In the strong heat and light of the cirrus-hazed sun, a red and white helicopter flies low over the pale calm sea close to shore, west to east, accompanied by a dinghy and an orange modern lifeboat.

7.30pm   22°   The sea is flat, pale grey-blue, marked by very shallow ripplings. Above the blue-white horizon, a deep bank of mushroom-pink haze merges into the pale blue sky. The sky is patched and streaked in zigzags and serpents of riotous white cloud capriciously tailed downward or diagonal.

*Monday 24 August*

4pm   22°   The faded light blue door is being painted.

*Tuesday 25 August*

9am   21°   The door is a bright light turquoise blue.

*Sunday 30 August*

10.15am   20°   The sea is a monochrome silver-grey, almost flat, with scarcely any discernible tidal movement. Waves appear as fleeting dark metallic-looking splinters.

*Friday 4 September*

11am   21°   In bright sunshine, a Mercedes Benz, a pale sort of platinum colour, draws up at the top end of the square. White ribbons meet in a yellow bow at the centre of the front of the bonnet. The driver, in a dark suit, fastens the bow, sprays the hubcaps, smokes two cigarettes and moves the car to the west side where, along with a grey-haired man in a beige suit with a carnation, a bride is guided into the rear seat, while two women in identical olive green, low-neckline, knee-length, breeze-ruffled flared dresses and delicate high-heeled shoes get into the taxi in front, and both cars leave.

*Monday 7 September*

10am   22°   About half a mile out, alone in the pale blue crystal sea, in bright hazy sun shining warmly through high soft white clouds, a long tall sailing ship, its dozen or so white sails glowing in three tiers, waits for a while, then moves and turns to the south-east, soon out of sight.

*Tuesday 8 September*

6.30pm   23°   About a quarter of a mile out in the flat milky blue sea, a ship is anchored: a broad vessel with two or three decks rising to an oval funnel and two tall mast structures towards the pointed prow. As the light fades the fine white cirrus cloud formation turns bright pink, and for a short time the sea is pink. Very gradually the ship turns, clockwise. By eight o'clock it has turned 180°. Soon its many conspicuous lights are a bright pale yellow-green, reflected in the surrounding water.

*Saturday 12 September*

12.30   21°   Crowds lean on the railings, looking down to the lower road, as roars from engines erupt from speed trials.

*Sunday 13 September*

12.30   The promenade pavement is covered in motorbikes and bikers. Constant streams of motorbikes pass.

*Monday 14 September*

In a fairly calm sea, and a clear though clouded light, the eighteenth or nineteenth century type of ship – unless another, very similar – has reappeared. All day it has been about a mile away. No sails can be seen. The masts accentuate the slender form of the structure, especially so in the morning when the vessel was pointed south towards the horizon. By the evening it is pointed east, parallel with the shoreline, and in the darkness its lights gently glow.

*Tuesday 15 September*

The blue agapanthus balls have turned green. The ship has left the scene.

*Saturday 19 September*

9.30am   19°   In the balmy air and milky light, a shiny white cloth marquee begins to take shape low  in the main garden, nearly the width of the grass. Rows of chairs are put inside.

A young cat from a west-side house, medium-sized, very fluffy, indistinctly tabby, lively and with a great interest in the environment, is on the roof of the garden shed. She tries walking on the top of the hedge but struggles and sinks a little and soon abandons the attempt.

22°   From  three o'clock to five o'clock, a celebratory funeral reception takes place in the marquee.

*Saturday 10 October*

6pm   The screen of sky beyond the sea is bright light blue, adorned in pink, white and lilac with very lengthy smoothly curved blocks, plumes and swirls.

*Thursday 15 October*

1.30pm     15°   The gardener sits on the ground, pulling plants from the area around the centre bush.

*Wednesday 21 October*

7.30am   13°   In dim, clear air, on the horizon, between pale green sea and crowded grey puffs of cloud, a bright white light continually flickers.

*Saturday 24 October*

3pm  16°  Along the coast road a postman, in a big durable red uniform jacket and dark shorts, cycles into the wind.

*Sunday 1 November*

11.30am  16°  In the murk of heavy rain in a powerful gale, a large veteran car, well over a hundred years of age, drives west at a speed equal to that of the present day vehicles.

The hedge, tidy, tall, snakily gyrates in the greater gusts while the softer of the high-flown plants are driven to swivelling and stooping. The sycamore leaves look small and scarcer.

*Monday 30 November*

11.30am  8°  Following a dry spell lasting two or three months, rain has fallen almost daily throughout November, often prolonged and heavy, often with gale force winds  and usually squally. This morning a blanket of grey fills the sky, and the rain is incessant. The sea, less tumultuous than on many recent days, is churned into a pale green-brown. The wind, volatile in strength and variable in direction, plays with the smoke lightly pouring from one of the tall chimney stacks – quadruple serried terra cotta pillars on high heavy unpainted stucco bases.

The saturated grass is vivid green. The sycamore is leafless.

*Sunday 13 December*

11am    7°    Triangular, silhouetted, the sailing boats glide swiftly on a flat silver-grey sea, lit by the unseen sun caught among the great white grey-centred clouds powering from the north-east. In front, a thick curtain of light rain falls.

3.45pm    5°    Over the horizon, rounded crusts of pale turquoise-blue lie under billowing lilac-blue banks, topped by broad pink and mauve cushions, creased and furrowed, floating slowly from the east.

*Thursday 17 December*

11.30pm    0°    Snowflakes fall, more and more heavily, settling. Two or three inches pile on the road, the pavements, cars, railings, balconies, canopies, hedge, grass, bushes and tree. Vehicles crawl along the coast road.

*Friday 18 December*

10am    1°    The snow, in places four or five inches deep, shines in the sunlight. The sea, rippling south-easterly, glistens, uniform, blue-silver.

In the garden, a mother and child in overcoats and hats play with the snow. Cars occasionally creep round the square. A female blackbird surveys the garden.

10.40am    The father, hatless, replaces the mother, gently lobbing big snowballs.

The sea blazes in a flood of dazzling platinum light.

10pm    Stars pierce the south sky. In the clear darkness, lit by the street lamps and windows, the snow is lustrous. Unseen footsteps crunch the freezing slush.

*Saturday 19 December*

2pm    1°    In the sunlight a long oblong shadow is cast up the garden gradient from the central bush.

*Sunday 20 December*

Noon    2°    The water has turned westerly. Over the thoroughly trodden snow, the elderly cat carefully and unsteadily crosses the garden. Some gulls return. One stands on a chimney top while smoke wafts into its face from the neighbouring chimney. The brown blackbird enters the central bush. A sparrow stops briefly on the brown hydrangea heads. When the occasional pedestrian or two step on to the main road pavement – a broad strip of crinkled ice – they slide, and most of them immediately retreat.

*Friday 25 December*

11am    5°    Wrapped up, some people stride, some stroll, along the front.

*Saturday 26 December*

11am   7°   Alone on the empty seafront pavement a child, aged perhaps six or seven, runs in long leaping steps as fast as he can, until just as he reaches the ornamental shelter to sit on the sea-facing seat, his adults appear. When they reach the shelter he jumps out of it and they all walk on.

*Friday 31 December*

6pm   2°   One firework flashes – too sudden to be located – either in the west beyond the roofs or reflected in third floor windows.

During the evening a sparkle of orange flame travels, not very slowly, across the sky, above the sea. Shortly before midnight two such flames go by, one apparently quite close to the land and like a kite, the other distant and more like a star.

At midnight, the full moon is almost directly above, just visible from the window. Soft clouds pass below it, and the ceiling sky is a bright dark blue.

# SECRETS
# &
# SAVIOURS

# SECRETS
# &
# SAVIOURS

BEVERLEY ELPHICK

# Dedicated to:

Darryl Wratten, Lyn Hayward, Julie Windless,
Selina Junega and Jennifer Pulling

# Author's Note

I wish to thank my editor for her unstinting effort on the second and third books of the trilogy. Catherine Stewart believed in me, brought sense to my disorder and kept me going when I flagged. I would also like to thank Amanda Deadman who created my website www.beverleyelphick. com These two books would not have come about without their sterling work and generous encouragement.

## By the Same Author

Three Round Towers

Retribution

Details, including a list of characters at www.beverleyelphick.com

# PART ONE
# June 1801

•   C H A P T E R   1   •

*Elecampane: (Inula helenium). One of the
most beneficial roots nature affords for the help of
the consumptive. It is under Mercury.*

*Culpeper's Colour Herbal*

I am not sure I believe in God, particularly in a loving
God, but when things go wrong then I ask myself how
can I believe in a deity who seems to be working deliberately to create chaos and unhappiness in my life. I don't
know who that deity is. Some might say it is more likely
the devil and if that is so I wish he would stop meddling
and leave me be.

I am no longer alone. I have a husband: Doctor
Bartholomew Grieve. I have Beth, the child of my best
friend whose suicide triggered the chain of events that
led me to where I am today and to the troubling repercussions that have affected us all and will probably continue to do so for the rest of our lives. I have come to learn
what love is: the love of a husband who treats me as his
equal (unusual even in this new century of 1800), the
unqualified love of a child and the support of my friends
who have been with me through so much.

Nowadays I live in Lewes in the county of Sussex in an elegant house near the castle. My life is comfortable with fine furnishings, good-quality clothing and, most importantly, plentiful food, whereas many others in the town and surrounding villages go desperately short. We have a housekeeper and gardener to tend to our needs, though I consider and treat them more as dear friends. With the able help of Mr. and Mrs. Jenkins as well as Bartholomew, my midwifery practice goes from strength to strength.

As I stand at the bedroom window, I happen to glance down towards the stables and see Mr. Jenkins leading Brown Betty round to the front door. She is saddled and ready to take Bartholomew off to his meeting with John Elwood. As Beth has been staying at South Farm overnight, I could go with him and spend a happy morning with Cecilia and the children. But not today. Today I must prepare for the arrival of Enid: she comes tomorrow and we must be ready.

∞

It was just a month ago that Bartholomew and I were sitting in companionable silence around the breakfast table when Mrs. Jenkins came in to clear, carrying a black-edged package for my husband. Anxiously, I watched him open it. His long sensitive fingers broke the seal and I held my breath as his brow furrowed, his lips compressing into a thin line.

'What is it?' I asked. 'What has happened?'

I had recognised his sister's handwriting as she wrote a tight, upright script but I couldn't read any of it from where I was seated. Little did I realise that this unwelcome missive was going to upset my hitherto happy life as the wife of Dr. Bartholomew Grieve, coroner, physician and occasional chirurgeon to the townspeople of Lewes. Two happy years we had been wed. Prior to that I had endured courtroom accusations of murder; experienced malice and the violent death of my first husband; kidnap and unlawful transportation - all at the hands of my distant relatives the Coad family and my mother's sister Aunt Tilly Kempe who had been the leader of the local smuggling gang but was now in Australia, transported for life.

Dr. Grieve (I still called him that when I was trying to make a point or if I was cross with him, but at all other times he was Bartholomew or Barty) looked up from the letter before giving me the bad news, news that he knew would be unwelcome to me.

'Enid is coming to stay. Her husband has been killed in a riding accident and she wants to return to Sussex. She proposes living with us and reminds me that this is our family home, with great emphasis on "our".'

My heart sank. Enid McGovern was Bartholomew's elder sister and she had been a thorn in my side throughout the two years of our marriage.

'Oh,' was all I managed to get out in my dismay.

'She expects to be here by mid-June. She travels alone. Her daughter is staying with her husband's aunt in Edinburgh.'

I breathed a tiny sigh of relief. Enid's daughter Beatrice, wife of George Mackintosh MP, was held up to me as a paragon of womanhood who had married within her own class, who behaved as the dutiful wife of an MP should, who didn't work outside the home and who got on my nerves every time her name was mentioned.

When I accepted Bartholomew's offer of marriage, I had no idea that he had a sister. In the past I don't think she intruded much on his life as she lived in Scotland and rarely returned south. It was only when the Lewes gossips who remembered Enid from girlhood wrote to tell her of my history and that I was a most unsuitable wife for Dr. Grieve that she decided I was not good enough and did everything she could to express her disapproval by whatever means at her disposal. I had been thankful that she and her daughter lived so far away.

∽

On the day of Enid's arrival, I ran downstairs to kiss Bartholomew goodbye and was relieved to see that he seemed untroubled. He knew we were unlikely to get on but would choose to ignore any irksome tendencies that his sister might display, appreciating that I would do my best to make her welcome and try to offer words of comfort on the loss of her husband. He knew I would also overlook the spiteful words she had written to him when she had discovered the facts of my background and the events that led to our engagement. He trusted me to do my best and I was proud of that trust.

In the weeks following the arrival of the letter, I had striven to see Enid in a friendly light; and once Bartholomew had departed that morning, I went to the kitchen to confer with Mrs. Jenkins on the arrangements we had made to ensure our guest's comfort. Although the couple had been with Bartholomew for many years, they had never met Enid. We had given her a pretty room on the second floor and refurbished it to include a writing bureau and a comfortable wing back chair; I had also made some new cushions and hemmed a pretty counterpane to match the rose-coloured damask curtains. I went up with Mrs. Jenkins to check that everything was perfect. In a dainty glass vase, I had displayed some dried flowers harvested from last year's colourful garden and also placed a cake of lavender soap of my own making on the pillow. The fragrance was refreshingly delicate and I hoped she would appreciate these small tokens of friendship.

'Mr. Jenkins will be right happy that you preserved his flowers,' said Mrs. Jenkins. 'I will take them down now to show him, if that be all right with thee, Esther?'

'But, of course,' I replied. 'I love to press and dry tokens of our memories. It was such a beautiful summer and we have it still, here in our hands.'

I couldn't settle to anything after that and eventually went back to the kitchen once Beth was happily ensconced with Mr. Jenkins and our pony Flossy. 'I think I will make tomorrow's bread,' I said to Mrs. Jenkins. 'It relaxes me, and after I have thrown the dough, I hope I will feel better. Do you mind?'

'Of course not, lass. This be your kitchen and to be honest your bread is better than mine,' she laughed. 'Even Mr. Jenkins prefers yours! What time do you think she will arrive?'

'She is coming on the coach from London - the Chailey route, so I imagine by mid-afternoon, all being well. I will go and meet it. I hope Charley's pa is driving - it would be lovely to see him again.'

'Is he the coachman you came down with when you returned from your adventures?'

'I wish I could think of them like that,' I said. 'My adventures, as you put it, were the most terrifying events of my life. I nearly lost everything and everyone. I sometimes wake in the night thinking that I am on that tiny wherry again with the water slapping against it and I swear I can still feel the cold side of the transport ship with its sharp little barnacles scratching my hands as I clamber up that rope ladder. Sometimes I even dream I can smell the stench of the convicts' quarters and see Aunt Tilly's glare - she is always haunting my dreams. I try to put these things behind me, Mrs. Jenkins, but our dreams are unmanageable, aren't they?'

She reached out to me, putting her hand on mine and prising my fingers from the table edge. 'I'm sorry, Esther. I didn't mean to remind you. Come, let us check we have everything we need. Are you still wanting me to serve four courses? Mrs. McGovern might prefer something light after all that bouncing up and down in the coach.'

'Well, if it is prepared, she can eat or not as she desires but Bartholomew will be wanting a decent supper. He is doing a full day at the coroner's court and has a late visit to a patient as well.'

Talking of food reminded me of a plan I had. 'I was thinking of inviting Cecilia and John Elwood to dine next week. I know they have never met Enid and it might be pleasant to have them over. What do you think?'

'I should wait and see how she is disposed before you invite anyone. She hasn't long lost her husband, has she? She might not want to socialise yet.'

'Oh yes, of course,' I replied, but if the truth be told I had been so anxious about Enid's arrival that I had barely given a thought to her plight, other than wondering why she wanted to return to Sussex when her daughter lived in Scotland.

Bartholomew had rarely mentioned the husband and I had rather got the impression that he didn't like him which is perhaps the reason why Enid had never visited. But now he was dead - and here she comes, straight back to Lewes and talking about staying! We had discussed it over dinner a few days after the letter arrived and agreed that Enid must be made welcome for as much time as she needed, but both of us were hoping that it wouldn't be for long. We had such an easy and comfortable relationship; I didn't want to put it under stress over family loyalties. I determined not to hold on to the nasty comments she had made in the past. I wanted to start with a clean sheet and fervently hoped she would do the same. What mainly worried me was that she would be unkind to Beth whom she had called the 'by-blow of disreputable, low people'.

I shook myself and said: 'No matter, Mrs. Jenkins. Let's put to with some energetic bread-making and I will attend to my herbs while it proves.'

Also, I thought to myself, I would take the opportunity to read a bit more of my copy of Mr. Culpeper's Herbal book. Bartholomew had given it to me on our first wedding anniversary. It had come as a surprise that such a strict man of science should have acquired for me a book that was so far removed from his own beliefs. He must have gone to great effort too to track down a reprint of what was originally penned in the 1600s. He couldn't resist pointing out however that Culpeper believed in the 'nonsense' of planetary influence relating to each and every disease and its healing plant. I knew my mother and great-grandmother would always note the influence of the moon and the great planets, so I made no comment but thought to myself that their ways were so much nearer to nature than Bartholomew's science. I sometimes felt very torn between these two distinctly different practices of medicine but quietly I was more drawn to the old ways.

I was astonished to discover that this Nicholas Culpeper grew up in nearby Isfield and came to school, it's thought, in Lewes; and, most importantly for me, that his early foraging would have been local. My own herbal knowledge had been gleaned partly from my father who was an apothecary, but also from my dear mother - her own learning having been passed down from my great-grandmother who'd had the reputation of being a witch. It was fascinating for me to compare what I knew myself against Culpeper's detailed notes. My receipts were made up from readily obtainable local herbs whilst his skill extended to plants that I had never even heard of, let alone seen. By and large, I relied on my tried and tested knowledge, but it was wonderful to find that he had similarities of use in the areas where our knowledge and supplies crossed over. But what I loved most about the book, and I know Bartholomew did too, was the little caustic comments he added to many of his receipts. Mr. Culpeper clearly did not have much time for medical men; it seems that he was a radical and often extremely outspoken. Bartholomew told me that Culpeper had once asserted that there are three kinds of people who cause disease in the poor: the priests who diseased their souls; the physicians who diseased their bodies; and the lawyers who diseased matters belonging to their estate. Bartholomew seemed to find this very funny though I could not but see the truth of it myself.

When I asked Bartholomew why (aside from making free with his insults) Culpeper had become so unpopular with the physicians, he became quite thoughtful. Then he explained that it was because Culpeper was trying to help the poor to help themselves by educating them in the easily found natural medicines that could be grown in their gardens, and that this of course damaged the earning potential of apothecaries and physicians. He also wrote his books in English and sold them cheaply so they were available to all.

'The great mystery of the physicians' Latin was debunked,' said my husband. 'The College of Physicians as a body did not like it and it seems they actively sought to prevent him printing books that everyone could read and learn from. The Society of Apothecaries was also incensed by Culpeper's cheap herbal remedies as opposed to their own expensive concoctions. Eventually Culpeper took advantage of the chaos of the Civil War to finally get his books into print.'

Bartholomew looked straight at me. 'In fact, something not dissimilar is happening today, Esther,' he said, 'with the physicians who are trying to drive out the midwives because they see them earning money from each confinement that they think should be theirs. Even though I am a member myself, I have to acknowledge that there is a venal aspect to our profession that is shameful. In addition, I am aware that many physicians have little knowledge of the female reproductive system. There have been a number of notorious deaths where physicians have been directly involved. One poor woman I heard of had her entire womb pulled out instead of just the infant.'

I had heard him mention this dreadful incident before so I wasn't shocked, but I did want to defend my family against the accusation of expensive concoctions.

'My papa was an apothecary,' I protested. 'I don't think he charged great sums for the tinctures and creams that my mother and I made.'

'Perhaps not everyone is as honest as was your papa, Esther.'

I had been delighted to find reference in Culpeper to the herb elecampane, which I had found at St. Michael's Church in Lewes where we were married, but also at St. John's in Piddinghoe, both round-towered churches, as it happened. Strangely, I felt such affinity with the many churches in Lewes and nearby, despite the fact that some of the most catastrophic events in my life had occurred in a church setting. Yet I was not religious, finding that people who espoused strong religious beliefs were not always kind and frequently judgemental and quarrelsome.

As I sat leafing through Culpeper, I remembered that tomorrow morning Beth and I were going to settle ourselves at South Farm's nursery to begin teaching Freddie his letters. Beth was already reasonably sure of the ABC but not in which order the letters came, so I had made up some easy rhymes and a tune to help them both along. I decided to put Culpeper away as I could not settle: my mind kept wandering and in particular to an earlier conversation with Barty in which he had suggested that Beth should be encouraged to address Enid as 'Aunt'. I was not so sure that Enid would welcome that direct connection. Beth called Bartholomew 'Papa', and it hadn't needed an instruction; it had come about naturally and we were all content with that.

∞

Thus it was that at last I found myself sitting in wait for the coach at the Star Inn, which offered a comfortable room suitable for ladies. My friend Mrs. Makepiece accompanied me as she had known Enid from years ago; more importantly, she knew just how anxious I was. The coach was as near to time as a coach can be when travelling so far, though improved roads and design had shortened the time it now took to get from London to Lewes. I rushed out of the hotel, delighted to see Charley's pa driving the great brown and yellow coach, sitting atop resplendent in his matching livery. There was a great deal of quivering and snorting from the beautiful animals as he carefully brought them to a halt.

I stepped forward, held up my hand to shake his and expressed my pleasure at seeing him again before asking, 'Is Charley well?'

'Aye, Miss Esther, so he is, and it be right good to see thee so chipper too. Charley said to say hello if I saw you.'

At that moment Mrs. Makepiece nudged me and I remembered why we were there, so I turned towards the coach's interior and registered a disdainful look from the only woman on board. I reached over to open the door and was surprised to find a hand from inside placed over mine on the handle.

'Miss Esther, what a treat to see you again! Or should I call you Mrs. Grieve now?'

For a moment I wondered who could be addressing me in such a familiar manner and whose hand remained covering mine. Then I realised it was the entertaining travelling companion who had accompanied Mrs. Campbell and myself from London when I returned as a free woman after being transported. Sir Magnus Crisp was a barrister and was in Lewes regularly for the assizes and other local work which he undertook on behalf of 'the great and the good' - a term he often used and seemed to find amusing.

'Sir Magnus,' I exclaimed, as he sprang to the ground, 'I had no idea you would be visiting Lewes today. Are you here for the week?' Regrettably, I blushed with pleasure at seeing him again and at the same time saw that Enid had taken due note of this, disapproval etched all over her face. She gave a curious little smirk, as if I had been caught in a disreputable act and she had been the only witness.

She alighted, and I was immediately struck by how unlike Bartholomew she was; perhaps because she was entirely dressed in mourning black which made her look thin and small. I stepped towards her, taking the opportunity to introduce her formally to Sir Magnus who grinned and said, 'We dispensed with formal introductions in London, and now I know all about this visit of Doctor Grieve's sister. She has been telling me of her many connections in the town and that they are her regular correspondents.' As he turned away, he gave me a wink, and I knew that Enid had been railing against me as the unwise choice of her foolish brother, not realising that Sir Magnus Crisp and I were well acquainted. He clearly had not advised her of that fact.

She sniffed and said, 'I was not aware that you had a prior acquaintance with my brother's wife.' It was an awkward moment but Mrs. Makepiece tactfully stepped in and welcomed Enid, as I should have done myself. Belatedly, I added my voice to hers, and within minutes we women were all walking towards the house. I had arranged with Charley's pa to have the luggage left until Mr. Jenkins could collect it. There were rather a lot of trunks - clearly this was going to be an extended stay though I prayed not a permanent one.

We took tea together in the drawing room before I offered to show Enid to her room, telling her that we had given her a chamber on the second floor with lovely views over the castle bowling green and the downs beyond, at which point she said in an incredulous tone, 'The second floor? My room has always been at the end of the passage on the first floor, and that is where I intend to stay. Bartholomew should have informed you that it was always my room.'

I saw Mrs. Makepiece swallow nervously and for a brief second I felt like sinking through the floor before I recovered myself and replied steadily, 'Bartholomew thought Beth should have that room when we first came to live here and we have had it redecorated for her. We did not know that you would be returning to visit, which is of course,' I added hastily, 'a great pleasure to us all.'

'Visit?' she spluttered. 'I have returned to my family home to stay, not "visit", as I made clear to my brother when I wrote. And where might he be? Why is he not here to greet me?'

'Bartholomew is busy this afternoon, Enid. He said to tell you that he would see you at supper.'

At that moment the door opened and Beth came in. She stood in the doorway and looked anxiously at the woman she was supposed to call 'Aunt' before turning to me.

'Mama, I heard loud voices. I would like to go and pick some raspberries with Mr. Jenkins. Please? He said I could.'

With some relief, I hurried Beth out of the room while Enid composed herself; clearly, she was upset and angry. I had no idea that Beth's room had originally been hers and wished Bartholomew had told me, so that I might have been a little more diplomatic. As it was, I could hear Mrs. Makepiece's soothing tones and thanked heaven that she was with me. By the time I had delivered Beth to Mr. Jenkins and made sure that he had indeed invited her to help him, I was able to return to the drawing room fully intending to hold my ground against this disagreeable woman. But as I hurried back, I remembered her loss and how tired she must be and resolved not to react to anything she said. I flung open the door with a pleasant smile on my face and asked if anyone would like more tea. Mrs. Makepiece was looking rather strained while Enid sat working her mouth grimly. Nobody replied, so I sat down on the window seat and tried my best to make conversation that one or both could join in. I decided that I would sit there, if necessary, until Bartholomew made an appearance; however, after fifteen minutes or so of light chat between Mrs. Makepiece and myself in which she refused to engage, Enid rose and said she would find her own way to the room she had been 'allotted' and rest before supper. We both jumped to our feet, making pleasantries about her settling in comfortably, having a much-needed rest and reviving her spirits after a difficult journey, before she forcefully snapped the door shut behind her, leaving us quite astonished at the fractious atmosphere that had pervaded the drawing room.

Mrs. Makepiece was the first to say something, which she did with a giggle: 'She hasn't changed a jot, then. She was always finding fault with folk. I'm surprised she ever married at all. Her husband is probably glad to get away.'

At that, I couldn't help laughing too and I felt a great relief come over me as the tension in my neck and shoulders dropped away. 'It's a bit far-fetched to say he died deliberately to get away from her,' I said. 'I'm fairly sure he fell from his horse, unless he encouraged the animal to bolt.'

She laughed again. 'Aye, perhaps that's it. I was hoping that marriage and having a child would change her but not a bit of it. You'll have your work cut out, lass, to bring her round. One look from her would sour the milk. I wonder if her daughter is the same?'

Mrs. Jenkins came in after a light tap on the door. 'Beth has picked and eaten most of the fruit. Shall I give her a bit of tea now or will you want to keep her ready to meet Mrs. McGovern?'

'Yes, please do,' I said. 'I will be down in a moment, and we will leave formal introductions until tomorrow. Enid is very tired. I think you were right - just three courses tonight, please. Bartholomew might like some cheese after his sister has retired, though.'

Mrs. Makepiece rose from her chair, saying, 'Well, I'll be away, my dear. I hope Enid will settle down and regain her temper once she has recovered from the journey. And, if she doesn't, then let Bartholomew deal with her.' She reached out to me and I gave her a hug.

'Thank you so much for coming with me,' I said quietly. 'It would have been so difficult without you.'

## CHAPTER 2

*Violet (Viola odorata). A fine pleasing plant...*
*of a mild nature, and in no way hurtful.*
*Astrology: a plant of Venus.*

Culpeper's Colour Herbal

Enid didn't reappear until supper and I spent a while acquainting Bartholomew with her reaction to Beth now occupying what she regarded as *her* room. I didn't tell him about giggling with Mrs. Makepiece and the 'sour milk' comment. I hoped that she would be pleasanter when in the company of her brother.

When she finally appeared, she had changed from one black gown to another but with the addition of an ornate black lace collar with jet beading. I watched carefully as brother and sister greeted each other, trying to judge the depth of feeling between them. Bartholomew was, as always, extremely polite and put himself out to understand the difficulties of Enid's situation now her husband was gone. Even so, I couldn't feel any warmth between them. She complained about everything relating to her journey, including that I had been 'hobnobbing with the coachman' rather than helping her alight. He laughed at this and ventured to explain why Charley's pa was known and important to me, but she didn't want to listen.

Rather than let her carry on repeating her grievances, most of which were about how she thought she had been slighted by all and sundry on her trip south of the border, I interrupted and commented to Bartholomew that Sir Magnus had accompanied Enid to Lewes. I also suggested that we invite him to supper with Mr. and Mrs. Elwood as soon as Enid was feeling up to it. Bartholomew looked at me with gratitude and enthusiastically tried to jolly our guest into acceptance of this plan. She coldly declined, however, saying that as she was in mourning, she would be unable to contribute to any such plans for at least a year and, she implied, neither should we! Fortunately, Mrs. Jenkins came in then to announce that supper was ready. Bartholomew introduced her as his 'trusted housekeeper' but Enid simply swept by, all but ignoring her.

When she was seated at the dining table, which had been dressed beautifully, she said, 'Bartholomew, I don't know how you have lived your life up until now but I am not in the habit of encouraging familiarity with servants. Our poor dear mother would have been astonished at such laxity. It is quite unacceptable.'

At this point I was about to remonstrate but didn't need to; unfortunately, Bartholomew had already had enough. He slapped his hand down on the table and declared that while Enid was in his house, she would be expected to live by the standards he had maintained for the many years of her absence and, furthermore, that he would not tolerate any belittling of people, servants or otherwise, whilst she was a guest under his roof.

Enid pursed her lips and reddened but said no more. We sat in discomfort through our three courses with Bartholomew and I both feeling the undercurrent of seething resentment. I tried to introduce some small talk but neither of them would respond. Finally, she flung down her napkin and got up. Bartholomew did not rise as he would normally do when a lady leaves the table, and as she left the room Enid turned and said, 'Clearly you have been mixing in undesirable circles for you to have become so impolite and boorish.' Once again, the door was forcefully shut as she retired from the room.

I rose and went to Bartholomew, putting my arms around his neck and whispering words of love and comfort. He sighed and pulled me down on to his lap before saying, 'I don't know how long I can put up with her in the house. She was always insufferable, and she hasn't changed. My love, it is you who will have to bear the brunt and I am sorry for that. We have enjoyed two wonderful years of contentment and now *this*.' He shook his head in what looked like despair.

'Come, Bartholomew,' I said, 'we can deal with Enid over time. She has recently suffered a great loss and today must have been difficult for her.'

I leaned back and looked into my husband's clouded eyes before saying, 'Barty, forget Enid, I have some news that will cheer you. After our other disappointments, I have been waiting a while to tell you, but I am - I believe - pregnant. And, Bartholomew, I feel so confident this time - I have none of the feelings of insecurity or sickness that I had before. I really feel I am going to be able to carry this little one to term.'

He pulled me back into a tight hug and buried his face in my neck, saying, with his voice muffled, 'Esther, this is such wonderful news, and I couldn't ask for a better end to a difficult day. How are you feeling, can you describe the difference from what happened last time?'

'Yes, I can. On both the previous occasions, I felt wretched from the outset and whilst I know many women experience such symptoms and accept them as a normal part of pregnancy, I felt there was a fragility within me that couldn't be explained by nausea and general malaise. I remember having very bad headaches and a limpness that seemed to take me over, almost as if the life was being sucked out of me. I felt ill throughout, so that it was almost a relief when the end came.'

'But you bounced back so quickly,' he replied, 'physically, I mean, even though we were both despondent at our loss. And now? Tell me, how do you feel now, and from the beginning?'

'It is as if I am a different person. My first inkling was the tenderness in my breasts which didn't happen before, and I stopped my courses; but, even then, I didn't dare believe that this pregnancy might be different. When the second month passed with no bleeding, I felt almost euphoric - but not so euphoric that I dared tell you. I was terrified that if I mentioned it to anyone, it would all go wrong. Every morning I woke up in dread that I might see or feel blood. It has been a tumultuous time over these past few weeks, but now I am so happy to share the news with you.'

Despite Enid's presence in the house, we went to our room with happiness in our hearts and as I lay in bed listening to Bartholomew's steady breathing, I hugged myself and whispered, 'You are loved, little one. You are and will be loved.'

I was gratified that my news was of comfort to Bartholomew and that we had so much to look forward to. I wouldn't allow Enid to spoil things for us.

## CHAPTER 3

*Oh! What manner of woman ought a*
*midwife to be! With what knowledge, skill, care,*
*industry and sincerity ought she to perform her*
*office? Let every honest woman that takes this*
*charge upon her, take care of it; and when she*
*comes to deliver a woman, let her know that for*
*that day or nights work, she must another day*
*give account before Jehovah....*

*A Directory for Midwives. Nicholas Culpeper*

We were a familiar and friendly household, with just Mr. and Mrs. Jenkins as gardener and housekeeper, Wini, our maid of all work who came in for three hours a day, Bartholomew, Beth and myself. We had our own particular rituals and ways of doing things, thus it was with trepidation that I approached the next day, wondering what impact Enid was going to have on our lives. We always broke our fast with Beth in the morning as this was sometimes the only opportunity in the day when we were all together, so I was relieved when Mrs. Jenkins came in to tell us that Enid had rung the bell to say that she required breakfast in her room. I said to Bartholomew that if this was to be a regular occurrence then we must employ Wini, the maid, for longer and more convenient hours. I didn't want to change our morning pattern but we couldn't expect Mrs. Jenkins to run up and down three flights of stairs to accommodate Enid, particularly as she was getting on in years.

When I pointed this out to Bartholomew, he nodded and agreed that we should try and preserve our normal way of life. We decided not to mention my pregnancy to anyone until I was further forward, so Enid being here became a convenient excuse to employ Wini for longer hours without explaining why. I knew she would be happy to do so as she was the mother of five children and working for us brought her some much-needed income. I did, however, explain to her that it was a temporary arrangement until such time as Enid settled into the household when, God willing, she would play her part and not just expect to be waited on hand and foot. As I explained the new duties to Wini, I didn't have much faith that Enid would ever contribute to the well-running of our home but by then I hoped my pregnancy would be established and Wini could keep to the extended hours. She was a good sort and hard-working.

Fortunately, I was not particularly busy just then, so I managed to combine the roles of nursing assistant to Dr. Grieve and midwife to a few Lewes ladies who were in need but had not the money to pay a physician. I also acted as governess to Cecilia and Farmer Elwood's son Freddie. My role at South Farm was to take charge of his basic education in tandem with Beth's, leaving Cecilia with just little Felicia to care for. I loved being at the farm. Beth and I rode Flossy over most days for one reason or another, though I had told Cecilia that I would not be over for a couple of days, just until Enid had found her feet.

On that first morning, she eventually appeared near noon and I had used the extra time to tidy up Bartholomew's surgery and transcribe some of his notes - jobs that I would normally do as and when I had time, usually in the evening.

She came downstairs in her black dress, with a cloak and bonnet over her arm.

'Good morning, Enid. I trust you slept well?' I said as pleasantly as I was able as I took her outer clothes and placed them carefully on a chair. I opened the door to the drawing room and indicated that we should go inside. I stood back to give her precedence.

She said in a clipped tone: 'Yes, thank you. I would prefer to be in my own room but...'

I cut her short by saying, 'I will call Beth and you can satisfy her excitement at meeting her papa's sister. I would mention, Enid, that Beth has suffered some distressing experiences in her short life and we seek to keep a quiet and gentle environment around her, with no raised voices. But before I fetch her from Mrs. Jenkins's domain, perhaps we can discuss our household arrangements so that we are all aware of where we stand.'

She was looking blankly at me, so I carried on, determined to keep control.

'I don't like to give Mrs. Jenkins any extra duties so Bartholomew will extend the hours of our maid Wini to enable you to have breakfast upstairs and perhaps join us for a light dinner, usually at about midday as we are very early risers. We also normally have our tea or supper anywhere between five and seven o'clock - Mrs. Jenkins always knows when. If either of us is called away, as is often the case, she will advise you, and I expect that everyone is given the respect they are due.'

Still Enid said nothing but her nose had a pinched look and she didn't appear to be breathing. Undaunted, I explained that I would be absent from the house most mornings and possibly during the afternoons too, depending on my midwifery practice and Mrs. Elwood's needs at South Farm.

'And when do you find time to care for my brother?' was her waspish comment.

'Bartholomew has cared for himself for many years and together we have developed our own ways of doing things. Mr. and Mrs. Jenkins manage the house and garden and, as Bartholomew explained last night, they are an important part of our household because they enable both of us to do our work, important work. Oh, and finally, Beth is never to be left unattended.' I didn't go to the trouble of explaining why as I couldn't imagine this woman putting herself out to look after her anyway.

'Now, on a lighter subject, would you care to take a meal with us before we leave to go to South Farm?'

She inclined her head which I took as a 'yes'.

'Good. I will fetch Beth and ask Mrs. Jenkins to serve. Bartholomew won't be joining us, but tea tonight will be at half past five, subject to any emergency calls from his patients.'

I left her standing in the drawing room and went down the stairs to the kitchen where Beth was helping Mrs. Jenkins make pastry.

'Come along, my love, we are going to meet your...,' I started to say "aunt" but then found I couldn't and changed it to "Papa's sister". 'Let's wash your hands. You need to be a very good little girl, so can I rely on that?'

'Yes, Mama,' Beth replied. 'Mrs. Jenkins has told me about Papa's sister. And that I need to be quiet and behave as she is very tired and unhappy.'

I smiled. 'Come along, then, we will go and meet her upstairs. Can we have dinner now, please, Mrs. Jenkins?'

I took Beth's hand and looked at my friend; I saw her mouth the words 'good luck'. I nodded and smiled back.

Beth, for all her six years of experience, was quite an old-fashioned little girl and when she held out her hand to Enid and said in her lisping voice, 'Good morning, Papa's sister. I hope you won't be unhappy for long,' I nearly wept with pride, but hoped that she would not understand the look in Enid's eyes which was plainly disdainful. To give Enid her due, however, she did acknowledge her with a tilt of her head and a brush of the fingertips. I expected nothing more, but fervently wished it was the start of an understanding that Beth was a significant part of our household and that, if Enid intended to stay, she must acknowledge it.

We ate together with Beth chattering away as normal. If she noticed that we grown-ups were not active participants, she gave no sign but just continued to inform Enid about Freddie and how they were both learning their letters, explaining that she knew most of them but forgot which way round they came. She also went on to describe how Flossy was sometimes naughty when we were riding out, wanting to crop the grass when she should have been trotting.

As Beth continued talking, I could see Enid's face stiffening with disapproval: she probably thought that Beth should not be eating with us at all. In Enid's early years, and it was still the case in many households today, children ate in the nursery with a governess or maid in attendance, but Bartholomew and I had decided that this was not to be our way.

Enid finally broke her silence to inform me that she would be calling on her various acquaintances in the town and leaving her card. She added that she would be available to receive calls on a daily basis between the hours of eleven of the clock and half past, as was proper for 'a lady in her situation', meaning that she was in mourning.

I had no option other than to acquiesce, realising that Enid certainly intended to use our home as her own and felt she had prior claim to it.

'I will inform Mrs. Jenkins of your plans, Enid,' I said. 'You are welcome to entertain in the breakfast room which has a nice sunny aspect and looks over the garden, or in the drawing room, if you prefer. However, Bartholomew must have privacy for those of his patients who call on him here, so I would ask you to keep the doors shut to protect their privacy as well as your own. Patients do not always care to have it known that they are visiting a physician.' I looked at her intently, all the while wondering who was to dance attendance on these callers. Wini and Mrs. Jenkins were already fully occupied and I was not about to start serving casual callers myself.

She replied coldly: 'I am perfectly well aware of the position and aspect of the breakfast room, thank you. It was, after all, our mother's favourite room; she had decorated it in the latest style. Our mother was, unlike so many others, a woman of taste and decorum. However, you clearly do not know that "entertaining", as you put it, is only appropriate in a drawing room. But I can't expect that you would know that, given your... past and upbringing.'

'What a wonderful memory to have preserved for you, Enid,' I said quickly, 'that the breakfast room should be just as your mother left it. Unfortunately, Bartholomew has not had time to refresh the decoration in the house, but it is in our thoughts to refurbish soon as it has begun to look very dated. Now, we must leave you, I hope your visits are satisfactory.' With gritted teeth, I left her to her own devices.

We hurried to the stable where Mr. Jenkins was waiting with Flossy groomed and ready for our ride to South Farm. He helped me up and then lifted Beth into my arms before I settled her in front of me.

'Take thou time, ladies,' he said, causing Beth to giggle and deny that she was a "lady".

It was a pleasant afternoon with the June sun high in the sky and we were both glad to be wearing bonnets to shield our faces. Once we had got down to Southover, we were able to put Flossy to a trot and eat up the way at a good pace. Beth was humming to herself and pointing to the swallows as they swooped in joyous flight. I felt the difficulties of the last few days drop away from me. All I wanted just then was to find Cecilia, tell her all about Enid and give her my good news. Even though Bartholomew and I agreed we should keep it quiet for now, that didn't apply to Cecilia to whom I told everything.

∽

And so it went. Later in the day, as we sat in her little sitting room with the children close by and Cilla bringing drinks and tiny sweetmeats for everyone, I described Enid's arrival and the disagreeable words subsequently spoken between her and Bartholomew before telling her about the calling cards and visits.

'She is not so much in mourning that she cannot invite visitors of her own choice, then,' remarked Cecilia, sipping her tea. 'Who are her friends?'

'I have no idea,' I replied, 'but I am fairly sure they will be no friends of mine.'

'Perhaps you should be present at some of her "at homes" just to keep her in her place and, of course, to see who visits - after all, you should be aware of who is coming into your home. Get Bartholomew to pave the way, and then perhaps you could also invite Mrs. Makepiece and Miss Wardle? I would come along too, if you needed moral support. And if you really want to upset her, invite Mrs. Jenkins. No, perhaps not, that is a step too far.'

I laughed and agreed with her. 'Yes, you are right, I should do that, particularly as Beth is still so vulnerable.'

'I am sure Beth would not be at risk from any of the ladies Enid invited, Esther, but people do gossip. These visits might lend an insight into your routines - and that's what enabled the smugglers to snatch Beth before.'

'Oh, don't remind me, Cecy,' I said. 'It still makes me feel sick when I remember that day and how easily she was stolen from us.'

'How is Beth when you are alone together now? Have there been any moments when the past has come back to her and she's talked about it?'

I glanced at Beth who was busy playing with Freddie before I replied, 'She does mention Job often – or "Joe" as she calls him - and occasionally Martha, but not so much recently and I try not to let anything remind her. It helps that she has Freddie to play with her and obviously we never leave her unattended. I think that now Aunt Tilly isn't around to manipulate the Coads, they haven't got the wits between them to pull anything off. And why would they? Beth would be just a nuisance to them.'

'Revenge, Esther – it's a powerful motive. You must always be vigilant. They'll also have added the loss of Job to their list of grievances - he was another body to work the farm and without him they have to work harder themselves. More to the point, he betrayed them by taking your side and hiding Beth for all that time.'

'I wish I knew where he was. I would like to tell him how Beth is getting on and perhaps say that I could put in a word for him with Captain Campbell.'

'I expect he will get in touch when he is ready. We know he has one good friend in Lewes, the person who let you know that Job had Beth safe. Now, you said you had some other news. The children are playing happily enough, so tell me what it is?'

'I am pregnant again, Cecy, and this time, I think it will hold. I feel so much better than I did both times before.'

She leaned over and grasped my hands. 'Oh, my dear, I am so happy for you! And you won't believe this, but I think I am expecting too. We will have our babies together.'

'Oh, my goodness,' I cried out, 'that is wonderful, Cecy.'

We carried on chatting for as long as the children allowed us and by the time I left, I felt much happier. Telling Cecilia all about Enid had cheered me up and put everything in perspective. I was thrilled that we would be having our babies, all being well, with just a month between them.

As I spent so much time at South Farm, I was able to keep up with all the people who had cared for me during the difficult times, so it was with great pleasure that I found Billy-alone waiting for me in the stables before we went home. Cilla had told me he wanted to talk privately so we made for the rooms that had been Beth's and mine when we lived at South Farm.

'I wanted to catch you alone, like, Esther, as I have some news that I think you should know.'

'Oh,' I said nervously. 'Tell me?'

'There be a boy goin' round askin' 'bout thee. I ain't seen him, but Pot says he looks like the fella that spoke up for thee at the trial, that smuggler, Digger - he that got a knife in his back sometime after it were all over.'

'Like Digger?' I asked, surprised. 'Is Pot sure?'

'Aye, 'e is,' said Billy. 'Pot says he got the same long face and big teeth.'

'Did he say what he wanted me for?'

'No, but he don't reckon it were a kindly enquiry, like.'

'Did Pot tell this boy where I live?'

'No! But he probably does know, anyway, as you is so well known 'bout Lewes. I just wanted to warn you, Esther, that I don't think you should drop yer guard.

There's a whole lot of people out there who 'ave got it in for you.'

'But why now, Billy? I hoped it had all blown over with Tilly gone away - and she certainly won't be coming back.'

'Times is 'ard lately, even for smugglers. You have messed up some of their lives and they don't like it. People is always looking to blame someone for their troubles.'

'You are such a wise soul, Billy,' I said. 'I have been wondering, though, and kept forgetting to mention it, have you seen anything of the Coads recently?' I asked.

'No, they be keeping quiet since it be known that they let Tilly stay with them all that time and there still be talk about Missus Coad dying so unexpected, like. They ain't leading things, though, someone else is.'

'Who do you think is likely to fill Tilly's shoes? I can't think of anyone amongst the men I saw who would be capable.'

Billy just shrugged his shoulders as he had not experienced all the events that I had, nor known any of the people or places that were involved. I changed the subject to one that I knew would interest him.

'Did you know that poor Martha has been sent to Bedlam, Billy? Doctor Grieve says she is unlikely to be released. It's sad, but perhaps it is better than some of the other options. You know that we offered some testimony on her behalf, saying that she killed her husband in self-defence and in order to save Beth? Surprisingly, though, Martha at least has money available to pay for privileges. It turns out that Chalky White was quite well-found and the money seems to be hers now, even though she's unaware of it.'

'Na, I didn't know that. What's Bedlam, be it prison?'

'Sort of. As I understand it, it's for insane or criminally mad people but it was a hospital to start with. I don't think it is a very nice place but then neither is prison, is it? Anyway, Billy, my friend, thank you for letting me know about Digger's son - I just wonder why he is looking for me. But no more of that. How are you and Cilla getting on? Will you be tying the knot soon?'

'We will, that, as soon as Farmer Elwood finds us a place to live on the farm.'

'Wonderful, Billy. You deserve some good fortune - and don't forget you have my bed to start you off when you are furnishing.'

I had given Billy and Cilla the bed that Wilf and I were to have on our marriage. It had belonged to his parents and Wilf had carved our intertwined initials into the head-board. Wilf had died in my arms from the gunshot wounds inflicted on him by Aunt Tilly at our wedding. She had been trying to kill Beth, but Wilf threw himself in front of her and the bullet shattered his chest. He took a month to die and I had nursed him night and day until infection got the better of him and he gave up the fight. It was a time of terrible pain for all of us; something I have tried hard to put behind me.

'Aye, Cilla be really excited about making our home,' said Billy, 'so it can't come soon enuf.'

∽

Enid had been with us near a sennight and we had fallen into an uneasy pattern whereby we all simply avoided each other. Bartholomew was privately resentful of the intrusion into his comfortable life and I was uncomfortable at having to act as a go-between. Everything seemed to be out of sorts and I knew it could not last.

I had been called out on several occasions to expectant mothers, leaving Beth in Mrs. Jenkins's charge. Previously this had all worked well with some give and take around bedtimes and mealtimes, but Enid made no allowance for my work and her demands on the household were, I considered, unreasonable. She had taken to carrying a little bell around with her and whenever she wanted something, she would ring it vigorously. I knew that Mrs. Jenkins and Wini did their best to do her bidding but sometimes it was just not possible to produce refreshments or attention at a moment's notice. She seemed to think that Wini was there for her sole use: for dressing and to fetch and carry. The poor woman wasn't a lady's maid and found it stressful to have to run round after Enid when she had other duties to complete before she could go home.

One evening, I returned to the house tired and unkempt from coping with a difficult labour during which the mother, Bess, had endured agony because her baby had become stuck, prolonging her labour beyond what I would consider safe limits. I had had to carefully put my fingers inside her to protect the child's head before making a deep cut in the tender and taut tissue that would allow the baby passage into the world. Later, I would have to sew her up and then pray that no infection would get into her through this necessary intervention. I knew that cutting would cause pain and risk to the well-being of the mother, but it was either that or let her tear; and if she didn't tear because she was losing strength, the baby could die.

I usually entered the house through the back door so that I could discard my stained work clothing in a little closet where I would also change and make myself presentable, but on this occasion the back door was locked and I knocked at the front door instead. Mrs. Jenkins opened it for me and I was met with exclamations of horror from Enid who happened to be standing in the hallway, though not with any intention of opening the door to save Mrs. Jenkins the trouble. My cloak had unfortunately parted and revealed some slight staining of my working dress. I had of course taken off my apron but on this occasion the apron had not been enough to save my dress from soiling.

When I finally entered the dining room, having scrubbed myself down and changed clothing, I was given a tirade of abuse about my consorting with low people and bringing their squalor into her house. *Her* house! I was worn out and in no mood to dissemble, so we had words over the dining table. Fortunately, Bartholomew was not there. I had to bring home to her that I was now mistress of *his* house and that she should have some sympathy for women who were struggling to birth their child. I reminded her that she too had once been a new mother and must recall that the very act of giving birth was not a decorous procedure. Finally, I said that if she was unable to fit in and live by our ways, then perhaps she should consider finding her own home. My words were met with an abrupt silence and, as an ugly rust colour began to flood her neck and face, she stormed out, almost knocking over Mrs. Jenkins who was coming in at the same time carrying a tray of food for me.

I was terribly upset. I couldn't bring myself to eat so instead I went up to the bedroom before Bartholomew came home. I knew I had said some dreadful things to our guest and felt quite awful about it. I should not have let her madden me, but everything had come together at once and I hadn't held back. After a while I crept into Beth's room and sat beside her bed until my breathing returned to normal. Watching her sleep was one of the pleasures of being her mama and I had missed so many nights with her when I had been confined on the transport ship and she had been hidden away in a forest by a man who had then decided to get rid of her. Now, thankfully, all of that was over; Beth was safely back with us and I made the most of every moment. But as I sat there, I was drawn into reliving my argument with Enid and realised that everyone in the house was upset now including Mrs. Jenkins and Wini who were both just trying to do their work but being endlessly scolded because it wasn't good or quick enough. Beth was becoming nervous too because of the tensions that swirled around; she sensed that Enid didn't like her and whenever they met, she hid behind me. I simply couldn't have that. I would have to speak to Bartholomew and try to find a way that would enable us to live together in harmony, or else we would have to find another solution. In just a few short weeks the pleasure and comfort of our life had been replaced by turmoil and anxiety.

When Bartholomew got home, he came straight up to our room after Mrs. Jenkins told him that I had retired with no food, too upset to wait up for him.

'What is it?' he said, his tired eyes full of concern.

'I can't go on like this, Barty,' I said. 'You'll have to speak to Enid and make sure she actually listens and changes her behaviour. I know you have been at work all day and the last thing you want is to come home to a disagreeable atmosphere. But if we don't do something, then Mr. and Mrs. Jenkins might choose to look for an easier life while poor Wini is at the end of her tether from being treated one minute as if she were a lady's maid and the next scolded for not being quick enough with the tea things. Enid won't even stoop to putting the coal on her fire. And, worst of all, she is making Beth very unhappy.'

'You look pale. I understand you haven't eaten?' He took my hand and kissed it before wrapping me protectively in his arms. I collapsed against him and started to cry, then hated myself for being so weak.

'We had a terrible row,' I blurted out, 'and I told her that if she didn't fit in with our routines then she should find somewhere else to live. She said I was bringing disrepute on us all with my "antics" and that I shouldn't bring my work inside *her* house.'

'I see. And the Jenkinses, are they part of all this? Have they actually complained?'

'No, but Mrs. Jenkins is getting very red in the face every time Enid rings that wretched bell, and Wini is too. Enid is so rude and cantankerous that I am afraid they will leave us. Then where will we all be? No one in this house is happy anymore - it is horrible.'

'Esther, I want you to calm down. Come, get into bed now, and I will bring you something to eat and drink. No more tears. Remember, you have our baby to cherish, and all this upset is not good for either of you. You have already lost two babies and we must do everything in our power to keep you well, mentally and physically.'

I nodded and clambered meekly into bed as he left the room. He looked very glum.

A few minutes later, he returned with a glass of warm milk with cinnamon and sugar along with a little of the supper that Mrs. Jenkins had kept warm. I must have fallen asleep shortly after that (Bartholomew had probably put a few grains of sedative in the milk) because I didn't hear him come to bed later on. I didn't always sleep well - too many anxious memories from our recent history returned to haunt me by night - so it was good to wake the next morning feeling rested and calm.

Mornings were hectic at home, so it was always pleasant to break our fast together and talk over the day's plans. Beth was looking forward to having a riding lesson with Mr. Jenkins before we headed over to South Farm to take Freddie up to the nursery for their lessons and give Cecilia a bit of time on her own with Felicia.

I hadn't told Bartholomew that Cecilia might be expecting again; we women sometimes liked to hug our secrets to ourselves for a little while. I remembered that there had been some worries during her third pregnancy and, of course, the death of her first child was the dreadful event that had thrown us together at the beginning and bound us tightly as friends ever since. Cecy had worn her tragedy like a cloak ever since and I didn't think it would ever fully leave her, nor her husband John. On the occasion that I first met her, when she'd been leaning over the uncovered well in the garden, contemplating ending her life, it was as if a strong thread had stretched between us that could never break. Thereafter, we were both in mourning: Cecilia, for a precious first child, and myself, for my best friend Becca, Beth's natural mother. That day we met, in such tragic circumstances, was also the day I first encountered Bartholomew and John Elwood, and our collective lives had altered from that moment onwards. When I looked back, I felt it was fateful.

I didn't bring up the subject of last night's confrontation with Bartholomew. I was feeling well and wanted just to sit with him and Beth with no discord; however, he suggested that after breakfast we go to his surgery and talk things over. When we had finished, I cleared away some of the dirty dishes, taking them down to the kitchen before following Bartholomew to his surgery.

'There be no need for you to be doing that, Esther,' said Mrs. Jenkins. 'I can manage and you have other things to be getting on with. So, off you go now and see if you can have a good rest today. Be sure to put your feet up when you are at South Farm.'

I looked at her wondering if she had guessed that I was with child, but, if she had, she was not giving anything away.

Bartholomew's surgery was a welcoming room. The early sun warmed it and, if there was no sunshine at all, Wini would light the fire as soon as she arrived. When I first became his nursing assistant, it was chaotic in there. Bartholomew knew where everything was but nobody else could have made head nor tail of it. Now we had in place a system of filing and a system of sterilising; a cupboard for instruments already sterilised; and a more general cupboard for larger pieces of equipment. I had furnished the examination area with muted pastel curtains that matched a moveable screen for patients who required some privacy. At one time Bartholomew had been seen locally as quite the lady's man, and before he married me was considered a catch. I was aware that some of his female patients did not seek privacy at all and there were those who were a long way from being shy! In those early days, I was so far below them socially that I wasn't even noticed. In fact, I used the screen myself more than the patients did. When it wasn't in use, I put it round the skeleton that hung in the room. It was male, though most people would not know that, and where he had come from was never disclosed to me.

Fanciful patients occasionally asked me if it came to life at night as a ghost and some were most discomforted by its presence. Bartholomew was very fond of it, however, and found it useful to explain the workings of the body. I thought it fascinating, myself; it helped me a lot to fully visualise the human body, be it male or female. I understood why people could recoil from it, though; after all, it was once the internal structure of a real human being. I did ask Bartholomew once what the cause of death had been but he appeared to think it unnecessary for me to know, so I never mentioned it again.

I shut the door quietly behind me and slipped into the chair more commonly used by Bartholomew's patients before looking up at him expectantly. I could see him cogitating for a few moments before he spoke in a calm, measured voice.

'Well, Esther, after I left you last night, I went up to Enid's room. She had not yet retired so I asked her to come to my study.'

I nodded, though my heart quivered anxiously. I really didn't want to revisit my argument with Enid but I knew we had to resolve some issues, no matter how distressing they might be.

Bartholomew was standing by the window and turned with a reassuring smile before saying, 'Enid and I are far from what one would hope a brother and sister might be to each other and it is because of this that I know what to expect from her and to a degree how to manage her. Even so, I have never seen her as bitter and spiteful as this and must presume it originates from a difficult marriage and being left with absolutely no means of support, which is why your suggestion that she find somewhere else to live hit her at the point where she is most vulnerable.' He broke off for a few minutes, mustering his thoughts.

'Eventually she disclosed what was behind her worries. I gather that her husband was a gambler, and that once he had got through his own money, he helped himself to hers which of course he was fully entitled to do. She was left a substantial legacy in our mother's will, stipulating that Enid should have some of the capital as well as the investment income whereas I would receive the property. This was all well and good for her - in the early years, at least - though less so for me, as I had to make my way with a limited income but at least I had this house and two cottages in the town. Enid's household was large, with a lot of staff, and she enjoyed the social position she had acquired through marriage, never anticipating it to diminish so ignominiously.

'So, Esther, the crux of the matter is that she has no money and nowhere else to go. Her daughter Beatrice is married to an MP who would not tolerate his mother-in-law living with them because of her difficult nature and the bad feeling between them. I know this because I occasionally communicate with my niece - though my sister does not know about that, so discretion is necessary.

'Our interview last night was forthright and I have told Enid that she must change her ways and manner. As you will imagine, she was extremely voluble with her opinions and I found it necessary to threaten that she would be asked to leave should she upset either you or Beth again - or me, for that matter. I have further stipulated that she is not to expect everyone to wait upon her and that she must play a full part in the household. I gather that the last few years of her marriage were in straitened circumstances, with only a cook and a yard man, so having to work in her own home is not unknown to her. She seems to have thought that she could return here to live the life she was used to as a young girl. She now understands this is not the case. It is not going to turn her into an amenable woman - she will never be that - but I trust her spite will be reduced as a consequence of our forthright discussion, and she knows what will happen if she lets me down.'

He took my hands in his. 'None of this is your fault, Esther. Enid inherited my mother's propensity to control: she too would turn spiteful if thwarted, so whoever I married would have received the same treatment. The fact that you and I had a colourful history together prior to our engagement and that you were thought notorious by some elements of Lewes society, all only added, I am afraid, grist to the mill.'

'Oh Bartholomew,' I said, 'what a horrible situation for her. I must have caused her so much distress by telling her to leave.'

'There you go again, Esther, always putting the best construction on people's behaviour. I would warn you not to give an inch in your dealings with Enid. She would take your kind heart and shred it to pieces if she could. If, by means of the threat I have laid down, she turns into a half-way decent person, then I will consider that I have really achieved something. And, you never know, she might even find some widower who will take her on – though, somehow, I don't think so. I am afraid she must remain with us whilst she keeps to the bargain. If she doesn't, then I will have to provide for her elsewhere.'

I nodded. 'How will we bring this new Enid into our way of life, then? Will she go to the kitchen and prepare a pot of tea if she wants one? Will she put her own coal on the fire? Will she help clear the table rather than summoning Mrs. Jenkins with her horrid bell?'

'Yes, to all of that. As I explained, she is more than capable of doing those things and perhaps her main difficulty will be in curbing her tongue, but now she knows the terms. I do not want you to pander to her at all. If you do, you will make a rod for our backs, Esther. It is better for us all to set out as we mean to go on, and that includes you. I have already spoken to Mrs. Jenkins. Now then, I have a patient due shortly, so off with you. I hope Beth enjoys her lesson, and we will all have dinner together later today.' He smiled gently as he dismissed me.

As I left Bartholomew, I noticed Enid's bell sitting on top of his bookcase. I smiled, wondering how on earth he had got it off her.

## CHAPTER 4

*Martha Ballard was a midwife - and more.*
*Between August 3 and 24 1787, she performed*
*four deliveries, answered one obstetrical false*
*alarm, made sixteen medical calls, prepared*
*three bodies for burial, dispensed pills to one*
*neighbour, harvested and prepared herbs for*
*another. A Midwife's Tale: The life of Martha*
*Ballard based on her Diary 1785-1812*

*by Laurel Thatcher Ulrich (USA)*

Bartholomew examined me and we both worked out that
I was approximately twelve weeks pregnant and in excellent health. There had been little or no sickness and apart
from some indigestion I had experienced no maladies.
When I eventually told my friends about the pregnancy,
they were so happy for us. Mrs. Makepiece and Mrs. Jenkins knew about the two earlier miscarriages so they understood well just how much I wanted this baby.

Beth, who was my legal responsibility (not by formal adoption but at the direction of the judge who had
found me not guilty when under the malicious charge of
the murder of her mother) was just one day old when I

first met Mrs. Makepiece. She had come to my aid when I was struggling to find somewhere to spend the night and feed the baby with all that I had on me - just some goat's milk. Earlier on that horrific day, I had found my friend Becca with her beautiful long golden hair matted and dulled by the muddy river water covering her face as her body drifted between the reeds and on the tide. I knew she had given birth all alone in old Hamsey Church but I'd had to search high and low before I could find the baby. Becca had made a tiny cradle out of waxed rushes and her intention had clearly been to let it drift with the baby down to Lewes, and for the little one to be claimed eventually, she must have hoped, by a childless couple. This was her last deliberate act, other than to lay herself down in the river because she knew there would be no place anywhere for her and a baby. She knew she would be violated again and again if she returned to Coad Farm where we both worked: if not by Farmer Coad himself, then by his sons.

The last year of Becca's short life was so distressing, it was no surprise that she should begin to lose her mind. When she went missing, I had to put myself into her thoughts to find and protect the child, then get as far away from Coad Farm as I could. I had waded and searched through the reed beds near the church until at last I heard a faint cry that could have been a seagull mewling high in the sky, but I knew better. The fragile cradle was lodged against a clump of rushes. It was still dry inside and, wrapped in a piece of flannel, I saw the tiny child lying unharmed if a little cold; but that was soon remedied by my shawl as I tied her to my chest, feeling an instant bond of overwhelming love for the little scrap.

I had returned to the farm, avoiding the missus, to look for the disgusting man who had fathered the child. After threatening Farmer Coad with the law, I forced him to drive me to Lewes where I hoped to find shelter for us both. The first thing I did was to find Becca's pa and tell him the sorry tale. He couldn't take us in because his new wife hated Becca and would have no truck with an illegitimate baby of hers. He gave me some directions, though, and by evening I found Keere Street where he told me I must ask for a Mrs. Makepiece who might take us in as lodgers if she was so inclined. I bless the day that we met and have counted this middle-aged woman as one of my dearest friends ever since. Without her, neither of us would have survived all the troubles we have seen.

∽

Bartholomew chose to inform Enid about our good news, with a firm comment about my need to rest as much as possible. He didn't have to tell her that he would hold her responsible if I was made unhappy; she already knew it.

Truthfully, she tried to fit in with us and I was thankful for that; but I knew I could never be a friend to her because that would have needed a complete transformation of her character, which was, plainly speaking, arrogant and nasty. She didn't talk to anyone much. I think she retained her angry thoughts but didn't dare articulate them for fear of drawing down Bartholomew's ire and threats upon her. When she first arrived, Enid had left calling cards at the homes of her acquaintances and for a while her calls were returned, though I couldn't help but suspect that this was more from a desire to see how I behaved as Bartholomew's wife. Despite Cecilia's good advice on the matter, when I knew someone was likely to visit, I chose to simply stay out of the way and keep Beth close by me. Over time, these acquaintances fell by the wayside and Enid was left with only us, her immediate family. Occasionally she received a letter from her daughter which she would wave under our noses, reading out any parts that showed her daughter to be a woman of substance, style and manners.

∞

I reckoned our baby would be born in January - Cecilia's about a month later – and, as my pregnancy would soon show, I told Beth all about it. I drew some pictures of how he or she would look inside me. She knew of course that I was a midwife and that I helped other ladies give birth but, in her mind, having a baby brother or sister was completely different and quite unrelated to what happened when I went out to work. I didn't mention that Cecilia was also looking forward to another little one. With her pregnancy behind mine, she needed time to explain it all first to Freddie and Felicia but Beth was so excited by my news that she could hardly contain herself.

'Will you stop going out now, Mama?'

'I should hope so,' said Enid, sniffing loudly.

'No, poppet,' I replied. 'Expecting a baby is not like being ill. I will be going out for as long as I am comfortable. My tummy will get very big and that might slow me down a bit, but lots of women keep going as usual until they are ready to have their baby.'

'Will you look like Cecilia did, just before Felicia came?'

'I hope so,' I replied, 'because she looked very well, didn't she?'

'Have you no shame,' Enid interjected coldly, 'to be discussing such matters with a child? And surely Cecilia Elwood should be called Mrs. Elwood by a young person? She is the daughter of an earl, after all. Where is the propriety? It is disgraceful the way this child is treated like an adult. If it were my child, she would be seen and not heard!'

'Fortunately, she is not your child, Enid,' came Bartholomew's voice, 'and I would remind you to keep a civil tongue in your head.' He had arrived home unheard by us and was standing by the door.

He continued as he walked into the room: 'We do not need to justify our reasons for talking to Beth as we do, Enid. But just this once I will explain that Beth and our new baby will be brought up with science as the basis of their understanding, with none of the balderdash that most women employ, like storks and babies found under a bush. It is quite absurd.'

I smiled at Bartholomew, thankful that he had been listening. Often Enid would make some of her sour remarks when she knew he was out, probably taking it for granted that I would not tittle-tattle to him in the interests of peace.

'Esther,' said Bartholomew, turning to me, 'would you and Beth care to join me for a ride out to South Farm? I have some thoughts to mull over with John Elwood and I am sure you would like to see how Cecilia is. We can take the gig.'

I felt a little sorry for Enid that Bartholomew had begun to shut her out of our family events; but she had brought it all on herself and as he had told me "not to give her an inch", I didn't. I had noticed that he was wanting to be away from home quite regularly and I supposed it was because Enid was always there, sniffing, tutting and looking down her very long nose at us. It was all very sad.

∞

We saw July out with a tremendous thunderstorm, and I was relieved not to be outside, but later that day the oppressive clouds lifted and the sun shone brilliantly, with sparkling raindrops resting on leaves like tiny tears of glass. I was happy the weather had cleared as Beth had progressed with her riding and Mr. Jenkins thought she would benefit from having extra lessons with the head stable lad at South Farm. Today was to be her first formal lesson and she was very excited. After our earlier troubles, when she had been snatched from that very yard, I knew she was no longer in any danger there as large gates had been fitted to the entrance and the yard itself surrounded by a high brick wall. Mr. Jenkins would take her in the gig and then wait for her - he would doubtless be looking forward to a chinwag with the stable lads.

I put my bonnet on and made my way towards Keere Street for a chat with my friend Mrs. Makepiece, taking the back lane to avoid catching the dust from all the carriages charging up and down the High Street at great speed. But as I went through the twitten, I was accosted by a surly-looking lad who planted himself in front of me. I stopped, wondering if I should quickly turn back in the hopes that he wouldn't follow. It was just a few steps to Castle Ditch Lane and the safety of other people, but I knew my limpy leg would not allow me to turn and run fast enough.

'What do you want?' I asked, my voice unnaturally high-pitched.

He spoke softly and I had difficulty understanding what he was saying. Repeating himself, he said louder: 'I been waiting for you. I been waiting till you be all alone.'

'Why? I have no money. What is it you want?' I could feel my heart pounding as I tried to keep my voice even.

'I wanted to see why my pa chose you over my mother.'

'I don't understand what you mean. Who is your mother?'

'My pa walked away from all of we and gave evidence for you at the Justice's hearing. Why did 'e do that? He must 'ave known they would turn on him.'

The realisation of who he was came to me.

'You're Digger's son?'

'Aye, an' because of you, we lost our pa and there were none other to give us money, like.'

'I didn't know Digger was going to give evidence against Tilly. But I was told afterwards that he was paid for his information, a goodly amount of money, too.'

'Aye, he were paid all right, but not a goodly sum,' he said bitterly. 'It were but a pittance so as to get your aunt convicted. She were sentenced to prison on his say-so.' He spat at my feet and I hurriedly stepped back, knowing that this young man could easily overpower me. 'The money didn't last long, an' me ma took to the grog.'

'I spent some time with your pa, and I liked him. He looked fierce, but he was a gentle man underneath. He told me that he wasn't involved in the smugglers' violence, that he was just a lookout. When my cousin imprisoned me in the barn, your pa was placed there as a guard. He said he would never hurt me and I believed him. It wasn't his evidence that got Tilly convicted, it was mostly mine.'

'Me ma reckons you bewitched him. He were never the same after 'e met you. She can't understand it 'cause you ain't pretty, with the pox on yer face and you being crippled, an' all. She remembers hear tell yer great-grandma were a witch, though, and so must you be, she says.'

'I am sorry.' What more could I say? Then I asked, 'Tell me your name?'

'Youse don't need to know my name.'

'Well, Digger's son, what do you want from me, then?' I said, as firmly as I could manage.

'I want you punished. I want youse to suffer like me ma do, with no money and no one 'cept me to look out for her.'

I leaned against the flint wall for support as my leg was beginning to ache. 'Does your ma have other children to raise?'

'Aye, there be seven of us and a new one coming on account of she needed some money. Some men will pay her, like. You turned me ma into a moll - it were that or the workhouse for all of we.' He had started to shout and was going red in the face.

I wished someone would come and my voice wobbled as I made myself keep him talking. 'Look, Digger's son,' I said, 'I didn't even know that he was going to give evidence. Neither did I know he was paid to do so until much later. I was deeply upset when I heard he had been murdered, but it was the smugglers who killed him, not me. I am more than sorry, but I don't know what I can do to help you or your family.'

He took a step towards me, lowering his voice menacingly: 'I thought I'd kill you, or that brat that everyone has to look out for. You deserve to be dead for what you done.'

'Then kill me. Go on, it won't be difficult, I am much smaller than you. But don't you think of hurting Beth - she is just a little one and knows nothing about all this.'

We both stood looking at each other and then I thought I heard footsteps. I turned at the sounds behind me as an elderly man came into the twitten.

When I looked back, the boy had disappeared. We were in a long, narrow twitten and I hadn't heard him run, yet he seemed to have completely vanished.

'Can I help, Ma'am?' said the gentleman, raising his hat to me and smiling. 'Are you unwell?'

One minute I was expecting to die and the next there I was sharing a pleasantry with a stranger, a very welcome stranger. I took a deep breath and tried to respond evenly. 'Thank you. I am perfectly well, just a little short of puff. I thought to lean here for a moment.'

'If I may say, you look a little pale. It's Mrs. Grieve, isn't it? Can I see you home?' He crooked his elbow for me and I took his arm gratefully to retrace my steps.

I let myself into the garden, thanking my rescuer for his assistance, but not telling him what had happened. I let him think that I was just a little tired and that was also what I told everyone else when they wondered why I had returned so abruptly. I went up to our room and sat by the window trying to make sense of what had occurred and what I should do about it.

My head throbbed and it was a struggle to calm myself. It chilled me to think of yet another family suffering the effects of one man's wicked desires that all in all had brought about both Beth's birth and Becca's death; Aunt Tilly's comeuppance as leader of the smuggling gang; and the killings of my cousins and other smugglers when the law took its violent revenge. I remembered the agonies I suffered when Wilf was shot, taking the bullet intended for Beth; then, when Beth was kidnapped; and later when I myself was captured and wrongfully incarcerated on a transport ship. I thought of Chalky White, murdered by his own wife Martha as she tried to protect Beth from him, and she now in Bedlam: on and on it went. So many lives affected, so much violence and it was still not over.

This boy, the son of Digger, was part of the next generation to learn how to hate and to pursue the fight to destroy both Beth and me. How many more of them could be out there, lying in wait for us? Billy-alone had warned me that the past chain of events had left families short of money. The authorities were everywhere, fearful of being invaded by France, even though there was supposed to be a truce in place. French privateers were stalking the Channel, ready to pick off any British boat they could board, thus the number of runs that the smugglers could do was reduced. So much hardship and desperation everywhere you looked. As I sat there in my lovely bedroom, I felt a cold stab of fear for all our futures. My baby's life - would it be blighted by my past? Could I continue to protect Beth as she grew up?

Eventually I calmed myself and managed to carry on as before. Luckily, I continued in good health, and subsequently made sure that I was never alone when I went out, which was difficult as my expectant mothers did not always go into labour when it was convenient. I encouraged my friend Eliza to gradually take on more duties. Once I had explained that I was pregnant, she had willingly taken over whenever I asked her to, and fortunately I was now able to pay her something. She lived in Castle Ditch, having moved from the slums of Cliffe. Her new home was much nicer, with a little garden. It was not so crowded as her former home and, most importantly in my eyes, it was scrupulously clean, as she was herself. Eliza was fortunate that her mother lived in Lewes; it was her suggestion that Eliza and the family should move in with her, as Lewes itself was a lot more wholesome than Cliffe and there would be more room for the family.

When I needed to stay at home, Mr. Jenkins took her a message and a bag with all the carefully wrapped, sterilised instruments that she might need. Her mother looked after her little boy and I paid Eliza from my small earnings. Occasionally we would work together so that she could learn from me, or if it was a difficult birth when two heads were often better than one and the strength of two attendants necessary.

Eliza could neither read nor write but her common sense and good memory were invaluable to me and our mothers-to-be. Bartholomew did all he could to help her learn more through me, as he reasoned that it would help me as well as the women we sought to assist, but he never came with us, always preserving his dignity.

## CHAPTER 5

*The enlightening Full Moon is the visible
climax of the moon cycle with Lady Luna fully
lit in all her glory, banishing darkness while
feminine energy is active in the world. Tides
are at highest and lowest while plants are vital
and juicy. We feel intense emotions, reveal
secrets and see clearly into inner shadows. Full
moon urges us to allow some giddy madness to
prevail, to celebrate fulfilment and confidence
in honouring our truth.*

Yvonne McDermott of Forest Moons

Bartholomew and I were awoken in the middle of the
night by someone simultaneously thumping on the front
door and clanging the bell. Initially I was terrified by the
jolt from deep sleep at such a clamour, but was reassured
when Bartholomew, having risen calmly to look out of
the window, described a young soldier standing below.
We hastened down and found the young man to be very
wet and bedraggled as he asked Bartholomew to urgently
follow him to Newhaven where there was a terrible acci-

dent in the making that involved a number of ships and the likelihood of many injured and dead.

I dressed quickly and slipped over to where the Jenkinses had their rooms, waking them as gently as I could. Mrs. Jenkins looked a bit bewildered by this intrusion but quickly said, 'Aye, lass, you get off as soon as Mr. Jenkins has saddled up for thee. We will look after Beth and all else.' Relieved, I returned to Bartholomew who was in the course of hasty preparations.

'Esther, there is no need for you to come. I don't want you risking yourself, especially as we do not know what to expect,' he said as he fetched thick outer clothing and his medical bag.

'Nonsense, I can help you with lesser injuries and can carry supplies - you will need more than you can take in your usual bag,' I replied firmly, as I fastened myself into my heavy blue cloak and deep bonnet. It had been raining hard earlier on and there was a blustery wind which fortunately seemed to be subsiding, but you never knew what it would be like down on the coast.

Bartholomew mumbled something about there being no time to argue and we set off with me riding astride Flossy along with a roll of instruments, bandages, wadding and of course a selection of my healing herbs, all tied securely to my saddle. We each carried two leathern flasks of fresh water from our well. Flossy was sure-footed and as I was riding single file between the soldier and Bartholomew, I didn't feel at risk. Fortunately, there was a brilliant silvery moon which cast strong light but also deep shadows; the wind, however, was chasing scrappy, ragged clouds which frequently plunged us into velvety darkness before moments later lighting the way as if it were daylight. I took care to guide Flossy carefully in the steps of the young man who I noticed carried a gun as well as his sword: it was tucked inside his uniform to keep it dry but ready for action. The light from the nearly full moon was a boon; without it we would have found our journey longer and far more difficult. The track to Newhaven was reasonably drained and clearly illuminated by the white chalk of the Downs.

Between the noisy squalls of wind, and when the track was wide enough for us all to ride alongside, Bartholomew questioned the soldier who explained, at some length, that he was part of a platoon from Seaford Barracks on routine patrol along the coast from Seaford to Newhaven. It was an arrangement agreed between the military and the excise officers who were stretched thin in dealing with repeated landings by smugglers in the area.

One of the soldiers had seen five French privateers chasing four British merchantmen travelling in convoy towards Seaford. Our soldier, who told us his name was

Spinks, said that our ships were being driven dangerously close to the shore by the privateers and, combined with the turbulent weather, it was clear that a disaster was looming. At this, we urged the horses on to greater speed, hoping against hope that we would be in time to prevent loss of life.

Eventually we found our way to the foreshore where there was a lot of scrub, grass and a few stunted bushes and trees; below, they gave way gradually to sand and shingle. We came across a most shocking sight: four ships, jumbled all together on the steeply shelving beach where they had finally collided. The masts, rigging and timbers were all being relentlessly pummelled and broken up by momentous waves. There were men clambering all over the stricken vessels, but they were clearly not there to lend help to the poor sailors who had been thrown into the boiling sea or onto the brutally hard, cold shingle. No, they were stealing the cargo and piling it up near a stand of horses further along the beach.

'Smugglers,' declared Bartholomew, coming up alongside me. 'They never miss an opportunity to turn a catastrophe to their own advantage, regardless that it is their own countrymen under attack by enemy privateers. Cowards and blackguards,' he added in disgust.

Spinks was white-faced as he turned to Bartholomew saying that his comrades must have been driven off because a small platoon of men had been there on the beach when he left. His commanding officer had instructed him to ride hard for Lewes to summon the surgeon/coroner as there would almost certainly be lives lost and many casualties. Using his own initiative, Spinks had also tried to knock up some of the larger dwellings in the village of Newhaven to request help but no one would open their doors to him. Another soldier was despatched to Seaford with the request for more medical assistance and more dragoons from the Barracks.

I was looking as far out to sea as the moon and wind allowed and saw five more ships pitching and tossing on the waves. They were not far out but well beyond the danger of the breaking waves. I pointed them out to Bartholomew and the young man.

'Aye,' said Spinks, 'they be the foreigners. They look like they are trying to make a run for it now, but I can't tell if the tide be against them - I am a landlubber myself. I don't know where me mates could be,' he muttered, looking distracted. 'There were ten of us down here when we saw the privateers attempt to corral and board the merchantmen. The British boats were trying to get away but they were being driven towards the edges of the surf - and that was when I left to fetch help.'

The smugglers hadn't noticed us, so busy were they scavenging for booty that they could use or sell on. They worked hurriedly, with some men searching and others loading spoils onto the horses. We edged quietly back into the shadows and Bartholomew told me to stay there on Flossy while he and Spinks dismounted, hoping to find the missing soldiers without being seen.

I nodded. 'Be careful,' I whispered, sensing rather than seeing the disquiet in Bartholomew's face as he melted into the darkness with young Spinks. When they had gone, I slipped off Flossy and took the reins of the other two horses, gently fondling their muzzles to keep them steady and from giving us away with any sounds. There were some stunted trees nearby and I carefully led the three of them into a clearing within the cover, loosely hitching their reins to some wizened branches, before creeping back to where I could look out but not be noticed by anyone on the beach.

I waited, wrapped tight in my dark cloak, confident that no one could see me as I had pulled my bonnet down over my face. The enemy ships were in retreat: they at least would see their families again.

A little while later, Bartholomew returned and whispered that they had found the captain and the soldiers of the platoon tied up further along the beach. They had been stripped of their uniforms and looked a sorry lot, with their weapons and clothing all missing. Bartholomew had decided not to try and release them yet in case they were set upon by the armed men. 'I have no knife big enough to saw through their bondage,' he said. 'They are safer as they are, if freezing cold.'

'What are we to do?' I returned, hoping that his decision was the right one.

'We can't do anything. The smugglers have all the advantage, and even if the other soldier returns with more dragoons from Seaford, they will have to be numbering at least twenty fully-armed men to overcome this lot.'

'But what about the sailors down there in the surf? I can see at least three from here - one of them was crawling further up the pebbles until he got kicked back. Are we just to wait here, then, until the smugglers leave?' I heard a note of desperation in my voice as I pictured the cold, wounded men with their lives ebbing away under the onslaught of waves, wind and, perhaps, a still rising tide, though it was difficult to tell with the beach covered in froth as far as I could see. Balls of foam were rolling all around at the wind's behest, as if they were playing a bizarre game.

'It is not far off dawn,' murmured Bartholomew. 'They will be leaving shortly, no doubt hoping that their crimes will go unnoticed. The privateers will get the blame for all of it and the smugglers won't leave anyone on the boats alive to tell the tale. They will probably push those sailors in the surf back into the sea to drown.'

'Then surely we must try to frighten them off before they kill whoever is still alive? And what about all the soldiers, will they drown them as well before they leave?'

Bartholomew looked undecided and more than a little desperate before nodding and saying, 'Of course, you're right, Esther, we have to create a diversion.'

He thought hard for a moment.

'Right. Esther, I want you to go back to the horses and stay under cover while I strike a flint and set fire to those bushes back there.' He was pointing to a scrub thicket that was far enough away from our horses. 'The smugglers might not understand what it means but it will cause alarm. They will want to be away as quickly as possible once they realise that they've been seen. Hopefully, they won't have time to focus on either the sailors or the soldiers - I don't want even *one* of them on my conscience. I will come and find you as soon as they have given up and can't find me!'

'Where's Spinks?' I asked. 'If he does the same at a distance along the beach, then that might truly panic them to leave. Have you got a spare tinder? I could do the same.'

'No, alas. But I will go and explain to Spinks and then we can set our fires simultaneously. As soon as you see them leave - and we don't know which way they will go but, if it's away from your hiding place - then you can get to the injured men when you are sure the smugglers won't turn back. Promise me you won't come out of hiding until they have really gone? It will only be a few minutes to wait and that will not make any difference to the men on the shore.'

I nodded. 'I promise. But be quick, it chills my blood to think of those poor men - they must be frozen to the marrow.'

He vanished into the night and left me anxiously watching for the fires to take so that I could get to the men lying near the surf, and praying that the tide was on the turn. I looked to the horizon to see if dawn was coming and thought I could see a thin ribbon of greenish light. Surely the smugglers should be hastening away now, before anyone was up and about? I muttered under my breath, 'Hurry, hurry, please hurry!' At last, there came a spark and then flames which took but a few seconds to climb up through the scrub. I turned to see if Spinks had managed to get a fire going too and breathed a sigh of relief when I espied a similar tiny splutter of orange farther away which soon blazed. I thanked heavens the vegetation was dry; it was still August, after all. The vengeful sea would not have reached as far up the beach as the greenery but there might have been damp from the night's rain that could have held back the flames.

The smugglers had spotted the fires, now well alight, and were running for their mounts, dropping all the remaining goods. Within minutes their horses were picking their way towards hard patches of sand, avoiding the pebbles. Once they were on firm ground, I realised that some would be heading towards my hiding place and that I might not be able to escape. I flung myself down into the undergrowth with my dark cloak wrapped tightly around me and prayed they would not stop to see who was watching them. I held my breath as I peeked through the spiky vegetation. They passed, but one of the men happened to look into the clearing: I saw him take in the horses and then move to dismount. I was behind Flossy and almost buried in the scrub, but just as I feared I was discovered, I heard Bartholomew and Spinks shouting, echoed after a pause by more shouts coming from the captured soldiers. Between them all, they were trying to set up a further distraction, and thankfully they succeeded, for the smugglers abruptly kicked their horses into a quick escape.

Within minutes we were alone, with only the raging of the monstrous sea to be heard. I rolled over and extricated myself from the burrs and prickles of the undergrowth before heading down the beach, trotting as fast as my limpy leg would allow towards the injured men.

We searched the shoreline and found eleven men in all, one a very young boy. For a horrible moment I thought he might be Job Coad - but he wasn't, and I felt deeply grateful for that, at least. Then we released the soldiers. They had told us where their clothing and weapons had been dumped, so after we cut their bindings with a sword from the pile of weapons, they were able to retrieve them and join us as soon as they could, still shivering from the cold, to help revive any of the stranded sailors. We were able to assist five but the rest were dead, mostly from drowning. It was left to the platoon captain to order a round-up of their scattered horses and then send out a search for the soldier who had been despatched to get more help from Seaford barracks but had not returned.

We picked up the injured and laid them gently well back from the shoreline as Captain Carruthers and his men set about building a bonfire from dry materials they salvaged. Bartholomew was optimistic that the five would survive once we had warmed them through. There were broken bones, grazes and cuts, some very deep, as well as extensive bruising. As we revived them, they began spluttering and vomiting from all the salt water they had swallowed. Bartholomew and I did as much as we could to patch up their wounds but we needed to get them back to Lewes to sew them up and splint the broken bones. The young boy was one of the dead. I wept for them all but for him in particular - his pale face was so calm and unlived-in. Apart from a great gash on his hairline, he looked as if he were simply sleeping; I couldn't begin to imagine the terror they must all have suffered. I felt for the lad's mother who would surely grieve for the loss of her beautiful boy. Perhaps I would write to offer some comfort that her son had died with peace reflected in his face.

Gradually the dawn crept up on us, tinting the sky with soft pinks and gold while the wind was ceasing its clamour as a rising sun chased it away. Spinks returned to us with the sorry news that he had found the missing soldier just beyond Tide Mills, sprawled on the ground with his throat slit, cut down before he had been able to get to the barracks. The poor lad had delivered the request for more men but was greatly distressed, white as a sheet and shivering pitifully. I tried to comfort him, but the captain told me that he didn't need soft words but activity, and then brusquely ordered him into Newhaven to find a horse and cart to take the injured to safety. The captain himself had the task of tracking down the local controller of shipping to turn this dreadful incident into something manageable and to find someone to take charge of the dead bodies, including those that might be washed up later. Bartholomew also gave Spinks directions to a physician's house between Newhaven and Southease where the injured might get more immediate help. Spinks replied that he had called there last night before coming on to us in Lewes and that the residents had not responded to his knocking. Hearing this, the captain shouted at him, saying that he should tell the inhabitants that they *must* open up in the name of the law.

'Put some force into it, man,' he bellowed.

Poor Spinks nodded and ran to his horse before making off as fast as he could, clearly charged with new resolve. I thought that the captain had been a bit harsh on him - he was just a young lad, after all - but perhaps that was how young soldiers were taught to become hardened to ugly sights and difficult situations. I wouldn't want a child of mine to enter the army or navy; the military world was such a brutal environment.

Bartholomew commented that the small population of Newhaven might well be too frightened to open their doors in the dead of night.

'This area,' he said, 'is rife with wrong-doers and smugglers. Many prefer to turn a blind eye.'

In fact, it was more than possible that the men appointed by the Excise Office were themselves agents of corruption, working hand in glove with the smugglers. The reputation of the revenue services had been tarnished by those officials who took bribes to look the other way, or, as in this instance, not to open their doors to help out in a crisis. At the same time ordinary citizens feared being seen to help a deeply unpopular government agency, with the lawless ever ready to take revenge on any neighbours who didn't toe the line.

I recalled coming down here to help rescue Billy-alone from the soldiers who wanted to put him on a ship to go and fight the French. I had been hiding in wait in a warehouse when a large band of smugglers rode into the area to rescue some of their own men. Billy got away by his own quick thinking, as did many others when it was a case of soldiers in a straight fight with the smugglers. The smugglers always won.

We eventually got away, leaving the captain and his men in charge of everything: organising the dead and injured alongside the search for the savage men who had capitalised on this tragic outcome of war and ferocious weather combined. The captain had a lot to do, including directing the extra help from the barracks to search the tideline in expectation of finding more bodies and then, in the safety of daylight, to round up the people to sort out the legal repercussions from such a disaster. There was also the question of what would happen to the remains of the ships and their cargoes. As we left, we saw Spinks returning with a flat-bed cart and a disgruntled-looking carter. The young soldier's musket was drawn. I waved and was gratified to see him smile, already looking more capable. I suppose that is what brandishing a weapon does for you.

It was still early morning but we were exhausted by then and anxious to get back home. Bartholomew, as the nearest coroner, would have a great deal to do but for now it was food and rest that were required. With the arrival of the cart, the captain could now arrange delivery of the injured men to us. They were bandaged and splinted temporarily, and we would make appropriate arrangements for their reception and lodging when we got back to Lewes. We rode home in silence, unable to take any further responsibility for the time being. There would be a reckoning in the days and weeks to come but for now we just needed to recover from our exertions.

∞

I slept for hours, exhausted and aching. When I finally woke, I lay for some time going back over everything that had happened last night. Should I have stayed at home? With hindsight I knew I really should have. There wasn't just me to look out for anymore: there was Beth and the new baby on its way. I had to be more responsible from now on, and in all things. Billy had warned me that wherever I went, the people who would do me down were watching and waiting, knowing that their time would come. I had taken too many risks in the past - including last night - though I could not but feel that I had played my part in coming to the aid of the injured. But no more. I kept seeing the boy-sailor's face and wondered how I would find his mother to tell her that he had acquitted himself well and died bravely.

Poor Bartholomew was already up and endeavouring to treat the wounded, a greater number than he expected as some of the soldiers had also been roughly used, and it seemed that the Newhaven physician had not turned out after all to lend any help. It also fell to Bartholomew as coroner to ascertain the cause of injury and death: the shipwreck or the smugglers. Eventually, he came to the conclusion that the men had died primarily because their boats had been forced into a ship-wrecking collision. Some had drowned after being knocked unconscious and fallen into the sea; some had died as a result of wreckage falling on them; others had simply disappeared into the raging waters. The survivors described how the vessels had been driven too hard by the privateers and that in the end the wind and sea had swirled them together into an almighty pile-up. It was a calamity and nothing anyone could have done would have improved the outcome. The privateers were to blame along with weather conditions that were almost unheard-of during August.

The cargo not taken by the smugglers was to be auctioned off as damaged but useable. One of the ships, the *Margherita*, had been carrying timber, which would find a ready local market and serve to defray the losses the owners suffered. The smugglers had taken items that were easily carried and saleable, particularly bacon and household goods but, in the end, no one had really benefited from this tragic incident.

The injured men were billeted in the town until they were fully recovered and were shown great kindness by the townspeople of Lewes. With the men's help, we were eventually able to identify all the dead and missing sailors and notify the shipping authorities who would inform the families - if they were lucky. I wrote to the mother of the boy whose name turned out to be Jonas. I never heard back so I suspected that she was illiterate and perhaps had not been able to find someone to read the letter out to her. I couldn't believe she didn't care.

The inhabitants of Newhaven who had refused to open their doors to Spinks were perhaps, I thought, ashamed afterwards of their lack of action, particularly the physician who might have offered help. Bartholomew was, however, surprisingly understanding, saying, 'It's possible, but not necessarily. They might have simply been afraid, and not without justification. Just think about it. If you lived in an isolated place like that and were knocked up in the dead of night by persons unknown that could include smugglers or robbers, you might think twice too before opening your door.'

I thought to myself that *we* had opened our door, though, straight away, and then ridden many miles to help. I had the aches and bruises to prove it.

The dead were all buried in one large plot near Newhaven and a public subscription was raised to erect a stone memorial for them. I understood from Bartholomew that the physician who might have helped us contributed a generous sum. I wondered whether someone had twisted his arm.

## CHAPTER 6

*Lavender (Lavandula angustifolia)*. *It strengthens the stomach and frees the liver and spleen from obstruction. Mercury owns it.*

Culpeper's Colour Herbal

I felt my baby flutter in the womb for the first time. It was perhaps the most wonderful moment of my life. I longed for Bartholomew to experience the same magic but as he was some distance away, I had to keep it to myself. On reflection, however, I decided that I couldn't, so I asked Mr. Jenkins to fetch the gig and then flew off to Cecilia's as I knew she would understand and share my excitement. Mr. Jenkins came with me. I thought it was an important enough matter to take him from his work, and he didn't mind; he always liked going over to South Farm.

∞

Two letters arrived for me. I had never had any letters through the post at this address before, so to receive two at one time came as a great surprise. I opened them slowly after studying them for a while. The outside gave no clue as what was inside as neither were overwritten and I wondered which to open first. One was neatly written, with a clean outside slip, black ink and no blots; the other less so. I broke the seal on the other:

*My dear Esther*

*You will be surprised to hear from me I know but you are the only person who will help. I was not cut out to be a mother, Esther. You knew it and I knew it, but I did try.*

*The thing is, I can no longer do it and I am leaving Charlotte with Mason who will not know what to do. Captain Campbell is at sea and won't return to London for at least three months. If Prickship (and I do remember why you called him that) comes to you, then I am begging you to help him, for Charlotte's sake. She didn't deserve me as a mother. Her real father is not the captain, but he does not know that, and it is best he never does. The real father is looking for me and I can't have a child in tow. He is not a good man.*

*I know you have a kind heart, Esther, and that you will do your best to protect Charlotte. I won't contact you again. Thank you.*

*Mrs. Campbell*

I gasped in horror at this message and then immediately broke the seal on the other letter, guessing it was from Mason.

*Dear Esther,*

*I don't know where to begin but I awoke this morning to find a little girl delivered by coach to my lodgings in London. It is Charlotte, Captain Campbell's daughter! Her mother has just left her for me to care for. I don't know what to do. I have been on leave for the last few months because my broken leg has not healed properly. Fortunately, I have seen a physician who swears he can help. That woman Mrs. Campbell knew where I lodged, and just dumped Charlotte on me and disappeared. The coachman was paid in advance by a lad who says he knows nothing about the child's mother nor her whereabouts.*

*What am I to do, Esther? I don't know how to care for a baby and she keeps crying.*

*I have taken the liberty of booking a coach to Lewes so I can bring Charlotte to you. I know you hold the captain in high esteem and will want to do your best for his daughter. Mason*

I reached for the edge of the table to grip on to. 'Oh good heavens, poor Charlotte,' I cried out. 'What must she be feeling?' I hurried down to the kitchen and explained it all to Mrs. Jenkins who wondered if there was a date on Mason's letter. I searched the close script and found nothing to indicate when the letter was written, which meant that he could have been due imminently, but as he had mentioned "booking" a coach, it was more likely to be tomorrow. It was then late morning and I had to go out shortly after dinner to check up on one of my mothers who might give birth shortly, if I was reading the signs correctly.

'Shall I prepare the little room next to Beth's?' asked Mrs. Jenkins. 'It might do for the time being until you work out how to find her mother and dissuade her from this unnatural course of action.'

'There will be no dissuading her, I fear. She is a very selfish woman who thinks of no one but herself. No, I will have to try and contact Captain Campbell, and, in the meantime, we will have to look after Charlotte here. Mason is incapable of doing so and, in any case, it is not appropriate. Let me think, Charlotte is between two and three years old now, so I think we will have to prepare the truckle bed. Do you think we should put her together with Beth? It might comfort Charlotte to have another little one nearby. Or we could put her in the cot until we see how she does since I won't be needing it for a few months yet?'

'Aye, the cot will be the best plan. I will ask Mr. Jenkins to move it into Beth's room when he comes in for his dinner.'

'And I will go and tell Beth that she will have a new playmate sharing her room. She will be surprised - and so will Doctor Grieve when he hears about this. I hope he won't be put out by it, nor Enid. I will explain everything when we have dinner. The earliest Mason could arrive is mid-afternoon but it will more likely be tomorrow. Mrs. Jenkins, I need to go out this afternoon, so will you ask Mr. Jenkins to be ready to fetch me back from just over the bridge in the Cliffe should they arrive today? I do hope they won't, though. It is so warm, and I am already a mite weary.'

Concerned that I was overdoing things, Mrs. Jenkins promised to have the cot cleaned and made ready by this afternoon just in case Mason arrived early. 'Did the gentleman say whether he would be staying or should we book him a room at the White Hart?'

'Yes, that's a good idea. I will call in when I am passing and see if they have a room. I don't really want him staying here but we must invite him to eat with us. It's the least we can do, and I am sure Bartholomew will be pleased to see him again. I'll go and speak to Beth and Enid now, if I can leave the preparations to you, Mrs. Jenkins. I will be as quick as I can this afternoon, though

I hope my patient is not in a hurry to have her baby. It is her first and she needs me.' I will call on Eliza, too, I thought, to see if she can help.

As I went upstairs to our room and collapsed into my chair, I realised I was out of breath and knew I had to calm myself. I felt unwell and quite distressed by the news; Mason's reappearance in my life was disconcerting as well. There was too much going on and I was wondering if I could cope with any more. I would ride Flossy down to the Cliffe. I couldn't face walking in the heat; though it was not far to go, I just didn't feel up to it. I took a gulp of water, hoping it would help me to settle. I would ask Mrs. Jenkins to make me some of my special tea after dinner. I was missing working with my herbs. I felt that if I just had time to prepare them, I would feel much better in myself, and I worried that if they weren't properly dried then my whole year's harvest would be ruined. Some of the drinks I made could be so soothing but Bartholomew was concerned that their properties might be too powerful for the baby growing inside me. Enough, I said to myself, things are as they are, just get on. Pulling myself together, I went to find Beth who was delighted to hear that she would shortly have a companion whereas Enid was horrified, saying that the child should be placed with an appropriate family somewhere else.

'And what do you mean by "appropriate", Enid?' I asked.

'A family of the same class as the child's parents,' she said pompously. 'Isn't that why we have a workhouse - for all the waifs and strays?'

'But Charlotte is the daughter of a naval officer - a captain, no less. Furthermore, he is known to us and I have had the care of her in the past. I am not aware of many naval families who would be considered "appropriate" nearby.' I ignored the workhouse comment as too ridiculous to waste my breath on.

Enid blustered, muttering on about my "antics" again, but I refused to listen to her insinuations and left the room just as Bartholomew returned from his morning calls.

'Bartholomew, will you look at these?' I asked, pushing the letters into his hands and fidgeting anxiously as he read them. Before he could respond, I made a point of saying, 'I have asked Mrs. Jenkins to prepare the room next to Beth's for Charlotte's use until we can contact the captain, her father. She is also cleaning the cot which could go in with Beth if she is unhappy.'

'As you think best, my dear. The good captain has been away for a long time and I am sure he will be happy that his daughter is with us. If the girls get along, then perhaps they should indeed share a room - it might bring some comfort to the poor little thing.'

Inwardly I blessed Bartholomew for his ready acceptance of my decisions in a difficult situation, especially when he was tired and simply in need of some peace and quiet. Enid, however, was unable to contain herself, fury spitting from her.

'Bartholomew, from what I have heard, you do not know if the captain is indeed the child's father, and the mother is clearly dissolute. How can you entertain the idea of introducing such a child into our family? Who knows what she will grow up like, *and* in the company of your precious Beth whose own parentage is scandalous?'

As Enid spouted her poison at us, I remembered that Beth's biological father was the despicable rapist Farmer Coad. I felt the chill of her words travel through my veins like ice.

'Charlotte will benefit from our steady influence, Enid, and I am sure that, like Beth, she will be a delightful child regardless of any parentage. That is all I have to say on the matter.' He turned his back on Enid and headed for his study, his face a picture of anger. I breathed a sigh of relief, safe in the knowledge that one of Bartholomew's deepest beliefs was in the innocence of children.

Dinner was a silent affair and immediately afterwards I hurried down to the Cliffe, stopping only to book a room for Mason at the White Hart. If he and Charlotte arrived today, I would not be there to manage everyone and Bartholomew would be out too. Who knew what Enid would say or do?

Thankfully my mother-to-be was not yet in labour so I was able to return home reassured within the hour, well before the London coach arrived. Mr. Jenkins was later recruited to go to the Star and see if a man of military bearing who walked with a limp was on board, accompanied by a very young child. Mrs. Jenkins and I laughed at the description we had given to her husband. When he returned, he was able to describe everyone who alighted, none of them with a limp! We relaxed and I uttered a prayer of thanks that we had more time to prepare.

∞

Mason and Charlotte arrived the following day and, accompanied by Mr. Jenkins, I was able to meet them personally as Eliza had taken over delivery for the young mother. I gathered Charlotte into my arms and felt her snuggle against me. She was tearful but wanted to be cuddled and as I looked down upon her delicate face with the long, wet eyelashes showing her distress, I wondered at Enid's sour mentality. I felt a prickle of tears myself and knew I would do anything to protect this sad little girl from her mother's neglect.

'Come, Mr. Mason,' I said, 'I have booked you accommodation at the White Hart but perhaps you would care to dine with us tonight? It is good to see you again and I am so sorry that you are still not comfortable after the injury. My husband will, no doubt, be able to advise you. Can you walk the short way to our home later on? We are just beyond the castle, through the archway.'

'Yes, indeed. In fact, my problem lies more in the twists and turns needed for life on board a turbulent ship. Esther, I am so grateful that you have taken charge of Charlotte. She is a sweet little thing and I'm afraid her mother shows her true colours by abandoning her to *me* - hardly the most suitable of parents.'

'Mrs. Campbell wrote telling me what she had done,' I said. 'She also told me that she was certain you would ask me to take charge.'

Mason looked perplexed. 'Well, why didn't she just send Charlotte to you in the first place?'

'She probably thought you were simply the nearer,' I replied. 'She'd have had to bring Charlotte here herself, and as I imagine she is hiding in London just now, perhaps she thought it would be easier for us to track her down if she came within ten miles of me.'

We stopped outside the hotel. 'Well, here we are. Please do come along to eat with us at about seven o'clock. I have written down the directions. I would warn you though that Bartholomew's sister is staying with us. She can be a little difficult, so please ignore anything she says, should she join us. Mr. Jenkins here will help me get Charlotte home along with her luggage, if she has some.'

'Yes, she has this small valise containing her clothes and one rag doll. I will see you shortly, then, Esther. I am so glad to meet up with you again. I have greatly missed you and our days together on board the *Lady Charlotte*.'

For a moment I thought he had tears in his eyes, but abruptly he turned away and left us. I chose not to dwell on his words; I did not want to have to acknowledge his pain.

∞

Bartholomew had the presence of mind to send an invitation to Cecilia and John Elwood to join us for supper that night. I was thankful that their company would lighten what might have become a difficult conversation. Before I went down, I looked in on the two sleeping children. Beth had taken to Charlotte with delight, seeing in front of her a real live doll to be introduced into all her play schemes. After they had tired each other out, I put them down. Charlotte settled into the cot which we had decided to place alongside Beth's single bed and then fell deeply asleep. While tucking Beth in, I whispered that she was to look after her new friend but to let her sleep. 'No early mornings,' I said. 'If you wake up and she is still sleeping, then let her be. She needs her rest.'

'When will her mama come? Will she take her away from me soon?'

'No, I don't think we will see her for a while because she needs time to think about things. She knows that Charlotte is safe and will be happy with us, so we must do our best to be her friend, even if she is a little sad at times.'

In truth, I doubted that Mrs. Campbell had ever spent much time with Charlotte. After the wet nurse, there would doubtless have been just a nanny or a servant to mind her. But who's to say whether either were any kinder than the mother? Charlotte was not clean of clouts yet so we would do our best to help with training her.

Surprisingly our evening went well despite Enid joining us. She was so busy fawning over Cecilia, I concluded that she was a social climber along with all her other less than endearing qualities. None of us raised past events during our conversation which was probably just as well as it would have meant endless explanations that I wasn't prepared to share yet. If Enid had not been there maybe we might have talked more about the things that mattered.

Cecilia was quite taken with Mason and I caught her watching me when he talked. While the men took their port, we opted to take coffee in the drawing room and fortunately Enid declined to join us, pleading tiredness. I for one was glad to see the back of her.

'Well, Esther!' said Cecilia. 'You never told me that Mason had expectations of you?'

'Expectations! No, Cecilia, Mason had delusions. I had no interest in him as a man, just as a kind acquaintance during some difficult times. He, however, has taken kindness to mean affection and I have been trying very hard ever since to let him down lightly. I am sorry he has come back into my life - no good can come of it for him.'

'Ah, what do you think he intends, then? You are, after all, a married woman now.'

'I think he intends to ingratiate himself. Friendship is perhaps what he wants - maybe he sees that as better than nothing. But Cecilia, I'm afraid it irritates me no end.'

And it seemed that I was right. When Bartholomew suggested that Mason should put himself under his care to explore the options for improving his leg, he decided to move to Lewes and to take rooms at the White Hart. At least Bartholomew didn't suggest that he stay with us, so I supposed that was something.

Charlotte settled in well and loved her playmate Beth. We took her to South Farm to meet Freddie and Felicia and, mercifully, all of them seem well suited. In some ways it made my life easier, as I didn't have to keep Beth entertained every minute. When we were at South Farm, we did our lessons all together, and when we were at home in Lewes, Beth now played happily with Charlotte and was generally content to do so, rather than asking me to play with her all of the time. Charlotte, contrary to Enid's predictions, presented as a timid and shy child and I couldn't imagine her having a bad bone in her body.

∞

Once Mason became established nearby, I quickly realised that Bartholomew revelled in his masculine company and the adventurous tales of naval life that they talked about endlessly. I tried to look at it from Bartholomew's point of view and asked myself whether, being in a household of women (one of whom he disliked) and children, he struggled to enjoy life as much as we did before Enid came. As he also began to ride over to South Farm regularly to spend time with John Elwood, I often wondered whether he was just trying to get away from us all. I rather hoped that our new baby would be a boy as I was sure he would like that.

∞

Eliza had become an important part of my midwifery plans now that I was less able to minister to my ladies; and with that in mind I took to my sewing to make her a work-pinny to cover her clothes and protect them from spoiling. She was absolutely delighted when I presented it to her and promised another to be 'in the wash'. Instead of it being a drab colour, such as she normally wore, I added some coloured edge-binding and straps, which gave her a very smart look. I don't know what I would have done without her then, since my life had become so busy; and with the baby growing fast, my ability to rush around was further diminished. He was very active (I always referred to the little one as 'he') and I tracked his movements all over my extended belly. I often caught Bartholomew studying me when we were alone together; and, on occasions, he tried to hear the heartbeat which he said was for no reason other than that he had never before had such continuous, close proximity to a pregnant woman and that it satisfied his scientific curiosity! I felt very cherished when we were alone together and did everything I could to help him enjoy our time in peace with no domestic interruptions.

Mrs. Jenkins had more help in the kitchen now, while Pot, Billy-alone's young friend, helped out with the heavier chores. Wini was coming in for longer hours every day so I just about managed to keep on top of things. When I looked around me and saw women who were caring for seven or eight children with no help to hand, I did wonder how they managed it. I consoled myself with the fact that I seemed to be running a small empire that employed people to ensure that my husband was able to do his job properly with no domestic worries. But it also allowed me to help my expectant mothers as well as teach Eliza the skills to take over completely when I was unable to work. It is a matter of scale, I told myself, as I also gave the children their lessons.

## CHAPTER 7

*I spun some shoe thread & went to see Mrs.*
*Williams. Shee has news her Mother is very*
*sick. Geny Huston had a Child Born the night*
*before last. I was calld to James Hinkly to see*
*his wife at 11 & 30 Evening. Went as far as Mr*
*Weston by land, from thence by water. Find*
*Mrs. Hinkly very unwell.*

*A Midwife's Tale 1785-1812 USA  Laurel Thatcher Ulrich*

With the thought in mind of Bartholomew suffering from
a surfeit of femininity, Cecilia and I planned to have a
joint family picnic at South Farm. Everyone was invited
and the men were roped in early to carry everything and
manage the event. Bartholomew looked so much happier
directing operations alongside John and Mason (I tried
desperately hard not to think of him as "Prickship") that
the picnic took on the garb of a military exercise. The spot
chosen was where Billy and I had been some time ago
when we were discussing the likelihood of my Aunt Tilly
planning her revenge on me. But I didn't mind that, and
Beth and Freddy both recognised the place where they
had had such fun before.

Billy and Cilla came along as well as some of the senior staff from both South Farm and the outlying farms that were part of John and Cecilia's estate. Mr. and Mrs. Jenkins didn't come on this occasion but Mrs. Makepiece, Miss Wardle, and Beth's grandfather all took up the invitation. Enid declined to mix with so many of what she called 'the lower orders' but as the occasion grew and grew, I think she came to regret it. Bartholomew and I were both delighted, however, that she was not there to breathe her sour spirit over our innocent fun. And it *was* fun. Cilla and the nursemaids took turns to organise races and nursery rhyme dances: they particularly liked the one about the London bells. For the little ones, we had their own picnic blanket placed to the side of the main area; and there were a number of chairs for those of us who were not comfortable sprawling on the ground! The gentlemen all clustered together and there was some one-upmanship in the games played by them but eventually they settled down to team games and from that point on it was all very good-natured.

We, the ladies, had brought sun parasols with us, and it was a wonderful afternoon, giving me time to speak to everyone important in my life including Billy, Mrs. Makepiece and Beth's grandfather. Being so busy made it difficult to keep up with everyone on a regular basis, so this was a great opportunity for me. The stable lads had been prevailed upon to give rides to the children, which they all loved. Flossy was such a gentle creature that she never minded all the tugging and pulling on her mane.

The only cloud on such a beautiful day was the appearance of someone in the distance who appeared to be watching us. I pointed him out to Billy who set off to see who it was. The man clearly didn't want to be spoken to as he disappeared over the hill as soon as he saw Billy heading his way.

'I think it be that Digger's son, Esther,' Billy said in an aside to me when he came back. 'I know he hangs around the town - I have seen him near the Castle inn, which you know is not a good place. Has he approached you again?'

'No, not since that time in the twitten. I'd hoped he had given up,' I said, gloomily, not liking to be reminded of the threats to us.

Towards the end of the afternoon, Cilla and the younger servants took the children back to the house whilst we adults began to clear up. It really had been the most enjoyable day and I was so pleased to see Bartholomew back to his normal self. As we made our way home to Lewes, I said to him, 'Bartholomew, can we not establish a home for Enid in one of your cottages? She is having such a detrimental effect, and not just on the children and servants, but you and me, too.'

'I have considered it,' he replied, 'but I don't see how we can do so. The cottages are both rented out and they are mean little places in the Cliffe area which would not be suitable for her. I have even considered renting an establishment on her behalf, but nothing has come up that is affordable or in the right place.'

It was news to me that Bartholomew had been endeavouring to move Enid away from us. Whilst I was pleased to hear it, I was afraid that it also went to show just how unhappy he was, which I found worrying. Had I been so tied up in my domestic affairs that I had under-estimated the degree of his misery? I put my hand in his and squeezed it, saying, 'Perhaps something will happen to improve the situation for us.' I don't know what I thought that "something" might be but I was sorry that our day out had been sullied by this brief interchange. I resolved to put Bartholomew at the very centre of my world and not let anything else get in the way. I now had three people in that world, with Bartholomew at the heart, and soon there would be four.

When we got home and entered the drawing room, expecting to find Enid sitting in her usual solitary and disapproving state, we were surprised to find a dark-haired man with her who was pacing up and down, his features florid and his demeanour agitated. I slid out of the room with the children and ran down to find Mrs. Jenkins.

'Who is with Enid?' I gasped.

'Her son-in-law. You had better go back to the drawing room, Esther - he has a lot to say, and there has already been some trouble.' She turned so that I could see a broken vase on the table. 'I'll see to the children for you.'

I flew back up the stairs. I could still move fast if I had to.

Bartholomew was shaking the man's hand as I came in. 'George, this is my wife, Esther,' he said. 'Esther, my niece's husband, George Mackintosh MP.' I stepped forward to greet him, but he seemed too disturbed to perform the meanest of civilities. He nodded to me curtly. I knew he was not being disrespectful; his mind was clearly in complete disarray.

Bartholomew rang the bell and when a flustered Mrs. Jenkins came in, he asked her to serve some tea and bring a bottle of brandy. While she scurried off to do so, he said, 'Well, what is it you are here for, George? What can we do for you?'

'My wife is missing and I have come to see if she is here with that woman,' he pointed at Enid, 'her *mother*.' The look he gave her was poisonous.

Bartholomew said quietly, 'Will you accept my word that Beatrice is not here, nor ever has been?'

'If you will swear it as the word of a gentleman.'

'I do so swear it. Now, kindly explain.'

I was watching Enid as this exchange went on and I saw her face blanch before she broke in: 'I am sure there is no need to involve my brother in this discussion, George. I don't see how it can benefit you.' There was a slight tremor in her voice.

'There is every reason to advise Bartholomew about the shame my wife has brought down on my family - and on his, too, if the connection is made public!'

I could hear Mrs. Jenkins coming up the stairs from the kitchen, so I went to the door and took the tray from her. She whispered that she would bring the tea in a few minutes. I told her not to bother; I didn't think anyone was in the mood to take tea.

I poured a measure of brandy for both George and Bartholomew. As I handed the glass to George, he said, looking at Bartholomew: 'Your niece, *her* daughter, *my* wife has been having an affair with my stableman. She was caught in the act, in flagrante, and the details have been broadcast and gossiped about all over my constituency. I have been made to look a fool at home, and I am trying to prevent the gossip from getting to Westminster since I seem to be the butt of jokes in all the talking shops and bars in Edinburgh.'

He took a shuddering breath before continuing: 'What makes it even more demeaning is that she says she would marry the fellow if she could!' He dropped into a chair, his head in his hands, before muttering, 'A *stable-man*, of all people.'

Enid glared at George before getting up with her head held high, and then marched from the room. I hurried after her, but my overtures of sympathy were flung angrily in my face. She turned at the bottom of the stairs, hissing, 'Well, this plays into your hands, doesn't it - my daughter bringing shame and opprobrium on us all? I don't want your sympathy. You are not worthy to even *talk* about my family! It is *you* who brings shame on *us*, and more fool my brother if he cannot see it.'

I was both shocked and dismayed by her words as I stood at the bottom of the stairs, watching her determined tread as she stamped upwards, her back rigid.

I didn't return to the drawing room; I didn't want to hear the details. Instead, I went back down to the kitchen where Mrs. Jenkins was clearing up.

'How long has he been here?' I asked.

'About an hour, and I am glad it was no longer than that because I thought she would tear him to pieces.'

'How do you mean?'

'Well, she wouldn't believe him, called him a liar - and that wasn't the least of it. You could hear her screaming all over the house - she was completely hysterical. I am that glad you came home when you did. He was ranting and raving and blamed Mrs. McGovern for bringing her daughter up so badly. He said it was all her fault - down to false pride and pretending to be someone she was not. He called his wife a "cheap whore who had obviously learnt at her mother's table".'

'Good gracious,' I exclaimed. 'What did he mean by that?'

'He said that Enid had strayed from her own husband early in her marriage and bore a child, and that no one knew if the child was her husband's or her lover's, but it was passed off as her husband's.'

'Enid? He must be mistaken - how could anyone think that of her?'

'Well, according to him - and I couldn't help over-hearing, Esther, he was shouting at the top of his voice, they both were - that was why her husband had treated her so badly and spent all her money. As punishment.'

'Mama,' came a little voice beside me, 'can you read us a story, Mama?'

I clapped my hand over my mouth, having not real-ised that the children were so nearby. 'Yes, of course, I will,' I said. 'Darling girls, you go on up now and get ready for bed. You can help Charlotte, Beth, and I will be up as soon as I can.' Both girls made their way up the back stairs. I could hear them giggling as they went.

'Oh, I hope she didn't understand what we were saying.'

'Of course not,' said Mrs. Jenkins. 'You go on up and I will keep an eye on the drawing room, in case they come to blows.'

I laughed. 'Bartholomew wouldn't be so foolish. Has George got luggage with him? Is he expecting to stay here?'

'No, I heard him say he was staying at the Star.'

'Thank God for that.'

George did not stay long. Bartholomew persuaded him to go and that it would be best to leave town, promising to get in touch if his wife turned up.

Enid did not appear for the next two days. Bartholomew finally decided he should visit her in her room and reported back to me that she was sitting, fully dressed, in her upright chair. He eventually persuaded her to come down and she duly reappeared for dinner. None of us mentioned the debacle, but we were watchful and Enid was unnaturally quiet. I didn't tell Bartholomew about her spiteful comments to me, reasoning that they both had enough to deal with; but I didn't forget them, and I began looking about the town for properties that we might be able to rent for her. I asked myself whether her departure from our house was more important than the money it would cost Bartholomew. I decided that it was but for the time being we were all keeping our distance.

∽

I had been putting off writing to Captain Campbell about Charlotte, but decided that I must at last do so. My plan was to send a letter via the shipping agent in London who looked after us when we returned from Gibraltar. I tried several times to put into words what had happened but found it immensely difficult. Cecilia and Bartholomew both advised that I should keep the information to a bare minimum and make it more about Charlotte than his errant wife. Rather than sending the letter through the public post, I decided to entrust it to our friend the coachman whose son Charley worked for the shipping agent. I would not divulge any details but just ask the office to forward the letter to the captain as soon as possible. I wrote:

> *My dear friend,*
>
> *I am writing to tell you about some recent events that I believe you to be unaware of, but first I want to say that your beloved daughter Charlotte is with us in Lewes and she*

thrives in the company of both my ward Beth and Freddie, the son of Mr. and Mrs. John Elwood. You will remember that the Elwoods were my patrons and we continue our close association to this day.

Some weeks ago, I received a letter from Mrs. Campbell who felt that she was not best equipped to be a good mother to Charlotte. Bartholomew and I agreed to take Charlotte into our own family until you return and decide what is to be done. My letter might be short on details of how this came about but do be assured that we are all doing our best to ensure Charlotte is the happy child that she deserves to be.

Unfortunately, I have no news as to the whereabouts of Mrs. Campbell but it occurs to me that she might be in touch with your agent, as I understand from Mason (who is also here in Lewes) that she has access through their offices to financial arrangements you have made for her and Charlotte.

I know that this news will be of grave concern to you and we all hope that on your return you can resolve any problems that Mrs. Campbell may have. It has been my experience that a small number of women struggle to come to terms with motherhood in the early months, and possibly for years. Perhaps your good lady has made the best arrangement for Charlotte's welfare, if indeed she is of this number.

*To finish on a happier note, my dear Captain Campbell, I can tell you that Charlotte is a contented child and of a sunny disposition. She is starting to talk - much encouraged by Freddie and Beth. Bartholomew and I are very happy to care for her and please be assured we will continue to do so until such time as you return and then we can all discuss plans for her future.*

*I am pleased to tell you that I am expecting a little one myself in about four months. We are fortunate that we have friends surrounding us and that our home is a joyous one for children.*

*I hope that you fare well on your voyage. Please remember me to Jones, if he is still part of the ship's company, and to Sarah who recognised me at the beginning of our voyage. Mason will be writing to you separately once the treatment he is undertaking with Bartholomew is complete.*

*With our very best wishes, and we hope to see you safely back home in due course,*

*Esther Grieve*

As I came to write the direction on the letter, I realised that I didn't know Charley's surname, so I left the house for the Star just in time to meet the coach. It was a fine still day and I enjoyed the walk. I went into the ladies' room and waited for it to arrive. If it was the wrong coachman, I would come back tomorrow. Happily, it wasn't, and after we had exchanged news, I handed the package over. 'Please would you give this to Charley, so he can give it to his employers?' I asked. 'It is very important, and I know I can trust you to make sure it gets there soon.'

'Aye, lass, don't tha fret,' replied Charley's pa. 'Mayhap I knows sommat 'bout it already, but we won't pick o'er the bones. I will be back two days hence, and if there be a reply, I will send for thee as soon as we arrive.'

'I will come down, anyway, and meet you,' I said, pressing his hand as he enclosed mine in his. For some reason, I felt tears come to my eyes. 'Give my best wishes to Charley,' I added.

As I walked back towards home, I realised that I had been out alone and had completely forgotten that I was supposed to be exercising vigilance. I looked behind me, but nothing seemed out of place and I wasn't being followed, so all was well. Delivering the letter was a weight off my mind but I wondered how it would be received by the poor captain.

## CHAPTER 8

*Sage, common garden (Salvia officinalis).*
*Good for the liver and to breed blood. Astrology:*
*Jupiter claims it.*

*Culpeper's Colour Herbal*

The weather had broken, with the long stretch of late summer heat deserting us in favour of cooler winds and storm clouds. Fortunately, the harvest was taken in before the first rains fell. I was not sorry as the heat had been hard for me to endure.

One morning in early October, Bartholomew asked me to come into his surgery as he had some news. I did so and was sorry to hear him say that he had conducted an autopsy in recent days on a woman and her unborn child. I had no reason to make any connection with this poor woman and sat waiting for him to explain his concerns.

'Esther, I am sorry to be the bearer of bad news for you - as well as for the people closely involved,' he began, 'but I believe that this woman was the wife of the smuggler Digger whom you will remember was murdered after Tilly's trial. It is another dreadful tragedy for this very unfortunate family. She was bearing a well-developed child, obviously from a later relationship, and both died during premature childbirth. Her children have now been taken into parish care.'

I felt like a bucket of cold water had been thrown over me. I had not told Bartholomew about Digger's son, the young man who had threatened me, but I remembered him saying that his mother had turned to prostitution in order to feed them all and that she was then with child. I couldn't very well tell Bartholomew what I knew now because he would have been upset that I hadn't confided in him before. Somehow, I had got into the habit of keeping things too much to myself and it led me into difficulties when everything came out. Billy was the only one I had told.

Carefully, I said: 'I know Digger had a big family with some older children. Can they not provide for the family?'

Bartholomew was looking at me intently and I felt like guilt was shining out of me like a beacon for all to see. I hoped he could not read what was in my thoughts.

'Esther, some of the information I gathered when I was looking into this case came from young Billy-alone who seems, as always, to be a fount of knowledge and could tell me something of the family. He implied that this further tragedy might be a threat to you and Beth. His reasoning, which was mostly extracted in a roundabout way, was that the family might consider their downfall as being your fault. Were you aware of this, Esther?'

I couldn't lie, not outright. Again, I picked my words cautiously. 'Billy had told me that I was at risk from the remaining smugglers and their families. I chose not to dwell on things that had not happened and just took care to keep away from lonely places. But surely you knew this, Bartholomew?'

To my own ears I sounded defensive, but by not telling Bartholomew about the incident in the twitten, I was only withholding a half-truth. He did not seem satisfied but refrained from pushing me into further explanations. I fled the room as quickly as I could, aware that Bartholomew was not entirely convinced by my answers.

I decided I needed someone to talk to and asked Mr. Jenkins to bring the gig round to accompany me to South Farm a little earlier than I had planned. Both the girls were due to have a lesson with Freddie and afterwards I could have a talk with Cecilia. I had much to tell her, including the scene with Enid's son-in-law and the letter I had sent to the shipping agent for Captain Campbell. I had not seen much of her recently with so much happening for us and she had also been busy enjoying another visit from her brother.

We were lucky to get some time alone as John Elwood and Cecilia's brother were away from the house that day and not expected back soon. Once the children were playing happily after their lesson, we sat down for a long chat. I explained about Enid's fall from grace - according to her son-in-law - and about the missing daughter who seemed to have fallen even lower. I also mentioned the nasty things Enid had said to me.

'Cecilia, I think we have to get Enid out of our house,' I said, feeling suddenly quite desperate now that I had put my thoughts into words. 'She spreads her poison and, even though we try not to listen to her, it just seeps into us and damages our happiness. Bartholomew is miserable, I am exhausted, and the girls are frightened of her. This should be such a happy time for us with the new baby coming and yet we are all walking round on eggshells. Since the shouting match with George, she has become even more haughty. She wears her disdain like a cloak and by turning on me I think she is trying to deflect censure from herself. I don't know what to do.'

My friend was astounded at what I had told her and seemed lost for words. After shedding a few tears of sheer frustration, I then launched into the story of Digger's son, adding that I thought Bartholomew suspected I had prior knowledge of the family and their predicament. 'I am sure he knows that I haven't told him the whole truth, and that implies that I didn't trust him. He was a bit distant,' I said miserably.

'Before we start thinking of what we can do, let's cover everything that's going on,' Cecilia said. 'Did you write to Captain Campbell, and is Charlotte happy with you?'

'Yes, to both your questions, and the shipping agent sent me a note to say that the package would be sent to the *Lady Charlotte's* next port of call which is, again, Gibraltar.'

After Cecilia had absorbed all the events that were causing chaos in my life, we took some tea and settled down to discuss our babies, happily tucked away within and protected by our bodies; they at least were untouched by any threat.

'Now,' Cecilia said, as we finished our drinks, 'what are we to do about Enid? Let us put our heads together and come up with a plan that draws the sting from her tail.'

'I would like to do that,' I said, 'but I think we must get home, Cecilia. The nights are drawing in so early now, it makes me nervous, even with Mr. Jenkins driving us. Can you think about everything I have told you and then we can put our minds to it?'

'By all means. We'll meet up again in two days and see what we can come up with in the meantime. And, Esther, do try not to worry so much. It is making you overly anxious and that is not good for the baby. Is Bartholomew keeping a close eye on you?'

'Yes, he keeps trying to listen for a heartbeat,' I replied, 'but he says there is no reason for it other than professional interest. Barty is so clever, Cecilia. He has made a sort of funnel by chopping up a hearing device which one of his patients used before she died. He pushes the widest part into my belly and listens through that. He says it is more effective than just laying his ear on my belly.'

Cecilia asked one of the stable lads to keep company with us on the way home, though I think Mr. Jenkins was none too pleased.

## CHAPTER 9

*Alder, common. (Alnus glutinosa). The leaves
gathered in the morning when the dew is on
them and brought into a chamber troubled with
fleas will gather them thereunto, which being
suddenly cast out will rid the chamber of these
troublesome bedfellows. Astrology: Under the
dominion of Venus, and of some water sign, one
supposes Pisces.*

*Culpeper's Colour Herbal.*

Despite all our good intentions and precautions for my
safety, an incident finally occurred, unexpectedly and in
broad daylight.

I had been on my way with Mr. Jenkins as my escort
to South Farm where Cecilia and I were going to discuss
Enid, as planned. He was riding Brown Betty and was but
a few paces behind me. The girls had stayed in Lewes as
Charlotte was a little grizzly: we had given her the newest
available inoculation against smallpox. Bartholomew had
been quite adamant that she was given the dose despite
Charlotte not being in her parents' care. He argued that

we were 'in loco parentis' and must do for her what we had done for Beth.

We were quite near the farm and almost upon the small copse where I had been affrighted once before. I had only a light hand on Flossy's reins as she was always very steady and didn't need me tugging on her. Suddenly, I heard Mr. Jenkins shout and when I looked back to see what was amiss, he was pointing to the trees over to the right. As I tightened the reins, I twisted sharply round in the direction he was indicating where a heavy-set boy with a long stave had appeared and, moving at speed, was almost under Flossy's hooves. Instinctively, I changed direction by pulling her away to the left and she responded by kicking her back legs at our assailant. I know she caught him because I felt the impact as I crouched low over her mane. By the time we had stead-ied, our attacker was running off. Mr. Jenkins trotted up to my side and laid his hand between Flossy's ears, gently calming her.

'Are thee hurt, lass? Did he get you?'

'No, Flossy kicked back at him, and it caught him unawares, I think. Did you see who it was?'

'It were no one I knew. He were quite young but looked as if he were a vagrant, sleeping rough maybe. I think we should turn back. We need to tell Doctor Grieve and he will want to call the constable.'

He took the reins and we turned slowly before retracing our steps, all the while looking into every bush and shadow. When we got to the house, Bartholomew came out, surprised by our unexpected return. Mr. Jenkins was already down and carefully helping me to dismount as he explained what had happened. Bartholomew disappeared off into the town as soon as I had told him that I was unhurt, even though I'd begun to feel a little winded in my side. We went indoors and Mrs. Jenkins fussed around us with a great deal of tutting and scolding me for riding about the countryside 'in my condition'. I asked her to make me one of my teas, went up to our bedroom and disrobed. There was an ache in my side and it was sore, so I took myself to bed. I thought back over the moment when the young man had almost got to me and realised that when I turned sharply, I had almost certainly pulled something.

By the time Bartholomew returned, having mobilised the constables who were already out searching for the fellow, I was quite settled in the warmth of my bed and enjoying a sedative tea that I had used countless times before for my pregnant ladies and, bearing in mind Bartholomew's strictures, knew to be safe. Mrs. Jenkins kept coming up to check on me and then going back down to reassure Mr. Jenkins who was extremely upset.

'He doesn't need to be upset,' I told her. 'It was his warning that saved me - his warning and Flossy's reaction to someone coming out of the trees at us. Please ask him to give her some extra nice hay and a good cuddle.'

'Shall I tell him to have some extra nice hay and a cuddle for himself as well?' She said this with a smile, but I could see she was worried and I knew that my riding days were over, at least until the baby was born.

Bartholomew examined me thoroughly and listened once again for the baby's heartbeat. Fearfully, I asked if all was well. I knew it was early to be trying to hear the baby's heartbeat but Bartholomew was still experimenting with various funnel-type instruments of his own devising, based on his dead patient's hearing aid. When it came to my own work with expectant mothers, however, I had always made do with just my ears, as had countless women before me.

'Yes, all seems well. I thought I heard a sound that I couldn't quite place, but I will listen again in an hour or so. I think you have just twisted a muscle in your side, unsurprisingly. Now, stay up here for this evening and we will check again a bit later. Would you like some more of your tea? I know that you would rather use your own blend,' he sighed. 'Mrs. Jenkins and I will see to the girls and then they can come up and sit with you awhile before they have their rest. Charlotte is a little happier and Beth is playing at being nurse to her and is excited to have two patients now. I've asked Mr. Jenkins to ride over to Cecilia and explain why you couldn't come.'

By the time the girls went down for a rest, I was more than comfortable but not yet ready to sleep; my muscles ached a little but nothing untoward. However, the fear of what I might have experienced was building up in my mind into something that truly frightened me. I knew my assailant was young and I was fairly certain that it was Digger's son. No one else had been threatening me, after all. When I first saw him, he was just a normal-looking lad, but this time he'd been dirty, unkempt, and his manner with the stick was truly menacing. I wondered if I should tell Bartholomew what I knew; then they might be able to properly trace him. Before his life had fallen apart, he'd once had a home here and a family: his father Digger - murdered, and blamed on me; his mother as well as her new baby, now dead; and his brothers and sisters taken into the parish care. I felt overwhelmed by it all.

Later in the day I fell asleep after some warm milk with cinnamon, but my dreams were fretful and it was a restless night for both of us. I know Bartholomew tried to soothe me when I woke him, but it was quite late in the morning before I felt able to rise. I went downstairs after gingerly feeling my waist and ribs. Perhaps I was dwelling overmuch on what was a minor incident in reality. After all, I had escaped with no real hurt to myself or the baby, and I had clearly needed the rest.

Billy-alone was in the kitchen with Pot and Mrs. Jenkins and jumped up as I entered, saying, 'I be telling Mrs. Jenkins that your attacker was most likely Digger's son, his name be Abe. He's been living rough, and I meant to come and tell you to watch out for him. I's sorry, Esther - if I had said before, you could have warned Doctor Grieve.'

Billy was looking at me closely. He must have realised that I had not told Bartholomew about the boy and his earlier threats. Once again, he had come to my rescue.

Mrs. Jenkins looked surprised that I was so quiet and didn't probe Billy for more information, but she was the soul of discretion and would accept the story that Billy was giving without going into the whys and wherefores. I breathed a tiny sigh of relief that Billy was covering up for me. I really had to start being more open with my husband: it was so wrong that I confided in my two best friends, Billy and Cecilia, but not in the man who would protect me.

No trace of my assailant was found and we all fell back into our usual ways except that I now used the gig whenever I wanted to go out. Mr. Jenkins or Bartholomew would always accompany me.

When at last I got to speak to Cecilia privately, we looked for a plan to remove Enid from our home. She knew of a house near the site of the old West Gate but of a better standard and larger than would be found in the Castle Ditch area. She proposed that a workman from John Elwood's estate be sent in to clean and bring the property right up to date. There was a tenant, but he was old and not making proper use of the house, so Cecilia thought it would be better and cheaper to provide him with a more suitable dwelling nearby. She told me that all his family had either died or moved away and that he was but one in a house that could easily accommodate four or five. The rent was not very high because of the old-fashioned decoration, and the neighbourhood wasn't very smart, but it was improving with more well-found families moving in recently.

'I wouldn't want to be the means of dispossessing someone of his long-term home,' I said in dismay.

'No, you wouldn't be depriving him. John had planned to improve the property and the elderly gentleman has already asked to be moved to somewhere smaller with a lower rent.'

'Have you asked John? Do you think he will agree, especially if this means bringing his renovations forward?'

She laughed. 'Of course, he will. Once it is refurbished it will be far more suitable for a genteel lady. There is enough room for a housekeeper-cum-cook to live in and Enid can always employ another servant, if necessary. It depends on how generous Bartholomew can be to his sister. John will want a market rent but the area is, as I said, not of the best but coming up. Better to get it now before the market rises.'

'At the moment I think he will be very generous indeed if it means getting rid of her! Shall I mention it to him? I wouldn't want you to go to a lot of trouble for Bartholomew to then refuse to pay the rent.'

'You talk to Bartholomew and I will talk to John. Who knows what they will say? We can but try.'

∽

I broached the subject the following morning. We had all breakfasted together, the girls were chirpy and the weather was fine, so when Bartholomew went off to his surgery, I followed him.

'Bartholomew, I have found a property that might be suitable for Enid,' I began, firmly. 'Can we talk about it now - or later, when you get back?'

'Have you, indeed? You must have more fingers in pies than I have, then, as there seems to be nothing available at a reasonable price.'

'Well, I don't know what you consider reasonable. The house is in need of repair and improvement - and if that is done, it will provide a property of goodly size without being over-large. It will be big enough for one servant - perhaps a housekeeper-cum-cook - who could live in.'

'Where is it?'

'It is quite near where the old West Gate was, in an improving area. John Elwood owns it and wants a new tenant to replace an elderly man who needs to move into something smaller.'

'Ah, you have been hatching this up with Cecilia.'

'We have not been "hatching it up", as you put it, just exchanging knowledge about what was available. John has been wanting to renovate the property but had not got around to it, and the elderly man is not paying a market rent.'

'Do you know what the rent will be? I am not a rich man, Esther.'

'Enid must have some money! She might not be telling you the truth about her circumstances. I do think we should explore this, Bartholomew. She is ruining our home life and, despite your threats, she is still being horrible.' Then I told him what she had said to me on the night when her son-in-law had turned up.

Bartholomew looked tired and dispirited, but I had to persevere.

'Please, promise me you will talk to John? If we can't afford it, then we can't afford it, but we don't know yet what it will cost and what Enid could possibly contribute.'

'I can't promise anything, but I will talk to John. Now please leave me to get on with my work.'

I went over and put my arms round him. 'Thank you, Doctor Grieve,' I said, as I walked away with a little spring in my step. It was a start, at least.

## CHAPTER 10

*Fennel (Foeniculum vulgare). The leaves or
seed boiled in Barley-water and drunk, are
good for nurses to increase their milk, and make
it more wholesome for the child. Astrology:
An herb of Mercury under Virgo and bearing
antipathy to Pisces.*

Culpeper's Colour Herbal

Eliza asked me to help her with one of our mothers-to-be, an older woman having a first baby. She thought she might be about thirty-seven but looked older, and we had become worried about her fitness to get through labour. Her husband was agitated and wouldn't leave us to do our work in peace and, while the family home was no dirtier than many we have visited, neither husband nor wife seemed to understand what was needed for a baby. There were no preparations, very little food in evidence and there was a strange relationship between them that made me wonder if enough love could be found to extend to a child. At one point, I insisted that the husband depart as he was interfering with our efforts to bring the baby safely into the world. He seemed to think that everything should stop in order to prepare a meal for him, or more worryingly, for his wife to get up and accompany him to the nearest public house for a drink while we waited!

I was finding it difficult to assist Eliza physically but I was able to advise and, as the birth was imminent, to help persuade the mother to stay in the right position; but she seemed determined to rise and follow her man to the alehouse. Luckily, her waters had already broken and a timely contraction threw them both into a panic. Once again, I asked the husband to leave us and suggested that he go out alone. He agreed, but it took ages to actually get him out of the door. Sadly, I began to think that both of them were soft in the head and perhaps not fit to raise a child at all.

Once he had gone, we pushed the mother into position and encouraged her, with some brute force, to stay put. The labour started and stopped repeatedly, and by the time the baby's head was showing, we were all worn down. When the husband came back, he took one look in through the door, a moment which coincided with a particularly painful contraction, and fled. Between times I tidied up the house and tried to make a space for the little one to call its own. There was a wooden crate being used for vegetables though it contained nothing fresh, just mouldy old bits, so I cleaned it out and lined it with my own shawl.

Mr. Jenkins was sent to collect me late in the afternoon as Bartholomew had become anxious that I had been gone too long. Eliza said she could manage for the final push and I promised to send some materials back to cover the child and make a nest in the rough wooden crate. Thankfully, we were not going to have to cut her and Eliza had all the instruments necessary to sever the cord. I was so worried about the family that I said I would visit after the birth to try and set the mother on the best path for the child. I hoped that once the baby was born the parents would be less absorbed in themselves and more in their child.

Eliza and I often visited a family after a birth as we have found that we can help with the many concerns that come up afterwards. I frequently thought back to Mrs. Campbell's experience of travail on the transport ship and fretted that I'd judged her too harshly when in fact she might simply have needed more help. I wondered if I had been too judgemental then because I lacked the medical and emotional expertise that I have now.

I still dreamt of being able to open a small cottage where we could take expectant mothers who, for whatever reason, function best out of their home situation. I had wondered if I could ask Bartholomew for the use of one of his two cottages, but having had the conversation about Enid and money, that clearly was not going to be possible. I tried to keep a mind that was open to all possibilities but, in reality, I was then just too busy and tired, so it would have to wait. Thank God for Eliza. I was pleased to be able to at least put some money in her pocket, as my earnings from teaching the children went towards our midwifery. Very few of our ladies could afford to pay us, so we didn't ask; but their genuine thanks and goodwill cheered us to the core, even though our work sometimes had tragedy attached to it. We often received small gifts, many of them particularly helpful for Eliza's family. A few eggs or jug of milk made a difference to her; and sometimes we would transfer a gift to another mother, particularly if it was health-giving food.

∞

Bartholomew seemed concerned about my pregnancy. I just couldn't understand why he needed to listen to the heartbeat so often. He swore there was nothing wrong and that the beat was strong and even, but would admit only to a sound that he is unfamiliar with. He said it was probably just a chance occurrence because frequently it wasn't there. I trusted him but I wished I could hear myself what he was catching. I struggled to imagine what other noise was being heard because sounds from the womb were not always clear-cut. Bartholomew had taught me all I know and, if he was unsure, I don't think I would have been able myself to diagnose an intermittent noise over and above the sounds from the water sac. Otherwise, our baby was very active. I felt I knew him already, simply based on how he moved. I tried not to worry, especially when Bartholomew reassured me that he had never before been able to study a live pregnancy for its duration, from conception to birth, and at any time of the day or night. I *did* trust him, but it was always on my mind.

I had not heard back from Captain Campbell, but it wasn't really surprising as he might not have even received my letter yet. I was sure he would be happy with Charlotte's development because she had blossomed and seemed far less shy; but he wouldn't know just how much of an improvement that was because the last time he'd seen her, she'd been but a few days old. To us, she was an affectionate child, and I have wondered if that was because we have been the only ones to show her love in her short life. When Captain Campbell returned - and if his wife was not coming back - what would happen to Charlotte, then? Even if Mrs. Campbell *did* come back and wanted to travel with him again, they wouldn't be able to take her with them, surely? It worried me. I felt we had to give her as much love as we could so that she would know what it was.

While I had been dwelling on all these matters, I little suspected that another bombshell was about to explode in our household - and once again, that it would involve Enid. We were at breakfast one morning and expecting to have a discussion later on with the Elwoods about renting their house: what needed doing, what the rate was likely to be and whether we would be able to afford it. As yet Enid knew nothing about our plans; if she had, she might have tried a bit harder to be amenable. I heard the doorbell ring and a few minutes later Mrs. Jenkins came in and asked Bartholomew to go out into the hall and meet the caller.

I heard a woman's voice before they went off into the surgery. There was nothing unusual in that except that most early callers were men, so I had no warning of what was to come. After sending the girls outside to play under Mr. Jenkins's supervision, once again I headed for the kitchen to find out who our caller was. Mrs. Jenkins said that the young woman had declined to give a name and, what was more, was not very well presented. 'In fact,' said Mrs. Jenkins, 'I think she has seen better days. She asked for Doctor Grieve by name and said that he knew her.'

I was intrigued and set about questioning my friend more. Unfortunately, unbeknownst to me, Bartholomew had come down the back stairs and heard my enquiries.

'Esther, leave Mrs. Jenkins be,' came his voice suddenly, 'and come along to my surgery, please. Your questions will all be answered.'

The young woman was indeed dishevelled, and with her abundant hair undressed, she looked as I imagine I did when I climbed out of the scrub during our recent escapade on the beach at Newhaven. Her clothing however was of good quality and some style. She rose and greeted me as I tried to assess who she was and why had she called. She was quite a lot taller than me but I sensed a retiring character rather than someone who would push herself forward.

Bartholomew said, 'Esther, I want to introduce you to Beatrice, whom you will know of as Mrs. George Mackintosh.'

I was completely taken aback. Enid's daughter? No, she couldn't be, I thought. How could these two be mother and daughter? I was so startled by this turn of events that it took me a while to find my manners. Finally, I held out my hand and looked her in the eye but didn't find anyone resembling Enid there at all. She was an extremely attractive woman, with good skin and a calmness about her that conveyed not a hint of the lemon-sour attitude that I attached to Enid.

Bartholomew was saying, 'You will remember, Esther, my telling you that Beatrice and I have communicated privately, unknown to Enid? And that it is better it remains secret? Our difficulty now is to introduce my niece back into her mother's life without a huge and damaging family argument, when things might be said that can never be retracted.'

I asked, 'Will your mother be pleased to see you, Beatrice? I know this might seem a silly question. After all, what mother would not be delighted to see her daughter after a long separation? But I'm afraid my grasp of Enid is limited. Frequently, I don't understand her at all.'

Beatrice did not reply straightaway. I looked at Bartholomew. This was the first time he had seen his niece and it must have been a shock to him but I could tell he was pleasantly surprised. I could see the admiration in his eyes; in looks and manner she was strikingly beautiful.

Suddenly, she sat down and I could feel the fatigue emanating from her. When she spoke, it was with a soft, rounded Scottish accent that had none of the harsh tones of Enid's, and I sensed a cultured lilt to it.

'It depends on how my mother took the visit from my husband,' she said. 'I am afraid she will not welcome me with open arms, especially as I bear the evidence of my shame. I'm sorry to tell you that I am expecting a child and that it might not be my husband's.' Her face flushed delicately as she gave us this unexpected piece of news.

I was dismayed, but I tried not to let her see that. A pregnancy as a result of adultery would make it very difficult to introduce Beatrice into society, let alone confront her mother.

'What can we do to help?' I said, as Bartholomew seemed unable to speak. Already I liked this young woman's manner; she was nothing like the picture I'd had of her in my mind. In the past I had come near to hating her as she had been held up as a paragon of class, virtue and womanhood: someone I could never aspire to be.

I glared at Bartholomew to urge him to respond, and quickly. Fortunately, Beatrice had been looking at me when she spoke and had not registered the look of consternation on his face. He's a physician, for heaven's sake, I thought; he shouldn't be surprised by this turn of events. Once again, it came to me that Bartholomew was inclined to put different interpretations on things when his own family was involved. My own use of herbs when pregnant was the first example I had seen of this attitude; and now he was doing it again, with his niece declaring a pregnancy out of wedlock.

'I have come to ask my uncle if I can take refuge here until my baby is born,' said Beatrice quietly. 'I have no options left to me. In fact, I have slept outside for these last two nights, my money is all gone and I have not eaten for a while. My husband has cut off everything from me, even access to my jewellery. I'd hoped to be able to sell it. I think he intends to drive me into the gutter, which is where he says I belong.'

I turned to Bartholomew and suggested, 'Why don't I take Beatrice upstairs so that she can refresh herself? We wouldn't want Enid to see her after two nights out in the open. If she is restored to her proper self, then we would avoid at least some of the anger that Enid will undoubtedly feel.'

I was trying to say that Enid would find it very, very shameful indeed if her daughter were not seen in the best light, regardless of any past deeds. I remembered what Bartholomew had said to me when we were in Gibraltar: that I must dress myself fittingly for the status I was claiming as governess and midwife to the Elwood family, rather than the one that had been imposed on me as a female convict. He told me that people only saw what was on the outside. I had taken his advice and spent some of his money on suitable clothing and shoes. If I had come back barefoot and dirty, I would not have met with the respect or kindness of the many people who helped me settle back in. It is, sadly, the way of the world.

Finally, Bartholomew found his voice. 'Yes, Esther, we should certainly do that. If you take Beatrice up the back stairs, there will be less chance of Enid coming upon her.' He smiled then at his niece and I thanked heaven he had recovered himself.

The back stairs were accessed from the kitchen, so I peeped outside the surgery and, seeing that the coast was clear, hurried our visitor down to Mrs. Jenkins's domain. Enid would never demean herself by coming down to the kitchen so I knew we were safe there, but neither did I want to bump into the girls who might innocently let the cat out of the bag.

'Do you know where the girls are, Mrs. Jenkins? We need to get Beatrice up to my room without seeing anyone.' I had briefly explained who our visitor was, knowing that she would not gossip.

'I think they went out to the stable to visit Flossy. I will go and check.' She returned minutes later. 'Aye, they are helping Mr. Jenkins groom the horses. I asked him to keep them outside for a while,' she added tactfully.

'Thank you, we will go up now. Could you ask Wini to bring up a pitcher of hot water? She can leave it outside my door, as the fewer people who know that Beatrice is here, the better.'

'Wini is occupied with Mrs. McGovern, so you have a good fifteen minutes or so before she comes back down. I will bring the water up myself and perhaps something to eat.' Mrs. Jenkins looked at Beatrice enquiringly and saw the gratitude in her face.

I led Beatrice up the stairs and checked no one was about before hurrying her into our bedroom. 'If you remove your outer clothing, I will tidy and freshen it up and you can conduct your toilet in peace.' She did as I suggested, disrobing down to her undergarments. I saw that her clothing was of the very finest quality and monogrammed, but when she turned her back to me, I was horrified to see some livid diagonal scarring. It was so shocking to see this gentlewoman bearing the marks of brute force that I sank into a chair.

'Do you need medical attention, Beatrice?' I said gently. 'I am quite skilled with herbs and Bartholomew is, of course, a physician.'

'No, thank you, Esther, the scarring on my back and shoulders is mostly healed. I do appreciate your help in assisting me and perhaps when I am ready to divulge everything, you will understand all that has driven me to this predicament. I had nowhere else to go but I realise my arrival is dreadfully difficult for you, particularly knowing that I am with child.'

She blinked a few tears away and my heart went out to her.

'I understand, Beatrice. Please don't think that we are seeking information in order to judge. I am a midwife and have seen many unwelcome things in the course of my work. Bartholomew is not happy for me to use my herbal knowledge on pregnant women – on myself, in particular – though he never worried about it before now. He thinks that we do not always understand the efficacy of some of the herbs, and while I have to abide by what he says in my own pregnancy, personally I have full confidence in my knowledge and I regularly use various herbs for maladies of pregnancy and to make soothing unguents. Let me know if you change your mind. I can help you, Beatrice. Please don't feel that we are unwelcoming in any way.'

There was a light tap on the door and I opened it to find a full jug of hot water left on the floor.

'Here you are,' I said, placing it carefully by my washing bowl. 'I will go into my little dressing room now and do what I can with your clothes.'

It wasn't too long before Beatrice was elegantly dressed, her hair brushed and pinned back with two lovely little combs. I had removed the mud and debris off her dress and cloak, then cleaned the clags from her dainty shoes. They had not stood up well to all the walking, the stitching on the seams splitting apart. My own shoes would not do for her because of the insert that had been fitted but I did, however, have some light slippers and offered them to her for the time being. She would have to buy some new footwear soon; but, after spitting on the shoes, they came up well enough and the length of her skirt covered the damage.

Mrs. Jenkins brought up a tray of my tea with some bread, cheese and cakes she had made yesterday. Beatrice was clearly very hungry and we sat together in companionable silence as she ate. I was dying to ask lots of questions but managed to refrain, other than asking if she knew how many weeks with child she was. When she had taken her dress off, I could not yet see the outline of her pregnancy. Then I asked, as delicately as I was able, 'Have you had any earlier pregnancies, even if they did not hold?'

'No, I have been married for quite some time, about twelve years, but no babies quickened. I wondered if there was something wrong with me. My husband certainly thought so.'

'Women always seem to take the blame for infertility,' I said, 'but it takes two to make a child. In your case, you are clearly fertile.'

'Perhaps we can avoid George finding out about it,' she said anxiously. By saying 'we', she clearly meant the three of us - I just hoped that Bartholomew would be able to live with that.

Later, when were alone, Bartholomew and I discussed what Beatrice's arrival would mean to our household, but not before we had reflected on the difficulties of her journey all the way from Scotland.

'I promised to let George know if his wife came here, but I could delay that information until we have some sort of resolution. I wasn't expecting to have to tell him that his wife is pregnant, though,' Bartholomew said ruefully.

'You were expecting her to arrive, then?' I asked. 'Do we have to tell anyone yet that Beatrice is pregnant? And when it becomes obvious, can't we let it be assumed that the child is her husband's?'

'No, I wasn't "expecting her" but it did cross my mind after she went missing that she might head for here. And to answer your other questions, it depends on whether the censure about George spreads down here. Enid won't want it known generally and neither would we, but gossip has a nasty habit of following people around. Beatrice is unknown in England, so she might be lucky; her husband's constituency is in Scotland and he probably doesn't go to Westminster too often. Some MPs barely warm the seats, they're so rarely there,' he added with contempt in his voice. 'Esther, I have a lot of work to do today. Can we postpone this discussion for a few hours?'

'Actually, no, Bartholomew, I don't think we can. The girls, the Jenkinses, even Enid herself could let something slip. We have to be prepared. Is it patients you need to see or town duties? What about an hour to sort out your urgent work? Meanwhile I will get my thinking cap on and make sure the girls are occupied.'

He agreed. I went downstairs to ask Mrs. Jenkins to take him some coffee - then I would sort out Beth and Charlotte and ask Wini to watch them. It was still early in the day and no patients were due until after dinner. I returned to the surgery at ten of the clock ready to discuss Beatrice and Enid.

'An idea came to me, Bartholomew,' I said. 'Couldn't we pass Beatrice off as a patient of mine whose pregnancy has to be monitored by me? That is, after all, what I want to do in the future: provide lying-in accommodation for vulnerable women.'

'But not in our own home!' Bartholomew looked horrified at the thought.

'Of course, I wouldn't expect to have unknown women here, but she is your niece. Surely that makes a difference?'

'Yes, but people won't know she is my niece. They will think I am running a home for fallen women - especially as there is no husband in sight.'

I wondered if he was worrying that the disdain that was coming Beatrice's way would fall upon him. Taking in a pregnant woman from an adulterous relationship would not be seen as an act of charity and might well affect our standing in the community. Any disapproval would be an extra load for Bartholomew to shoulder, not to mention giving shelter to yet another woman and child in his house. In my imagination, I suddenly saw him fading away or running off to sea again, so worn down by all the people living or hoping to live in his house, demanding his time, care and support. Until two years ago, he was living alone; perhaps he was wishing that it were still so. I shook these niggling thoughts away as I watched him anxiously moving his quill, diary and other objects around his desk. I could see the agitation in his stance as well as the obsessive way he was rearranging everything.

'We will have to tell Enid that her daughter is here,' Bartholomew said finally. 'If George was right that Enid herself committed adultery all those years ago, she might be open to creating a shield around her daughter.' He was clearly thinking aloud and not expecting an answer but I didn't let that deter me.

'Perhaps we could get them both to move into John Elwood's house near the old West Gate? That might resolve all the issues. After all, many women do return to their mother's care when their pregnancies are fragile, just as Cecilia did. Then we could keep Beatrice under wraps and find her some clothes that don't show a growing baby.' At the back of my mind, a doubt entered: no clothes could disguise my own pregnancy, I was gaining so much weight. I persisted nonetheless: 'We won't have to tell George because we can say we didn't know anything about it.'

'That is always supposing that Enid *agrees* to moving into the house and to having her daughter live with her,' Bartholomew said glumly.

'Do you think that George might be persuaded to support his wife?' I asked, going off at a tangent.

'No, you heard him rant. Even when he calms down, he is unlikely to agree. Pride and high self-opinion will prevent it. He's been cuckolded - no man likes to admit to that.'

'But surely he should send on Beatrice's clothing and jewellery when he knows where she is. Did she have a dowry, or some money of her own, perhaps?'

'I don't think that is likely. We could ask Enid - but if her husband was doubtful about Beatrice's paternity, he would be unlikely to have bestowed a dowry on her.'

'I think George should return her jewellery, at the very least,' I insisted, 'but the longer we can keep this quiet, the better chance we have of protecting her.'

Bartholomew fell quiet for a moment, then said, 'I know of women, usually in the families of my richer patients, being sent away for the duration of a pregnancy, and the offspring then placed with a childless couple. In fact, Esther, that is a good solution. Perhaps we should suggest that?'

I could see that he was looking at this entirely from a man's point of view and at the same time trimming his quill to within an inch of its life. I put out my hand and took it from him before saying, 'It might be a good solution for men, Doctor Grieve, but I can't think of many women who would voluntarily give away their babies. And let me remind you that I am qualified to say that - I have met a lot of pregnant women! And, where would she go, pray tell? We don't know anyone who would accommodate such an arrangement, do we? In any case, Beatrice might not want to farm her baby out to an unknown family. I certainly wouldn't!' I declared stoutly, though suddenly Mrs. Campbell flashed into my mind as an example of a woman who had done exactly that, albeit we weren't unknown to her.

'No, true, but it could be a solution.'

I could see him clinging to that convenient prospect, before he went on to say, 'Now, when are we going to bring the two of them together?'

'I think it will need to be soon. We can't hide Beatrice for long without explanations. Perhaps you should speak to Enid first? She listens to you. I could take Charlotte and Beth to the Elwoods while you approach the subject when you are alone with her. You will have to admit that

Beatrice is here in the house already, so the fewer people around to hear the likely hysterical reaction from Enid, the better. Or perhaps it would be more sensible - as the pregnancy does not show at all as yet - to bring Beatrice and her mother together but not mention anything to Enid about the baby for the moment. Actually, I think that might be the best way,' I decided. 'It buys us time.'

'When are you next due at South Farm?'

'Tomorrow. We can stay all day and keep Mr. Jenkins with us, too, which will leave only you, the two of them and Mrs. Jenkins. I will speak to her - we know she is discreet. I can also tell her to give Wini the day off. What do you think?'

Bartholomew agreed, saying, 'That is reasonable, but if, say, we did decide to inform Enid about the baby tomorrow, I would need to have an alternative plan in mind. In my experience, when people have to make difficult decisions, they react better when there is choice.'

One obvious solution came to me. 'Well, if you do feel it necessary to mention the baby,' I said, 'what about asking Mrs. Makepiece, as an alternative plan? She took me in with a child knowing that it was not mine. People know that she occasionally has lodgers and, as you said, no one knows Beatrice in this area. She could perhaps even suggest that Beatrice is affianced to one of her sons.'

'Mrs. Makepiece's sons are rough and ready from a life at sea. Beatrice is quite different - even with a change of clothing, she wouldn't fit that bill. But staying there is a good idea in the short term: no one would need to say what their relationship is. In fact, it would make an excellent alternative to Enid and her daughter being together whilst all this anger is swirling round - and until the renovations are complete, which might be a while.'

'Still, the best solution for us all in the end,' I said, 'would be to settle them together in a separate establishment. Enid might look on our plan to rent a property for her with more willingness once she gets used to the idea and that she would have her first grandchild with her.'

Bartholomew grimaced. 'I am not sure she will see that as an advantage! But, yes, in the meantime, just for today, Beatrice could stay quietly in our room upstairs. The children won't expect to go in there nor will Wini if you tell her not to.'

'I could go down to see Mrs. Makepiece this morning and ask her about it. Beatrice would be a lot safer there than with us, after all. There'd be no chance of George tracking her down - nor of Enid, the children and Wini accidentally coming across her.' I felt ready to go there and then, so keen was I to find a good solution.

I could see Bartholomew was relieved that Beatrice might not have to be hidden in our house for long, and

I have to say I agreed with that: it could complicate the outcome we wanted.

'I will go down to Keere Street shortly, and in the meantime, I'll ask Beatrice to stay upstairs until we have found a solution.' I rose, ready to put everything in place.

'Make sure you ask Mr. Jenkins to accompany you, my dear.'

'Yes, I will.' With so much going on, I found it easy to forget my own safety, despite the recent incident.

'Oh, and another thing,' Bartholomew said. 'Our friend Mason is planning on going down to Portsmouth as Captain Campbell's ship is due to dock soon. He hasn't got a date yet but I thought to warn you.'

'Good heavens, that was quick. I haven't even had a reply to my letter. Now, I must get to Keere Street in case Mrs. Makepiece goes out.'

I rushed out of the study and flew up to our room where Beatrice was quietly doing some of the hemming I had left lying about. She looked peaceful and I felt myself drawn to her. She must have suffered a truly frightful ordeal to have all that scarring on her body and surely even deeper emotional distress as well, so I was happy that she had escaped and was now safe with us in Lewes.

I sat down next to her and said: 'Beatrice, I am just going to see a friend who might be able to help us find a solution to our predicament. I won't be long. Please can you lock the door so the girls don't find their way in? Mrs. Jenkins will bring you up some refreshments if I am not back by our midday meal. It is important that no one sees you. Bartholomew is uncomfortable with lying to George but we don't want him to find out that you are in Lewes, least of all here.'

'Whatever you think best, Esther. I am so grateful that Uncle Bartholomew is prepared to help me, and you too. I know my mother has not made things easy for you.' She raised her beautiful eyes to mine, and I understood that she had heard the worst of her mother's tales and venom through the letters that passed between them.

I held and pressed her hand in mine, wondering that she could feel sympathy for me whilst suffering so much herself. Her reasons for the actions she had taken must have been powerful ones and I for one wasn't going to decry them.

'Mrs Jenkins will knock when she knows the coast is clear, so don't worry. I hope I will be back soon with good news. In the meantime, Beatrice, you are safe and in Barty's care. We are both so pleased that you came to us for help. We won't let you down.'

## CHAPTER 11

*Chamomile (Chamaemelum nobile).* *A stone that hath been taken out of the body of a man being wrapped in Chamomile, will in time dissolve, and in a little time, too. Astrology: The Egyptians dedicated it to the sun.*

*Culpeper's Colour Herbal*

Mr. Jenkins walked with me to Keere Street and then returned home when Mrs. Makepiece said she would accompany me back. All this security was a nuisance and I was beginning to think that Digger's son Abe must have left the area as I had seen neither hide nor hair of him since the day he tried to attack us on our way to Cecilia's, and of course it might have been him spying on us that day of the picnic. Our walk to Keere Street had been slow as there were so many people about, it being a livestock market day, according to Mr. Jenkins. The High Street was always busy but that day there seemed to be so many carriages and wagons kicking up dust, I kept having to step aside into shop doorways. However, we got there in one piece, despite my having to keep my skirts up rather higher than I would have preferred. I had a voluminous cloak that was perfect for advancing pregnancy: I didn't like to draw attention to myself and my condition as some people seemed to regard it as something that should be hidden. I still had two months to go before our baby was born and I was certainly not going to hide away for that amount of time.

'Mrs. Makepiece, I have to swear you to secrecy about something,' I said, as soon as I had taken off my bonnet and outer clothing.

'Why, what have you done *now*?' She looked amused by my declaration.

'Me? Nothing. But this morning we had a visitor who has thrown herself on our mercy and we are trying to think of a way to protect her.'

'Good heavens! Who from?'

'Her husband, and maybe Enid too.'

She raised her eyebrows. 'You had better sit down and tell me all about it then.'

It took quite a long time to explain and then to ask if she would take Beatrice in as a lodger for a while.

'But supposing Enid refuses to move into the Elwoods' house?' she asked. 'And, if she does, say, agree to move, but then won't give her daughter a home?'

I sighed at the thought. 'I think we will have to cross that bridge when we come to it. In the meantime, would you consider taking Beatrice in and keeping her secret?

Bartholomew would pay you a lodging fee for her, and she is really very nice - so nice, in fact, that it is difficult to see her as Enid's daughter. If she is here, we won't have to lie to George. It is all a bit delicate, but it would be very awkward for us if Beatrice was under our roof.'

'How long do you think she will be able to keep her pregnancy hidden? Is she showing?'

'No, far from it – ages, if she doesn't go out and draw attention to herself,' I replied. 'She has only to wear loose clothing in the short term. Cecilia's house might be ready then, so that Enid could take her in as a daughter who is in need of her mother's care. Bartholomew wants to try and negotiate both Enid's removal as well as George's return of Beatrice's jewellery and clothes.'

'Surely, if Bartholomew asks for the jewellery, it will imply that Beatrice is here under his care?'

'We were thinking that Bartholomew could tell George he has heard from Beatrice by letter, saying that she has gone abroad and is asking him to act on her behalf; she is, after all, his niece. No one need say that she is in Lewes. I am sure there is room to bargain, once all the shouting has died down.'

'You will have to tell Cecilia, as well,' said Mrs. Makepiece. 'Have you thought of that?'

'Yes, but she will help,' I said.

'Are you sure? It is quite a thing you are asking of her.'

I was surprised at this comment but went on to say, 'Cecilia is a very compassionate woman. She will understand Beatrice's predicament.'

'Well, I hope you are right.' Mrs. Makepiece rose and went into the kitchen. I could see she wanted a moment to think. After a while she returned, saying, 'I will let Beatrice stay here, as you ask, but we will have to make up a likely story about her until Enid can be persuaded to move and the house is ready. Have you thought, though, that Enid might tell George herself that Beatrice is here, out of spite?'

'No, she wouldn't do that,' I said firmly. 'She hates him as much as he hates her. But, thank you, thank you. I will go to see Cecilia tomorrow and stay out of the way while Bartholomew talks to his sister. When can I bring Beatrice down?'

'This evening, after dark. Now, I will walk you home. Then I must go and sort out some extra provisions and get back in time to air the bedding.'

We walked slowly back up Keere Street. It is very steep, with a cobbled surface that was quite tricky for me to manage. Mrs. Makepiece left me at the barbican and I gave her a kiss as she set off to prepare for her unexpected visitor.

Bartholomew was sitting in his study when I got home, his desk as always immaculately arranged, looking distinctly troubled.

'How did you get on?' he asked.

'We are to take Beatrice down this evening after dark,' I said, discarding my boots and bonnet and suddenly feeling rather weary. 'Now, I think I need a rest. I'll make myself comfortable in the breakfast room as Beatrice might be sleeping upstairs, and the girls can come in and play with their toys.'

After supper Bartholomew went out and prepared for the trip to the bottom of Keere Street. They could easily have walked but he thought it best to take her in the gig as she would not be so visible. In the end he introduced Beatrice to Mrs. Makepiece himself, as I was exhausted by all the excitement and it was easier for him to go out at night without inviting comment.

As I waited for him to return, I was amazed to think that it was only that morning that Beatrice had arrived. It felt so much longer than that.

∞

The next morning the girls and I took the gig to South Farm with Mr. Jenkins riding Flossy alongside us. It was quite early; the ground was still heavy and damp and I could feel autumn taking hold. November is such a variable month: you never quite know what to expect. After I had given a lesson up in the nursery to Freddie and Beth, I took them down to play in the stable yard where they were learning how to curry the ponies. Charlotte went up to have a nap with Felicia. They were near enough in age to settle down together and with luck Cecy and I would have at least an hour undisturbed.

Cilla brought some lemon slices and hot water to Cecilia's sitting room so we could make tea for ourselves. As soon as she left, I embarked on telling my friend all about our visitor: what she was like, her accent, how she had impressed me and how horrifying it was to think of her having to sleep outside on the journey to us. I elaborated on her travels from Scotland by coach with what little money she had, having to move in the final stages from an inside seat to becoming an outside passenger, only to suffer the ribald comments of the male travellers up top; then, having finally run out of ready money and with nothing to barter, how she'd had to walk from East Grinstead to Lewes - in all, a journey of hundreds of miles.

As I talked, I paced the room while Cecilia quietly made the tea. I couldn't just sit down and drink without having described how Beatrice had then hidden herself in a barn for her first night on foot; and, for the second, found a hayrick somewhere near Chailey. In neither place had she slept well, constantly afraid that she would be discovered and come to harm, alarmed by the squeaks of rats and mice all about her and worrying about being bitten.

Finally, I sat down and took a sip of the hot tea before saying that I had tried to imagine myself having to sleep in a hayrick and how it made my skin crawl. It was only after going right back to the beginning and recounting the whole story of Beatrice and George that, with some trepidation, I told her that Beatrice was also with child but unsure who the father was. I carefully outlined how Bartholomew and I thought that the pregnancy could be hidden for some time, or indeed until the child was actually born. By that time, George might have given up on making life difficult for his wife, as he had seemed more distressed at being cuckolded by a mere stableman than by losing his wife. I mentioned also that he had no idea as yet that a child was expected and that it would make him even angrier because his wife had not borne him a son and heir and he blamed her for the lack of one. I was becoming aware of the sound of my own voice, gabbling on; suddenly I heard again in my head Mrs. Makepiece's warning note and it came to me that her query might well be justified.

Cecilia rose from her couch and walked to the window, remaining there with her back to me as I enquired how the renovations on the house were coming along. Probably this was not the most tactful thing to go on to say because she guessed what I was going to ask of her; perhaps she had known much earlier in our conversation.

She turned back towards me but I couldn't see her expression as the light was behind her.

'You are hoping to move Enid in, and then settle her daughter and the baby with her in our house. Is that it?' she said evenly, but there was a stiffness in her voice and her body.

Cecilia didn't speak while I soldiered on, setting out Beatrice's sorrows and George's anger once more but it was only when I told her about the livid scarring that I caught a flicker of sympathy on her face as she returned to the seat beside me. I was beginning to feel uncomfortable and thought it better to confront the matter head-on.

I said, 'You are right, Cecilia - settling them all in the house was what I was hoping we could arrange with you. Would you find it difficult to agree to my plan? Would John disapprove, maybe to the point of declining the association?'

'For my part,' she said after a long pause, 'I would trust your judgement of Beatrice's character. But surely you can understand that we cannot be seen to condone this, Esther, even though we know it goes on in many families? It is difficult to know how John would see this. He might be sympathetic, or he might not. He is a conservative man who believes in the sanctity of marriage, and so do I.'

I looked directly into her eyes before saying, 'If we do come to ask this of you, Cecilia, what would you personally think?' I asked this because I knew that Cecy could talk John into anything.

'There are two sides to a story, Esther. And even if your Beatrice is more sinned against than sinning - though I am not sure whether that is the case here or not - the situation would have to be presented in such a way that everyone could accept what is in front of them at face value, so that there is no cause for suspicion or for anyone to start unpicking the story. If that were to happen, it would embarrass us all and at the very least show John and I to be complicit. I am afraid that would be unacceptable to us and under those circumstances we would have to ask them to leave.'

I nodded, feeling my spirits slump as she continued, her tone clipped: 'It is unfair that women are always cast as the promiscuous party, even though in Beatrice's case it appears that she is. Perhaps we expect too much by looking to people of privilege to be a model of good behaviour.'

Cecilia seemed to be following through an intricate line of thought in her mind; perhaps in a battle with herself, to be fair.

'But, in general,' she went on, 'one only needs to look at the affairs and peccadilloes of our royal family - the Prince of Wales is a case in point - and of the nobility, too, to see that they set no good example. The Duke of Devonshire has a beautiful and well-born wife, yet she has to compete for his attention with his mistress, who was once her best friend but clearly had designs on the duke from the beginning of their friendship. They all live together now in a ménage à trois, with the children from both women, hard as that may be to believe.'

I was so astonished by this revelation that I sat openmouthed as Cecilia continued speaking.

'The Duchess Georgiana knew she wasn't safe in her marriage until she had borne a son and heir, which she finally did about ten years ago. She understood that she couldn't demand or expect fidelity until she had done her duty but, even now, after all this time, she still has to put up with the duke's mistress in her own property and, seemingly, with equal status, except for the title. Mind you, it is rumoured that Georgiana has also had a child out of wedlock, with a politician (I won't say who). The baby, a girl, was sent away but is now being raised by her paternal grandparents. Poor Georgiana has to visit her in secret while her husband conducts his affair in full view of their circle and the world at large.' Cecilia shook her head in bewilderment. 'These things happen all the time and no one escapes scot-free, particularly the women, whereas the men seem to gain in reputation rather than lose it.

'However, Esther, my rather long-winded point is that while I understand the hypocrisy of this kind of behaviour, the fact is that the likes of John and myself are *expected* to behave with propriety. If we don't, then both family and public censure can be harsh and damaging. And, Esther, I'd remind you that if people of status distanced themselves from us, the repercussions would have an impact on our children and their position in society. People would not want to be associated with such disgrace and those who connived at it.'

I felt my face beginning to redden with the growing disquiet I was feeling. As the daughter of an earl, Cecilia would know at first-hand how her peers might react. Shaken, I tried to make amends: 'I am so sorry, Cecilia, I didn't mean to trouble you with other people's problems. But I do feel bound to try and help Beatrice - even more so, when I saw evidence of the beatings she has endured!

I realise now that I am asking a great deal of you, at little cost to myself or Bartholomew.'

'I am not sure you *do* understand what you are asking of us, Esther,' Cecilia snapped back.

Her face had paled and I could see she was upset as well as angry, though I knew any such loss of control would be abhorrent to her; I sensed her struggling to maintain her composure. I sat very still, troubled by what I had unleashed through my thoughtlessness.

'I will have to think about it,' she said, eventually. 'If we were to present this to the outside world satisfactorily - perhaps by saying that the child is her husband's - all might be well. You will have to enquire, carefully, if this is indeed a possibility - dates can easily get confused. You should also find out if Beatrice intends to keep the baby once born. If she doesn't, then there is no problem, is there? She will just have to hide the pregnancy and birth, though goodness only knows what would become of the child. I might find myself judging her solely on how she deals with that eventuality,' she added, rather primly.

We sat quietly for a short while thinking about the dilemma and its ramifications. There appeared to be no easy solution and I felt I had overstepped the mark in the friendship I enjoyed with Cecilia.

At last, she sighed and said, 'I won't mention anything to John until such time as we have more information. I must say that this whole affair is rather unfortunate for poor Bartholomew! I am sure he has ample fortune, but it is a heavy price for him to pay - to have to keep both his sister and his niece, never mind a baby, as well - and if this all comes out, it could seriously damage his professional reputation. However, we will carry on with the renovation of the house meanwhile. John has a great deal of time for Bartholomew, and that might sway his decision.'

Cecilia looked at me before adding, coolly, 'I would council you to great secrecy, Esther. Remember, people will know about this already. A woman such as Beatrice cannot move freely about the countryside without exciting comment; her looks and accent will define her. Anyone would wonder: who is she, where is she going, who does she belong to - and why is she travelling with the common people as an outside passenger when she clearly isn't accustomed to doing so?'

I wanted to interrupt but didn't. She clearly had more to say and I knew it would be better to bite my tongue and listen.

'Beatrice's arrival in a small town like Lewes will also not have gone unnoticed. There is another issue, too. Suppose her lover turns up here after we have all claimed the child to be her husband's? We would become embroiled in further scandal. I do not know this woman and I am not sure I want to take such risks for someone with whom I have no connection and whose behaviour has been so greatly wanting.'

I was dismayed to think that my grand scheme was flawed but the children were clamouring for our attention, so we ended our discussion, with each of us having a lot to think about.

It was a relief when we were called to the dining room. Mrs. Fisher made us a light and tasty dinner of pease soup followed by bacon pudding. I was quite pleased to see that her seasoning had improved, with some delicate herb flavours in both courses. This was finished with a lemon syllabub and Savoy biscuits which the children particularly enjoyed. Cecilia was very quiet while we were eating and I knew I had pushed her too far.

Later, on our return to Lewes after an awkward afternoon walk and a stilted goodbye, we entered the house via the back door. I had hoped to see Mrs. Jenkins so she could give me an idea of how the talk with Enid had gone but she wasn't in the kitchen and all was very quiet. Brown Betty was in the stable so Bartholomew was probably at home: his coroner's work was generally done in the morning unless something awful had happened in the neighbourhood. I led the girls upstairs to take off their outer clothing and left them there while I went to find something for their tea. Perhaps Mrs. Jenkins was having a rest in her own quarters whilst we were all occupied.

I soon found the children's tea things under a cloth in the pantry where it stays cold no matter how warm the kitchen gets. I took the tray up to the dining room and called them down. We three sat and enjoyed our food, though I took only a glass of milk and a biscuit. I kept returning to my conversation with Cecilia and the more I thought about it, the worse I felt. Cecilia was my best friend - and there I was, trying to inveigle her into a course of action that would be distasteful to both her and John.

As soon as the girls were finished, I went back upstairs to play with them before getting them ready for bed, so it was some time before I went to find Bartholomew in his surgery where he was sitting quietly with only one candle burning on the desk before him. He looked sad but made a real effort to smile at me.

'Well,' I said, 'how did it go? Did you speak to Enid?'

'Yes, we had words. It wasn't a pleasant conversation, as you guessed it wouldn't be. Really, Essie, my sister is a truly vindictive woman and it's because of that I am forced to remove her from my house,' he said, then correcting himself, '*our* house.'

I was stunned at his declaration. 'Oh Bartholomew, I am so sorry. Was it dreadful for you? What did she say?'

'She raised the matter of Beatrice's paternity before I even got half a dozen words out - she must have been stewing on it ever since George's visit. She brought up and denied his "wicked insinuations" in the most scathing language. I thought it might lance the boil, so to speak, so I let her have her say with no interruptions. Once she had got that off her chest, she seemed to calm down, so I told her that Beatrice was staying with friends and that I was proposing to rent a property for them here in Lewes so that mother and daughter could be together.'

'And,' I said eagerly, 'was she pleased?'

'Far from it, she flew into a rage. I am beginning to wonder if there is something wrong with my sister - some diseases of the mind can manifest in unreasonable behaviour. But I had underestimated the value she puts on living here in "our family home", as she put it. I think what really sticks in her craw is that you are mistress of what she thinks of as *her* house, and nothing will change that.'

'Did she not realise that she and her daughter would at least be together and independent? I take it you didn't mention the baby?'

'No, I didn't. Childbearing is such an unknown quantity - a first child, an older mother, the high level of early miscarriage - I thought it best to leave it until a later date. Anyway, I went downstairs and suggested to Mrs. Jenkins that she might like to go out and do some shopping. Then I came back, and I'm afraid it was as if we were children again but with the tone and language much, much worse. She does not want to see her daughter because she has brought shame on Enid by having an affair and, even worse, by being caught in the most embarrassing of circumstances. I think she held her daughter's marriage and position in society so high, and now it has all come crashing down - in front of you and me, as well - and she won't forgive that.'

'Oh, my dear. What are we to do, then?'

'Well, I have had enough, Esther. I am afraid she can no longer live here; she will have to find somewhere else. I have told her to find rooms and to use her own resources to pay for them. I do not believe that she is without income. Several things that she said originally, she contradicted today. In short, I believe she has told me a whole pack of lies!'

'But has she no compassion for Beatrice on the breakdown of her marriage?'

'No, none! I think it might be a case of having been found so wanting herself all those years ago that she has now become holier-than-thou - consequently, louder in her condemnation. She described Beatrice as a "whore and sinner" amongst other things which I won't offend your ears by repeating. Her hypocrisy is breath-taking. I am sorry to tell you all this, but you must understand what we are dealing with because there will be repercussions. There is no going back. Enid is now disowned by me as a sister. The sooner she leaves, the better, and I have no intention of funding her.'

I was flabbergasted by Bartholomew's tale and his evident displeasure at being taken in by his sister's falsehoods. But I was also sorry that there could be no happy ending for mother, daughter and grandchild.

I went to the dresser and poured us both a tot of brandy from the bottle Bartholomew keeps in his surgery. We sat for a long time consoling each other and thinking of how we could help Beatrice. As Bartholomew said, she was the person who needed help and was the most deserving. How I loved Bartholomew at that moment. So honourable and kind to a niece he had never even met before yesterday, not to mention one who was in great trouble and whose problems could have an impact on his own social position. I did suggest that Enid could cause him some damage once the news got out that she had been asked to leave his home. He responded that his reputation was more than resilient enough to deal with the mutterings of a "foolish and possibly deranged woman". 'Reputation is not worth a jot,' he said, 'if it can be lost so easily.'

After supper I went early to bed feeling terribly weary and saddened by our mutually difficult day. Bartholomew brought me up some warm milk with a small sedative and I tried desperately to get to sleep. I really couldn't understand how someone could have so much hate in them when there was no great cause. People from all walks of life have difficulties, but most learn how to overcome or put them aside. Tilly had hated me - but she thought she had strong cause in the loss of her two sons, even if their deaths were not my fault. Even the boy Abe thought he had good reason to hate me because he could blame me for both his parents' death. With Enid, on the other hand, it was all so trivial and vindictive. But at least she was leaving and I was so relieved to know that. At the back of my mind, though, I wondered how things would turn out now. Would Mrs. Makepiece keep Beatrice as her lodger now Enid had flatly refused the company of her daughter?

The following day, I stayed in bed until mid-morning. I had not felt I could burden Bartholomew with Cecilia's cold reception of my plans; nor had I slept well, fretting that I had seriously damaged my friendship for what appeared to be no good reason now that Bartholomew was throwing Enid out. The girls came in and played happily around and under the bed and soon encouraged me up, so I rose and got dressed to go out. I planned to visit Mrs. Makepiece and her lodger but not before writing a note to Cecilia to apologise for suggesting that she and John should put themselves in such an invidious position. I explained that Enid was no longer part of our family and that Bartholomew had asked her to leave. My excuse to Cecilia was that I was out of sorts but that I now realised that I needed to calm myself and stop trying to mend everyone's problems. I sealed the note and asked Mr. Jenkins to take it to South Farm as soon as possible, but not to wait for a reply.

## CHAPTER 12

*Elder (**Sambucus nigra**). The wholehearted
healer is bountiful and generous with sweet
flowers, juicy berries and healing properties in
all parts. Her vigorous growth, full of life and
death, reflects the majesty of Grandmothers,
traditionally keepers of wisdom for their
communities. They supported their tribe with
plant lore and compassionate guidance gained
from seeing the setbacks and triumphs of
generations.*

Yvonne McDermott of Forest Moons.

Bartholomew offered to walk me down to Keere Street
and we agreed a time for Mr. Jenkins to meet me at the
bottom of the steep hill an hour and a half later. It was becoming increasingly difficult for me to move around. My
baby was all out the front whereas some women seemed
to carry further back into the spine. It made moving so
uncomfortable that I felt unbalanced and vulnerable. I
compensated by leaning back, which wasn't very good for
my posture, but there it was. Bartholomew held my arm
and promised to send the gig with Mr. Jenkins later.

When I knocked on the door, it was opened quickly by Mrs. Makepiece who peered round the edge rather than opening it fully as she would normally do.

'Come in, Esther,' she said, ushering me in. 'We are both glad to see you and hopefully you can tell us what is going on. Bartholomew told Beatrice here that he was intending to speak to her mother yesterday, so we're agog to know what the next step will be?'

I had the impression that Mrs. Makepiece was rather enjoying her clandestine role. I wondered what to tell them but decided that honesty was the best policy. It took but a few minutes to outline all that Bartholomew had told me. Beatrice wept a few tears which threw us both into a fluster, so we made a great effort at settling her down and reassuring her that we were ready to help her, no matter what. She was very pale and looked drained. The last month must have been incredibly hard on her and God only knows what her married life had been like previous to that. Mrs. Makepiece produced a tiny glass of canary for her and suggested that I have one too. It was too early for me, but she had one herself to keep Beatrice company. In my mind's eye, I kept seeing those scars on her back, looking so very raw, and I was sure I could improve the healing with a salve from some of my herbs. I decided I would prepare something, no matter what Bartholomew said, and bring it on my next visit.

'I think you must make ready to stay here very quietly, Beatrice, avoiding all visitors until such time as we have a resolution to our dilemma. You are among friends,' I said, looking to Mrs. Makepiece for reassurance that it was the case. As I expected, the dear lady nodded vigorously and put her arm round her new lodger.

'Aye,' she agreed wholeheartedly, 'you will be safe here with me. We will invent a history and a reason for you being in Lewes, in case of busybodies.'

'I don't think we need plan any further than the next few weeks, as things can often resolve themselves naturally,' I said. 'Once Enid has left our home, we will be able to see things clearly and we won't all be walking on the eggshells that have paved our way for so long. Both the girls and I will look forward to that day - so will Bartholomew - because she has a way of poisoning the air that we all breathe.'

Beatrice started to try and explain how her problems had come about, but Mrs. Makepiece stopped her.

'You have no need to explain to us, dear. It will only upset you further and you don't need to be saddened any more than you already are. Now, I am going to make you two a pot of tea to serve with this lovely piece of lardy cake, and we will all cheer up.'

Unfortunately, there was a knock on the door just then which made us all jump like rabbits. Mrs. Makepiece pointed upstairs and Beatrice tiptoed up the narrow stairway. I was glad to see that she was wearing my slippers.

It was only Beth's grandpa, and as he was a regular visitor, he didn't seem surprised that there were three cups and saucers on the table.

'I've come just in time for tea, then,' he said. 'And how are you feeling, my dear?' He nodded at my rather ungainly frame.

'I am well, though I have had to slow down more than I expected. The baby is not due until January and we are only in November, so poor Eliza is doing all the midwifery for me now.' At that moment there came a creak from the floorboards above us.

'That's the house settling. It does that when the seasons change - the wood shrinks and expands in these old houses,' Mrs. Makepiece said, with no change to her demeanour at all. 'A piece of cake, anyone? There's plenty more.'

We all sat and chatted for the next hour or so until Mr. Jenkins was due to collect me from the bottom of the street. I felt a bit sorry for Beatrice who was being as quiet as a mouse upstairs and probably thinking of the lardy cake, as I would surely have been doing if it was me up there. When I pushed myself up and out of the chair, Grandpa rose with me and asked if he could come and visit Beth soon.

'Of course,' I replied. 'But what if I bring the girls down here instead, and then perhaps we can all go for a little walk to the Grange?'

The big house just close by wasn't open to the public but occasionally the owner would allow people to walk round the gardens.

'And perhaps have tea here afterwards?' I went on. I really didn't want him coming to the house in case the unpredictable Enid came upon us. I had no idea what she would say or do.

'Would you like that, Mrs. Makepiece? I don't want to put you out, but the girls enjoy coming to visit and with Grandpa being here too, it would be lovely. I can bring some biscuits from Mrs. Jenkins's pantry.'

'I'll ask the housekeeper,' said Mrs. Makepiece, 'and see if we can walk round the gardens if the family are away.'

We settled on a time eight days hence just as another knock came at the door. This time it was Mr. Jenkins. I kissed both my friends on the cheek and made my way rather slowly down the cobbled street to the gig.

As Brown Betty ambled home, I wondered what Enid was doing to find herself somewhere to live. Although I had no sympathy, I knew it would be hard for her to find rooms. She would have to work through her acquaintances who had been noticeable by their absence recently. If she had a reasonable pot of money, she could move into the White Hart which was cheaper than the Star. She could do that straightaway and save her pride a little. Being asked to leave was a devastating blow for her and I worried what she would do to retaliate. At least Bartholomew wouldn't have to fund John Elwood's house now, which must have been a relief for him. I had no idea how well-found Bartholomew was. Our style of living was not penny-pinching but neither did he spend money on frivolities.

When we got home, I entered again by the back door, the entry nearest to the stables. It was always pleasant to come into Mrs. Jenkins's kitchen where everything was warm and cosy. Tonight's meal smelled appetising though I was now finding it quite difficult to enjoy my food, except for cake. I craved sweet food with flavourings like vanilla and almond, and she knew exactly how to use my culinary herbs to get the most out of them. Bartholomew liked savoury dishes, but a lot more of them, sometimes with heavy sauces too, so I might eat only one or two courses to his four; then he would want some cheese as well. Mrs. Jenkins understood how little I wanted to eat so she would contrive special dainty dishes for me that would be nourishing for the baby as well.

After a brief rest and some time spent reading to the girls, I went into the room where my herbs were stored. Many of them were dried and hung; others were bottled in spirits, some in oil. I regularly lifted the dried ones to my nose to ensure that they were potent and not suffering any mould or infestation. I spent an hour preparing a receipt for Beatrice, one to calm and heal that my mother had used constantly.

I had no names for the potions Mother made; she just seemed to know what to use and the right proportions. She would then tailor them to the person and condition she was treating. I had simply copied her then but nowadays I used my own intuition and of course was able to check against Mr. Culpeper's findings too. She was taught by her grandmother who was known as a wise woman by some and a witch by others. My mother told me that her grandmother would sometimes cast spells and that she was much sought after by women of the same persuasion as herself. They would come and go in great secrecy, knowing of society's attitude to witches and the danger to themselves. Quite often these women were also midwives. I was so lucky to have had training in this field but also that I could bring to it my own natural skill with herbal remedies. However, my talent, if it could be called that, had come from all the women before me, possibly generations of them. Perhaps I should make a written record of my receipts, as Mr. Culpeper had done? It would be quite difficult, though, as most of the preparations were not measured precisely: I would need to test everything and find a uniform way of measuring. It would need time that I didn't have.

I decided to eat in my room rather than sit with Enid and Bartholomew at the supper table; I really couldn't face any more arguments. Mrs. Jenkins brought me up a letter delivered by one of the stable lads from South Farm. I opened it with some anxiety as my concerns about Cecilia had been like a thorn rubbing into me constantly whilst trying to get through my day. Quickly I read the message and then reread it. I could see that Cecilia was as disturbed by what had happened between us as I was. However, she went on to tell me about a relative of John's whose story had had a bearing on the proposal I had put to her.

*... There was an incident in John's family some years back in which a young woman was sent away in disgrace. When she eventually returned, she was ostracised by everyone to the point that it seriously damaged relationships within the family and also had financial repercussions. John was not old enough to know all the details, but he does remember the discord and bitterness as it was his favourite aunt who was effectively cast out and who subsequently was never fully reinstated as a daughter of the house. The child she bore disappeared and she never knew what had happened to the little boy. She lost her status and money as she was cut out of her father's will and became little more than a lowly dependent. She died very young, John believes, because she was heartbroken.*

*I know, my dear, that this was a long time ago and perhaps, because of that, John might be sympathetic to Beatrice's plight but, knowing him as I do, Esther, and that his views, as I said, are conservative, I really would not want to remind him of such sadness and then, if the worst came to the worst, for him to once more have no ability to influence other people's thoughts and actions as far as Beatrice is concerned. People can be very cruel.*

Cecilia went on to say that she understood why Bartholomew had decided to ask Enid to find her own home and that she was glad to hear it. She also promised to treat Beatrice with respect and kindness, should they ever meet. She signed her letter with love.

I was so relieved by her thoughtful and loving letter, I burst into tears. I couldn't bear for anything to damage our relationship. What frightened me most was that I'd had no idea what I was asking of her. My lack of social knowledge and understanding had led me floundering into a quagmire, unable to even see it, much less address it properly.

Bartholomew joined me upstairs later in the evening, reporting that he and Enid had sat in silence throughout the meal. He also had some good news which helped lighten our spirits.

'I forgot to tell you about Mason and Captain Campbell, Esther. It seems that the *Lady Charlotte* is going to put in at Portsmouth for some refitting and the Captain will then come on here if he can find a boat that is heading up the channel. I have calculated that he will be here in the first week of December. Mason has undertaken to explain about Mrs. Campbell and the provision we have made for Charlotte.'

'Wouldn't it be quicker if he takes a coach?'

'Well, you know as well as I do that if you have been on a ship for most of your life, that is the only way to travel. I am sure if there is nothing available, he will come by other means. We must warn Mrs. Jenkins that he will likely want to stay with us, as it would be better for Charlotte. We will need to prepare her carefully, Esther.'

I nodded before saying, 'I feel so guilty about this, but I haven't kept up with Mason's poorly leg. Were you able to help?'

'Fortunately, yes, and provided he does what I tell him for the next six months or so, he should return to full mobility. If he had stuck with the surgeon to whom I'd sent him originally, none of this pain and ulceration would have happened. One of the biggest problems a surgeon faces is that their patients think they know better, and then the charlatans get to work on them.'

The following morning, I sought out Bartholomew in his study and broached the subject of Beatrice's wounds by saying, 'Bartholomew, as we were talking about treatment of injuries last night, there is something I haven't mentioned before. Beatrice has some terrible scarring on her back – she has clearly been beaten, probably with a lash. In fact, the wounds look very similar to those I saw on the ship. She does not ask for help but it all looks terribly raw to me and I think we should prepare something to help the healing. I know you don't want me to use my preparations, so have you anything that would help?'

I should have realised that this revelation would be a terrible shock to Barty but, alas, I didn't, thus I was unprepared for his anger at the violence used against his niece.

He paced the room bristling with equal measures of indignation and disgust that George had used his wife in such a manner. I endeavoured to calm him because he had become very red in the face, which was most unusual for him. I knew Bartholomew to be a calm man with measured characteristics so this loss of temper was quite frightening. At one point he threw a box of notes on his desk and everything scattered. I hurried around after him trying to collect it all, only to find his favourite quill broken and in need of trimming or replacing altogether.

It was some time before everything calmed down and eventually Barty apologised to me for his display of temper. He was slumped at his desk looking quite melancholy and it took all my efforts to raise his spirits. I wondered if this information would have a bearing on negotiations with George in the future. I felt sure it would.

Later he said: 'My dear, Beatrice has not asked me to give her an examination so it might better if you undertake that role. I will give you a salve that we used on the sailors' wounds. It is a gentle formulation, so should be fine for pregnancy. I would rather you applied that, my love, as your herbal receipts are unknown as regards potency. They have not been tested in the long term whereas my preparation has been observed over many years by medical men. I have to remind you that what your mother taught you, Esther, has not been recognised by physicians, and although I accept that there is a place for your skills, it is not wise to use them on pregnant women. I'm sorry. I am not belittling you or your knowledge, I just think we should err on the side of caution.'

I was a little put out by his dismissal of my salves and tinctures but, in my own case, didn't dare go against his advice. Later, however, I did slip my little pot of salve for Beatrice into my reticule.

'How are you feeling, Esther?' said Bartholomew. 'You are pale.'

'I am just tired. All this excitement with Enid and Beatrice has been quite draining.'

'Well, it won't be long now. We are half-way through November then we will just have December to get through. I feel certain the baby will present in the early days of January, as you calculated all along. I'll listen to the baby's heartbeat later and check the position.'

'Have you any thoughts, Bartholomew, about whether our baby is a boy or a girl? And as to names, have you got any wishes - perhaps a family name?'

'I had this self-same conversation with Cecilia last week. I said no to her and I will say no to you too. My only concern is that the child is healthy and strong. There is a lot of a virulent sore throat about which affects children - some call it the Boulogne sore throat - and smallpox, too, though you have had the pox, so it should be protected from that.'

'I wish you hadn't said that, Barty,' I grumbled. 'Now I shall add that to my worries.'

Later, Bartholomew was able to reassure me about the heartbeat, even though once again he took ages listening. The position was right for this stage, which I knew anyway, but I felt a bit worried by how large I was. It is difficult to judge when looking at oneself but if I were commenting to any of my mothers-to-be, I would just say that the baby is "a good size" and "likely to be strong". In my mind, however, I would be thinking that I have seen the strong die and the puny survive; though, of course, I would never voice anything like that to an expectant mother.

∽

The next morning, I slept in again until Mrs. Jenkins appeared with a light breakfast. The sun was shining into our room and it warmed my heart to lie there in comfort and know that I was loved. The girls had been in to romp on the bed before going down to eat with Bartholomew. Beth asked me continually if the baby was coming that day - she had no conception of days let alone weeks.

'Esther, I have a bit of news that you might care to know,' said Mrs. Jenkins.

'What is it?'

'I have heard – well, gossip, really, but from someone who knows - that Mrs. McGovern has been around the town maligning you and Doctor Grieve with the most scurrilous tales. At the same time, it seems she has been asking all her acquaintances if she can take rooms within their households but they have all made excuses. She has also been to the White Hart to see if they can accommodate her for a month as of tomorrow.'

'Really?' I brightened up at the thought that she might be gone soon.

'Well, that's not all, Esther,' Mrs. Jenkins went on. 'She has said to some that she is thinking of returning to Scotland, where she still has property.'

'No! Are you sure?' I was astonished, resolving on our next meeting to pin down Beatrice to tell me what she knew about her mother's finances and find out whether Enid had been lying to Bartholomew when she'd said she was destitute.

I felt much better after I had eaten a lightly-boiled egg and had some small ale. By the time I got downstairs, the girls were washed and dressed, thanks to Wini chasing them up.

'Girls, we are going to see Cecilia today,' I said, 'so can you run and tell Mr. Jenkins we will be ready in half an hour?' Screams of excitement could be heard all over the house as they ran to do as I bid.

It was a lesson-day for Freddie and Beth, so Mary Jane looked after Charlotte while Felicia was sleeping. The alphabet songs had been a great success and we were doing some numbers-work, using the same plan but adding realistic examples. I really enjoyed making up silly rhymes to help them learn sequences and we would sing them much as you do nursery songs. Both children were bright and enthusiastic about everything I proposed, so they were a joy to teach. If the weather was fine, by which I mean it wasn't actually raining, we would often go outside for practical lessons. Beth wasn't my natural daughter so I was interested to see if my nature lessons were taken up. Would she be interested in plant-life and growing things, based on my teachings, or would it all go over her head? I had never quite forgotten Enid's insinuations that there was bad blood in both the girls and that they would therefore go to the bad themselves. It was a terrible thing to believe and even worse to say.

Cecilia and I managed an emotional hour together to catch up. I was very quick to emphasise that Enid no longer had Bartholomew's support and that there was no turning back. If she moved into the White Hart, as Mrs. Jenkins had heard, then the pressure on us would be removed and we would all be a lot happier. Our exchange of letters had cleared the air and neither of us mentioned the gist of our previous difficult conversation.

'And what about her daughter, Beatrice?' Cecilia asked nonetheless, but her voice was free of tension. 'Is she still living incognito at Mrs. Makepiece's, and is she well?'

'Oh yes, and they are getting on like a house on fire!' I laughed but I was keen to ask Cecilia's advice on a matter that kept pressing on me.

'Cecilia, can I ask you something?'

'Of course, what is it?'

I sighed. 'It's my herbal preparations. Bartholomew doesn't want me to use anything on pregnant women – by that, he means Beatrice and myself and probably you, too - as he says that their efficacy is not known and could be harmful. He talks with some respect of Mr. Culpeper, who documented all the herbs in this country and made drawings of them too back in the 1600s - as you know, Bartholomew found a copy of his writings and gave it to me on our first anniversary - but still he harks only to science. My problem is that my mother and her grand-mother would never have heard of or read Culpeper: all their knowledge came down through generations of wise women. I think it helped if the receiver of the wisdom was predisposed to use the knowledge. I know that my great-grandmother didn't bother to pass on her skills to Aunt Tilly, my mother's sister, because she was not of the right character. Tilly was quite angry about that - she was jealous of my mother.'

'Is it Beatrice's wounds that have brought all this about now?'

'Yes, it has brought everything to a head. I have agreed not to use anything of my own preparation on myself, except my tea, but now Bartholomew won't even let me use a simple and very useful cream on Beatrice's scarring. The thing is, I have previously used my skills with no ill effects on many pregnant women - so it seems as if he is saying that *they* don't matter but that the women close to him are not to be experimented on.'

'Oh Esther, I can't believe that your tinctures, teas and creams would bring harm to anyone. They didn't to me, or all the other ladies you have helped. Perhaps Bartholomew just can't reconcile himself to something that is not scientific.'

I reached into my reticule for the little pot of salve, saying: 'I have made this cream for Beatrice which I know will help her, but Bartholomew insists I use his cream which he declares is scientifically proven not to be harmful and was used for sailors' wounds. I don't really know what to do.'

'Well, if we don't tell anyone, why don't you use a bit of Bartholomew's cream on one area and a bit of yours on another? If it is on her back, she won't see anyway. Also, if Bartholomew's cream was suitable for war wounds, how many pregnant women has it been tested on? I would suggest none.'

'That's a good idea, Cecilia, but I can't not tell Beatrice! Or perhaps I could ask her to use mine but not tell Bartholomew?'

'Well, either way you would have to lie to someone.'

'I wouldn't lie to Bartholomew about this. It wouldn't occur to him that I would follow my own instincts over his, so he won't mention it again.'

Cecilia laughed.

'I will follow this with interest,' she said. 'But I must just mention before you go how relieved I am that Enid won't be living in one of our houses. The last thing John and I need is another difficult tenant and Enid really is quite dreadful.'

## CHAPTER 13

*Rosemary (Rosmarinus officinalis). It helps a weak memory and quickens the senses. The Sun claims dominion over it.*

*Culpeper's Colour Herbal*

Enid was gone at last and we all rejoiced. It was as if a dark cloud had suddenly lifted and the house were flooded with sunshine. She had told Bartholomew at lunchtime yesterday that she wanted Mr. Jenkins to fetch her trunks from the attic. As Mr. Jenkins was with the children and myself at Cecilia's, Bartholomew had to do it himself, which hadn't pleased him because he was busy; but he told me later he had felt that the sooner it was done, the sooner she would be gone. I hadn't told him yet that Enid was moving into the White Hart because it could have been just gossip; neither had I mentioned that she might return to Scotland where she apparently still had property. But later that evening, after the girls were in bed and we were enjoying a meal without her ill-natured presence, I told him what Mrs. Jenkins had said.

'Well, as I said before,' he replied, 'she clearly has some resources because she was contradicting herself whilst we were arguing. One of my patients has already mentioned some of her - frankly - vicious comments. The fact that none of her so-called friends want her in their homes speaks volumes. Let us put her out of our minds, Esther. I have had enough of her and I am sure you have too.'

'Even Cecilia said she was glad Enid was not moving into one of their properties!' I replied. 'Bartholomew, I am taking the children to Mrs. Makepiece's tomorrow so that Beth's grandpa can spend some time with her. We were going last week but the weather was bad. We might walk down to the Grange and then have tea back at her house. When we are alone, I will ask Beatrice if she knows about her mother's finances and whether she has property still in Scotland. Even though you are not supporting her now, it would be useful to know if she did tell us a pack of lies.'

'Don't let's talk about her anymore,' said Bartholomew. 'Just be glad that she has gone and we can go back to the way we were.'

I was so thankful that Bartholomew's spirits had lifted and we went up to bed with lighter hearts. When he slipped his arm around my waist, large though it was, all the warmth between us came back. Later that night, as I was lying awake, I thought how enjoyable our dinner together had been and how, hopefully, we would never have to look upon Enid's sour face again.

December had arrived and I was looking forward to my last month of pregnancy with just Bartholomew, our girls and me. We had decided to forego any big Christmas celebrations this year - the girls would be at the centre of our world but it would be a fairly quiet time.

Our trip to the grange was not possible in the end as it was raining again but Beth's grandpa joined us for tea, with poor Beatrice hiding herself once more in the main bedroom upstairs. Even so, she must have enjoyed hearing such cheerful laughter - I don't think she'd had much to laugh about in her earlier life. I couldn't help wondering whether her lover had brought her happiness and pleasure, and if she missed him.

Later, when Grandpa had gone home to his cold-hearted wife and the children were calm and playing alongside Mrs. Makepiece, I sneaked upstairs to tell Beatrice that her mother was now living at the White Hart and talking about returning to Scotland.

'Beatrice, did you know that your mother told Bartholomew she was penniless and had no resources to fall back on?'

Her eyes widened. 'No, I didn't,' she said, 'and that is not quite the case.'

She was looking downwards rather than at me and I sensed her embarrassment so I sat down and put my hand gently on hers.

'It is not your fault, Beatrice, how your mother behaves. No one in their right mind would think any less of you for it - *we* certainly don't.'

'You have all been so kind to me,' she said, 'I feel I must make up for the lies she has told.'

She took a deep breath.

'My mother has two small properties near to where she and my father lived. They were once part of the estate but when my father got into difficulties over his gambling, he sold off a lot of the farm and stock but kept the two cottages. One of them is the lodge at the entrance gates; the other was originally the farm overseer's house nearby. Both have tenants and the money from them belongs to Mother. She also has investments from her own mother that could not be cashed in by my father - they caused a lot of conflict. She is not a rich woman nowadays, but she is very far from destitute. When my father died, she found that the house they'd lived in was mortgaged to pay his debts, so she had to leave. The man who funded my father's gambling habit now lives there. Mother didn't want to stay in Scotland because it hurt her pride to have fallen so low. The new owners also bought most of the furniture and fittings which at least gave her some ready money - it is that which she is using now. I don't know how much she got, but if I know my mother, she would have extracted every penny from the sale. She also sold the horses - two of them were brood mares and quite valuable. One of them was the horse that threw my father. He died instantly.'

'Well, Beatrice, it seems that your mother told Bartholomew a great many untruths and we can have nothing further to do with her. I regret if this hurts you, but once Bartholomew has made up his mind, he rarely changes it.'

'I am mortified that she has treated her own brother so badly. She doesn't deserve the kindness you gave her in what you thought was her hour of need. It is despicable.'

'I must go back down in a minute,' I said, rising once more, 'as the girls will be wondering what I am up to, but before I go, I wanted to say that, if you wish, I will look after you and the baby, and act as your midwife when the time comes. I would also like to treat your scars with either some cream that Bartholomew has given me, or with my own salve. We can make a difference to your comfort, Bea - scar tissue can pull and tighten, so you would be wise to let us help. It is your choice, but please don't think you deserve to be uncomfortable. Your scars will be with you for the rest of your life and you might as well reduce the discomfort when you can.'

'Thank you so much, Esther, and I would like to be in your care for the duration of my pregnancy. Perhaps, when next you come, we could try and help the scars with your own preparation.'

'I have it with me, Beatrice, so I will give it to Mrs. Makepiece, because she will need to apply it. I think it wise to try both creams, perhaps Bartholomew's on your lower back and mine on your shoulders. We should see a difference very quickly and can then proceed on the basis of which works best. Of course, as far as your uncle is concerned, we will say that his was the most suitable, regardless.'

Her voice had been trembling and tears came to her eyes. I pulled her gently into my arms and held her for a few moments before I started to feel my own tears ready to flow. I always found myself crying when seeing others do so. A few minutes later I lumbered back downstairs, ready for Mr. Jenkins coming to fetch us.

When we got back home, the girls were more than ready for their beds. As I went up to kiss them, there came a hammering at the front door. Bartholomew opened it and was greeted by a messenger who looked a little bedraggled, the weather having clearly deteriorated badly. By the time I got back down again, Bartholomew was already putting on his heaviest cloak and hat, saying loudly, 'It would appear that Mason and the good captain are likely to make land this evening at Seaford. They are in a convoy of twenty-three merchant ships and hope to be taken off near Seaford Barracks. The messenger got delayed when his horse slipped a shoe - he should have been here yesterday. I will take the carriage and bring them back. Jenkins will come with me, so there is no need to worry if we are gone for some time.'

'Be careful, Bartholomew,' I said. 'It is a way to go in the dark and the weather is bad. Shouldn't you wait until tomorrow? They can always put up at the barracks.'

'No, I've a mind to fetch them,' said Bartholomew. 'I have other things to do tomorrow which can't wait. You can't go in your condition, and Jenkins needs someone with him - it is not fair to send him out alone. Stop worrying, Esther. I will be back before you know it.'

I knew in my heart that he relished the idea of rushing off: I think he saw it as a manly adventure. Whereas if I'd accompanied him, I would certainly have slowed him down in the worsening weather - feeling the cold, not wanting to be wet, anxious as to what I might find when we got there.

∞

Despite his reassurance, Bartholomew didn't come back. We waited all the next day and night, but still he didn't come and no messages arrived. Initially, I wasn't too concerned as he was often delayed in the furtherance of his work but on the second day I began to worry. I hated sitting alone at home and finally I resolved to find Billy and borrow Cecilia's trap, which was much bigger and better than ours, to go after them. I managed, with Mrs. Jenkins's reluctant help, to back Flossy into the gig, and with the girls tucked in beside me, I got to South Farm and explained, requesting that Cilla or Mary Jane look after the girls. Cecilia spiritedly refused to let me go, saying she would send Billy and one of the stable lads instead. After my initial spurt of energy, I realised that was the best thing to do. I collapsed onto the day bed, tired and anxious.

Cecilia sent a lad out to find John Elwood who came galloping on his horse into the yard before we had even finished our tea. Within ten minutes he had organised everyone: Billy and the lad were well mounted and John was riding his big horse Nero. As we stood in the doorway to wave them off, he looked down at me and said, 'Esther, for once in your life, please do as you are told. Do not leave here until either Bartholomew or I come back! I want your word on that.'

'I promise, John,' I said meekly, 'we will stay with Cecilia. But please hurry, I have a feeling there is something dreadfully wrong.' They were gone with a thudding of hooves and crunching of grit that sprayed up behind them.

Though Cecilia and I had plenty to do with all four children, I found myself still fretting. It hadn't taken long to tell her about Enid's duplicity and the slanderous things she was saying about us but after that I was constantly looking out of the window and checking on the time and weather. A weak sun lanced some rents in the now billowing clouds and I was more than grateful to see the light break through. The weather since I waved Bartholomew off had been foul: rain which had turned to sleet and, at times, a dense, cold fog had clung to the chimney pots, the air thick and sulphurous.

Cecilia and I compared notes on the state of our pregnancies. The month between us seemed more than that and I felt like a whale compared to her neat bump. I couldn't wait now for this to be over. My belly was stretched as tight as a drum; I could feel a grinding ache low down and a gnawing soreness in my lower back that was almost intolerable. I was constantly having to relieve myself, and my ankles were swollen. I had had enough of being pregnant, yet still had a way to go.

I went down to see Mrs. Fisher and Cilla in the kitchen while Cecilia took a rest. There was some bread proving so I thought to give them a hand to help them along with their work. I overheard Cilla whisper to Mrs. Fisher, 'She looks like she is going to pop!' I ended up having to sit down, breathless and struggling to inhale. The advice I would give to my mothers-to-be came to me with force: 'Walk if you can, stretch out. If you can't walk, lie down with your feet up, don't compress your belly. Forget the household, forget the dinner, focus inwardly on yourself, breathe slowly, harvest each breath, be calm.' But I wasn't calm.

## CHAPTER 14

*Alehoof (Glechoma Hederacea)* *The juice
dropped into the ear doth wonderfully help
the noise and singing of them, and helpeth the
hearing which is decayed. Astrology: It is a
herb of Venus and therefore cures by sympathy
the diseases she causes: and those of Mars by
antipathy.*

Culpeper's Colour Herbal

Billy-alone returned with a message to say that Bartholomew, Mr. Jenkins and John were well but caught up in helping the people of Seaford and Newhaven deal with yet another terrible shipping accident occasioned by the weather. I knew it had been a bad year for storms, but when you live seven or so miles inland it is easy to forget just how difficult and different it can be at the coast - Bartholomew had been called out many times to coastal villages in his capacity as either physician or coroner. I refused to allow myself the thought that Captain Campbell and Mason might have been hurt in the incident, reasoning that a great many ships passed by Seaford, and with no ill effect. Every time my thoughts veered towards visualising what was going on, I clamped down on my imagination.

I was thankful to see Billy and to get a message from Bartholomew to say he would return to me by nightfall and that I should go home if I was not too uncomfortable. Mr. Jenkins had also passed on a request to tell his wife that he was well, though greatly saddened by what he had seen. I was so relieved at Billy's coming that I burst into tears.

I bundled the girls into our gig and, with Fred, one of Cecilia's stable lads, accompanying us, we headed for home. We had not gone far - travelling slowly as I didn't want to jolt myself – when, without warning, we were set upon by two wild-looking men, one on either side of the track. They were brandishing weapons and sticks and charged at Flossy to try and grab her bridle. To my side, another man suddenly appeared. It was Abe, though looking much older, with unkempt hair and a thick beard. I saw him laughing excitedly as he lunged at the gig and thrust a stave in between the spokes of one of the wheels, forcing poor Flossy to an abrupt halt. She reared up and I could see the terror in her eyes as she fell heavily, crashing to the ground and dragging the gig over with the three of us flung beneath it. In a blur of pain, I heard shouting and horrible, ear-splitting sounds that could have been Flossy squealing as she struggled to free herself. Both girls were ashen-faced as they clung to me, whimpering. I was beneath them, so at least they were cushioned from landing on the hard track as I had.

The padded seat of the framework saved us from being crushed. I hoped that Fred was unhurt, but I didn't know if his horse was down as well. I couldn't bear the thought of Flossy hurt and in pain. I heard Fred's voice shouting shrilly but then there was a gunshot and I didn't hear him anymore. This blast went off very near my head and deafened me. I pulled the girls tight to me and whispered to them to be very quiet and still; we lay there too terrified to move but then I felt a warm fluid seeping round me. I tried to see if it was blood and if so whose it was, but found myself unable to move beyond swivelling my head. One of my hands was free, however, so I gently felt over the girls' little bodies. Beth seemed unscathed but Charlotte had a lump growing on her head and I saw her eyes roll up into unconsciousness. Momentarily I wondered if the poor child was dead or dying just as her father was coming to see her. All was painfully quiet now as I strained to hear every little sound above the ringing in my ears and the whirr of a wheel still spinning. After what seemed ages, I heard a man shout nearby. I knew he was shouting though his voice was muffled. I heard him say, 'What did yer bring it down for? We won't be able to get to 'em now afore someone comes.'

A younger voice came back which I recognised as Abe's: 'They probably be dead anyways with that cart on top. We could just point the musket under and fire to be certain, like.'

The older man replied, his tone scathing, 'You's a fool Abe. You planned all this, an' you didn't even do that proper. I ain't gonna be hung for killin' childer. Everyone within miles of 'ere will have heard all that row. I reckon we'd better run for it. I'm off.'

'Me too,' said a nasal third voice. 'I want none of this, I don't care what she done.'

'Wait, we should finish them off. Gimme the musket, will yer?'

'No, boy, you be mazed in the 'ead. Get out of here, afore we all get taken up.'

I heard a scuffling, footsteps running away, then silence. Terrified that it might be a trap, it took a while for me to pluck up my courage to call out.

'Fred, are you there? Can you hear me?'

I heard a groan and then a dragging noise along the ground near me.

'Fred!' I cried out in relief, as his white face peered in at us. He wasn't very old, no more than sixteen, and he had tears running down his face which was creased with pain.

'Where are you hurt?' I asked. 'Can you walk?'

'Don't reckon so, I can see the bone in me leg. Are you alright, an' the little ones?' He was sobbing with shock yet worrying about us. My heart melted for his kindness.

'I don't know,' I wept. 'Charlotte is unconscious, but Beth is frightened out of her wits. We need help. I have a terrible pain in my side - I think I am bleeding. Fred, is Flossy all right? I can't hear her. Can you see her? Is she all right?'

He didn't answer but that might have been because he'd seen people running towards us. Although I couldn't see anything, I could hear indistinct voices coming closer. At first, I thought it might be our attackers returning and sunk down on my side, the movement causing pain to rip right through me. I don't remember any more after that, though they told me later me that I was talking throughout the effort to lift the gig off us, but nothing intelligible.

After we were freed and I hazily came to my senses, I peered around me, trying to grasp what had happened. I was on the ground and Flossy was lying on her side, just an arm's length from me: she had been shot in the head, probably to silence her. I could see her foreleg was broken as well. I tried not to look at her, but repeatedly I was drawn back to her dear face, her eyes blank, her spirit gone. I felt sick with grief as bile surged up into my throat. Fred's horse had run off after throwing him onto the track and, luckily, had galloped back to his stable after dragging the poor boy for a short way until he slipped the stirrup. No one at the farm seemed to have heard the screaming or the shot; it was the return of the horse with a trailing bridle, reins and a broken stirrup that brought everyone running to find us.

Billy-alone was cradling Beth in his arms and she was wailing as loud as her little voice would go. Charlotte was with Cecilia who had summoned her carriage to come and help us. 'Cecy, I cried, 'is she all right?' Cecilia was laying the poor little mite down on the cushioned seat and I could see that she was limp. Billy clambered up into the carriage with Beth and I saw him gently stroking Charlotte's face with his other hand.

'Esther, thank God,' Cecilia cried, as she climbed down, her distress clearly visible on her face. 'I thought we had lost you - you were raving when I got here. I have sent someone for Eliza in case the baby is coming. Your skirts are all wet.' She knelt down on the ground despite her own advanced pregnancy and cradled my head in her arms.

'I don't want you to worry. I will see to everything - Bartholomew, the girls, Fred. And Esther, I will have this town turned upside down to find the men who did this.' Her voice cracked with a sob as she spoke but a thin little wail from the carriage took her hurrying back to Charlotte, once she'd been helped to her feet by one of the men who then placed something - a cloak, maybe - under my head and another over my body. I heard her tell Billy to take the girls to the house and return for us directly afterwards. I don't know how they got Fred back; I never saw the going of him.

Cecilia came back to me. 'Esther, Billy will take the girls back home now so that they don't become more upset at seeing you in difficulty. Then he will come back for you, my friend. Are you hurting anywhere else? Is the pain from your wound or have the contractions started?'

'I don't know, but I think there is pain that is different from a contraction. Can you send Billy to get Bartholomew, urgently? Poor Fred is badly injured - he needs Bartholomew.'

'I've already sent one of the lads. Billy wouldn't leave you - he was completely distraught that he wasn't here to protect you. Eliza is going to be with us soon. She was just finishing with a young mother when we found her. One of our men is bringing her to us.

'When Billy gets back, I think we must try and lift you into the carriage, Essie; you can't have your baby out here in the open. There are people watching, too. They've come from Lewes - they seemed to hear all the noise, though we didn't. I can't send them away - there are too many of them - but I am going to go over and explain what has happened and ask them to return to the town and help us track down these evil men. Our head stableman went to find the constable and he is organising a search party now. Be brave, Esther, we will do everything possible to get you home to South Farm and your baby born safely.'

If we had all the strong women who were my friends helping us, I thought, then we would surely survive. The pain in my side didn't feel like a contraction. Even though I had never experienced one, I knew how they built and affected the body. This pain was quite different: it was sharp and increased when I breathed more deeply. As I felt myself beginning to fade, I was thinking that I must take shallow breaths when they tried to move me; if I could just feel where the pain was coming from, I might be able to tell them how to lift me.

∞

I found myself back in my old bed, just off the kitchen at South Farm. I opened my eyes slowly, unsure of how I had got there. Turning my head, I saw Cilla and Billy sitting by my side, holding hands.

'Esther, you be awake!' Billy said. 'How d'you feel?'

'The girls?' I gasped. 'Are they safe?'

'Aye, they be well, and eating their heads off. Charlotte has a big lump on her forehead, but she didn't know it until Beth showed her in the mirror. Now they is giggling and Freddie and Beth want one too.'

'Bartholomew?' I whispered, desperately trying not to breathe deeply and set off the searing pain again. I was shivering uncontrollably as I tried to prevent the agony tearing through me. I knew I was in a state of shock and was terrified for my baby.

'On his way with the master. I'll just fetch Eliza and Missus Elwood, shall I?'

I nodded, but then regretted it. 'My head hurts, how long have I been here?'

'About an hour, Esther. You was well gone,' said Cilla, as she patted my hand.

The door was pushed open and Cecilia, Mrs. Makepiece and Eliza crowded into the room. Behind them came Mrs. Fisher with a drink and bowl.

'In case you feels sick, Esther,' she said.

Gathering around the bed, they started talking at once. I looked up into their anxious faces, bewildered by all the voices which kept fading in and out. Cecilia asked everyone to leave, except Mrs. Makepiece and Eliza. She took the bowl and cup and placed them close by me.

'Did I faint?' I whispered.

'Yes, but it was more than that,' Cecilia replied, 'because you have been unconscious for quite a while. When you passed out, we decided to lift you into the carriage hoping you wouldn't feel so much the pain of being moved. How are you, dearest? Can you describe where you hurt? Eliza says you are not in labour yet but, because your waters have broken, that could change at any moment.'

Mrs. Makepiece was gripping my hand tightly and I managed a smile as I my pulled my fingers free. She had a tear rolling down her cheek.

'Don't cry. Please, don't cry,' I said. 'We've all escaped and the girls are well, according to Billy and Cilla. Will Bartholomew be long?'

'No, he should be with us any minute now,' said Cecilia, 'and he already knows about your state of health because we sent one of the men to meet him with a note about your condition.'

I started to cry and then all of us were crying as the door sprang open and my husband came in, filling the room with authority and calm.

'Ladies, Ladies, please, enough of all these tears, kindly leave Esther and me alone. There will be plenty of time to talk once I have checked her over. Mrs. Fisher is ready to feed everyone and, Cecilia, your husband needs you after his heroic riding. Out, everyone out'.

He sat down beside me, lifting my hand and putting it to his cheek.

'Now, Esther, tell me where it hurts? I understand that you had one of the spokes of wood sticking in you, just below the ribs, and that it pulled out as you were lifted. We need to check there are no splinters left behind and put a dressing on.'

Someone must have undressed me because all I had on was my torn shift, which was soaked in blood. I could see a wad of material stuck to my side with a bandage tied round me to hold it on.

Gently, Bartholomew removed it and, though it tugged where the blood had dried and stuck, it was off in no time.

'Well, that doesn't look too bad. I was expecting worse,' he said, as he gently probed the area surrounding the wound. I knew he was looking for splinters or grit. 'It is relatively superficial though it will need stitching. I think you have also suffered some broken ribs just above. It is painful, I am sure. I stopped at Lewes to fetch some supplies as I used up most of the contents of the bag I took to Seaford. Now, before I patch you up, I just want to examine your head. Cecilia said you were talking about your ears?'

I nodded. 'My ears are ringing, and my head hurts, Barty. There was a shot near my head. I think it was what killed Flossy.' I started to cry again as I thought of Flossy lying alone and cold on the road, and clasped his arm.

'Will Flossy be buried, Barty? I don't want her chopped up.'

'Rest now, Esther, we'll talk about that later. It's not surprising your head hurts. You have had a terrible shock and undoubtedly hit your head as you were thrown to the ground. There is a big bruise on your temple and a lot of grazing. Are your ears ringing now?'

'Yes, will I go deaf?'

'No. There might be a bit of impairment for a while, though. But can you imagine how many deaf soldiers there would be if they all reacted like that to gunshot near their ears? Now, I want to examine you to see how the baby fares. I understand that your waters broke? I just need to check that is the case, because you could have just relieved yourself in the terror of the situation. It happens. Quiet, now, I will listen to the baby's heart first.'

I stopped sniffling and wished I could hear the reassurance of a strong heartbeat but all I could hear was my own heart thumping. After Bartholomew had finished his examination and said that all was well, he went to find some soap and a towel to wash me down. He was so gentle that I felt safe and reassured. When all was done and he was satisfied, he sat on the bed and took my hands in his.

'I don't think your waters have fully broken, if at all, and I don't think the bump on your head has done any serious damage. The cut is easily mended, as are the broken ribs, but we must keep you quiet until the baby wants to come out. You are not positioned for birth yet, so I want you to rest, and I think you must stay here for a few days at least. Cecilia will be happy at that, as she feels the need to keep an eye on you and I can reassure her that the baby is safe and not about to come out. She has been a good friend to you, Esther, and I know that she won't let you get up and go out, whatever you say. My dear, you will have to take things very slowly now - we do not want to precipitate events because giving birth through broken ribs is going to be very painful, I'm afraid, over and above the usual pains of travail.

'Now, I must go and see to Fred as he has a nasty open wound on his leg. I will come back later, and I'll tell you then all that happened in Seaford, which is why I didn't get home when you expected. Fred has told us all about the men who attacked you and they appear to have been local, so there is a good chance of them being apprehended. One of them is called Abe, and Billy-alone seems to know a lot about him.

'Now, lie patiently. I don't think you will feel like getting up anyway for a few days as you have had a serious shock, never mind all the cuts and bruises. We don't want you to catch anything either, as it will delay the healing and cause you pain. I will have a look at both girls as soon as I have sorted Fred out but Cecilia tells me they are quite recovered. When I come back, we can have dinner together here.' He leaned over me and gave me a kiss, saying, 'I won't let anything happen to you, dearest - you are more loved than anyone I have ever known. When I heard what had happened, I realised just how special our love is.'

I started to cry again as he left me. I knew how important he was to me but to hear him say that made my heart swell with love and tears come into my eyes. As emotion flooded through my body, I sank deeper into the bedding, my head, pulse and life-force all throbbing painfully.

Bartholomew did not return to talk later as I had fallen into a deep sleep and he thought it best not to wake me. He took Mrs. Makepiece and Eliza home in Cecilia's carriage with his horse tied behind. When I woke the following morning, I knew he was there again but at a distance, as if he were at the end of a tunnel. We did not have our talk for a few days as I was unable to concentrate; all I wanted to do was sleep. I had few visitors other than the children to kiss in the morning and the evening, though someone sat with me all the time. As I drifted in and out of sleep, I was always aware of one of my friends by me, holding my hand. I tried to stay awake but found it impossible to keep my eyes open.

## CHAPTER 15

*Comfrey (Symphytum officinale).* The
roots of Comfrey taken fresh, beaten small,
and spread upon leather, and laid upon any
place troubled with the gout, doth presently
give ease of the pains. Astrology: A herb of
Saturn.

Culpeper's Colour Herbal

I had lain abed for five days and only then felt able to catch up with all that had happened. There had been a steady stream of visitors, but I had had the impression that none of them wanted to talk about the course of events that brought me to South Farm and then to my ill-starred attempt to get back home. Finally, when Bartholomew came to have breakfast with me on the sixth morning after the attack, I asked him to tell me what had delayed his return to Lewes from Seaford and where Mason and Captain Campbell were. It was only yesterday morning that I'd remembered they were coming to see Charlotte.

My memory had been playing tricks on me and I was struggling to place things in their correct sequence. I supposed it was not surprising, all things considered.

Every now and then I experienced flashbacks, usually to the gunshot and the dreadful noise that came before it, but also to the thin little cry from Charlotte – it tugged at my heartstrings every time I thought of it. In fact, it was always by a sound that I was drawn back to the period when I lay on the hard track wondering if we were alive or dead. I resolved to ask Bartholomew why that was, but mostly then I needed to know what had happened in Seaford.

'Are you feeling stronger, Esther?' he said. 'Some of what I have to say might be hard for you to hear.'

'I think you must tell me everything, otherwise I will fret. I am stronger now, so much so that I realise bad things must have happened when you didn't come home. I would rather hear the truth instead of imagining the worst.'

'The messenger's delay in coming to get me was calamitous,' Bartholomew began, 'in that if I had heard the news sooner, I might have been able to save more lives. As it was, I arrived in Seaford in dreadful weather and at the end of a nightmare scene.'

'The beginning, Bartholomew?'

'All right, Esther, but it is a long story.'

I was not surprised when he pulled out his little note-book from his inside pocket. My husband was methodical and didn't allow things to slip from his memory - his mind was much more disciplined than mine.

He began again by saying, 'There was a convoy of twenty-three merchant vessels due to pass by Seaford Bay en route from Plymouth. The vessels were escorted by the *Harlequin*, a man-of-war sloop owned by the Royal Navy. Captain Campbell and Mason had joined the fleet at Portsmouth, sailing on the *Harlequin* which was under the command of Lieutenant Anstruther. She was armed to the teeth with a dozen six-pounder cannons and half a dozen twelve-pounder cannons. She had a crew of forty-five and six passengers: three men, including Captain Campbell, Mason and a civilian who had his wife and two children with him - a baby and a two-year-old. This warship was to protect the fleet from attack, particularly from the French privateers who plague these busy routes.'

I nodded encouragingly as I could see he was hesitant about giving me such a detailed account of events.

He continued: 'Later, Mason told me that the fleet had experienced turbulent weather on its way up the channel. As it's been a bad year for rough weather, this did not cause any great concern until Wednesday night when the vessels were hit by hurricane-force winds, freezing temperatures and driving sleet. In the early hours of Thursday, there was a change in that the wind subsided but it left a thick fog along with sleet and below-zero temperatures. The *Harlequin* constantly fired its cannons to alert the following convoy of her position. In effect, not only was she the fleet's protector but also her pilot. It was clear to Mason and Captain Campbell that there was no possibility of them being put off the Harlequin in such dreadful conditions; a hazard of travelling by sea, but one they well understood. Lieutenant Anstruther - and this is where the calamity occurred - was under the mistaken belief that the fleet had cleared Beachy Head,' said Bartholomew, 'so he changed his course to further inshore. The fleet all did likewise, and the six foremost vessels, namely *Eunice*, *Albion*, *Weymouth*, *February*, *Traveller* and *Mitbedacht* were then, like the *Harlequin*, unknowingly on course to run aground in Seaford Bay. The first the crews knew of their plight was when they found themselves heading into the violent surf.

'Esther, you have gone pale, are you sure you want to hear this? We could wait until you are stronger,' Bartholomew said, his face crinkled with anxiety.

'No, Bartholomew, I need to know what happened. Today, tomorrow, or the next day, your account will not improve. It is better that I understand, otherwise I will just lie here imagining even worse things.'

He nodded before resuming: 'Everyone on those seven ships faced terrifying and immediate danger. In the darkness and fog, those on board could only hear the dreadful sounds of splitting timbers, masts snapping and sails ripping, together with the crashing of vicious waves breaking right over the stricken vessels. The breakers and the surf of the tide were forcing the vessels to crash against each other, adding to all the confusion and damage. Despite all of this, the crew of the *Harlequin* continued to fire its cannons to warn the rest of the fleet of the error of navigation that had been made and of the danger they were in.' Bartholomew paused here before saying in a voice that was full of admiration, 'It was due to these efforts that the remaining sixteen merchantmen successfully continued on the correct course and would later pass Beachy Head in safety.'

'Captain Campbell and Mason?' I asked, afraid of what was to come.

Bartholomew did not reply but carried on with his account: 'The residents of Seaford who had been drawn to the beach by the sounds of the cannon were unable to do much to assist or even to assess the true situation with the fog obscuring so much of what was happening. In the meantime, those on board the stricken vessels were lashing themselves to the rigging, desperate to avoid being washed overboard. As dawn broke and the fog thinned out, the full horror was revealed.

'A barrel was lowered from the *Harlequin* attached to a rope and the action of the waves took the barrel ashore where the rope was then secured by the good people waiting to help. This then allowed those still on board to get ashore, including the civilian male passenger. Unfortunately, it was then found that his wife was still on board, holding both the children and begging that they all be saved. Then - and this is so heart-warming, Esther - two of the *Harlequin* crew who had just been rescued themselves got a small boat and went back through the breakers at great risk to their own lives. They managed to get alongside and then up on to the *Harlequin*, but the woman would not leave the vessel herself until her children were taken first to safety. The two sailors each took a child and lashed it to their bodies, and only then would their mother let herself be helped into the small craft. Happily, the sailors delivered the family without mishap to the shore, where the Harlequin crew were all gathered minus two of their number who were later reported to have drowned.'

'Why didn't the woman's husband help her off with the children?' I said indignantly.

'I don't know, Esther. I am telling you this as it was explained to me. Sad to say, perhaps it is a case of *every man for himself* in such circumstances.'

Bartholomew referred again to his little notebook.

'Of the *Weymouth*, with a total complement of eleven, all but four safely reached the shore. These four mariners all drowned trying to reach safety in a small boat. The *Eunice*: when she ran aground, a man from Newhaven, together with a number of soldiers from the 81st Regiment based at Seaford Barracks, rescued not only the master and his crew but a large proportion of the cargo. These same brave men also assisted in the protection of the cargoes that were washed ashore to prevent them from being stolen by some disreputable local individuals, wreckers known as the 'Seaford Shags', who had the temerity to try and steal cargo from under the onlookers' noses. Some of the soldiers taught them a lesson they won't forget in a hurry.

'The *February*: unhappily, the crew were not so fortunate, as fourteen of the total complement of sixteen men lost their lives. The mate and the ship's boy were the only survivors. Once the vessel was close to running aground, the crew took to the rigging; and as each part was washed away, they all took refuge on the main mast. However, sadly, the weight of sixteen men was too much and it finally gave way - they were all thrown into the sea and lost their lives.

'Finally, Esther, the *Mitbedacht*. Of the total of thirteen men on board the Prussian vessel, only one survived. A soldier of the 81st regiment saw this one man lose his grip on some wreckage and start to drift away. Lieutenant Derenzy plunged into the sea, grabbed the mariner by the hair and managed to drag him to safety. The *Albion* and *Traveller* sailors all survived, but a total of thirty-five men were lost.'

Bartholomew came to a halt then, shifted his balance and took my hand in his.

'Esther,' he said quietly, 'I am deeply sorry to tell you that Captain Campbell was one of the two from the *Harlequin* who didn't make it back. Mason did, and he is now safely back in Lewes. He is looking forward to meeting up with you and, of course, to seeing little Charlotte. Mason tells me that the good captain had not stopped talking about the child since he met him in Portsmouth.'

'Oh Bartholomew, no, I can't bear it,' I cried out as I fell back, feeling a clammy sweat flood over me. I began to heave into the bowl Mrs. Fisher had left me so many days ago. Barty moved up beside me and propped me on his shoulder, using his handkerchief to wipe my face and the back of my neck. I could hear his little soothing noises as I continued to spew before I managed to say, 'No wonder you were unable to return. Poor Charlotte, what will happen to her? Bartholomew, we must keep her with us. Did the captain have any other kin? Oh, Mother of God, I don't know what to do,' I sobbed as the sweat broke out again on my forehead.

'Calm yourself, Esther, please. All these questions will be answered in due course. Mason has knowledge of

Captain Campbell's situation and we will explore all of that. There is a great deal to do in relation to this tragedy and we can't make any decisions until we understand all the ramifications, and due process has been followed through. But rest assured, my love, Charlotte will be at the forefront of our concerns. She will be loved and cared for by us, and I will do whatever is necessary to ensure her well-being.'

I started to weep again. So much had happened in such a short space of time and I felt desolate for Charlotte, and for myself, too. Captain Campbell had been such an ally to me in my troubles; and whilst I don't remember the events on board the transport ship with any pleasure, I had found out a lot about myself on that voyage and made some lifelong friendships. I was unable to stop visualising his tragic death: my imagination took me to places I didn't want to go, and I didn't seem able to shut a door on that.

'But, Esther, there is more news, *good* news that will cheer you. The ship's boy who escaped from the *February*, along with the mate – the only two survivors - is known to you and wishes to be remembered to Beth.'

My mind raced as I took in his words. 'Job,' I said, 'it must be Job! Where is he? Can we see him? How is he? Oh Bartholomew, what a wonderful thing. It doesn't detract from the pain of losing Captain Campbell, but it feels like a miracle to have Job returned to us when he might so easily have been one of the dead.'

'He is now on one of the ships currently anchored just off Seaford, Esther, that turned about from Beachy Head to offer help. We didn't think it wise to bring him back to Lewes in case his brothers got to hear of it. Both he and the mate have been given a berth together. They are considered lucky omens - you know how superstitious sailors are. The remainder of the ships probably chose to sail on without an escort and would have set off as soon as they saw a break in the weather. Nothing was keeping them anchored nearby except goodwill to their lost and rescued companions. The men are deeply respectful of their shipmates.

'Now, are you feeling better, Esther? I am so sorry to have to bring you so much distress, particularly when our child is on the cusp of being born. I was concerned that all the shock you have recently suffered could well precipitate your labour.'

I dried my face and wiped my eyes, 'I am not overwhelmed, Barty,' I said. 'Having the good news as well as the bad helps.'

He continued patting my hand and wiping away stray tears as he went on: 'Mason is back in Lewes, as I said. He is still staying at the White Hart, and we are already discussing the consequences of Captain Campbell's death and Charlotte's legal status. He is in touch with the shipping agent. As soon as you are well enough to come home, he will call on you.'

'I want to go home today, Bartholomew,' I said. 'I feel so much stronger now - physically, I mean - even with this horrific news. The girls need to return to their normal routine, and I expect Mrs. Jenkins and Wini are missing us, too.'

'I agree. We will try and get you home in comfort so that your ribs don't give you further pain. Your wound is healing nicely now. I will go and see Cecilia - I am sure she will lend us her carriage for the trip. She and John have done so much for us, my dear, that I honestly don't know how we can ever repay their kindness.'

'I want to have our baby in my own bed, Barty, and it can't be long now. I am sure Cecilia will help and Eliza will be nearby if you are called out.'

'I am not going anywhere, Esther. I fully intend to be the first one to meet our boy in the flesh,' said Bartholomew, hastening to add, 'or girl.'

I laughed and winced. 'Ha, I've caught you out,' I said. 'You *do* want a boy!'

After he left me to find Cecilia, I lay back on my pillows and relived his words in my mind. Tears gushed down my cheeks once more as I pictured the terrible conditions at sea. I could not help but recall in detail the Newhaven incident with the privateers, so I had a good idea of what the scene would have been like in Seaford; but thirty-five men dying must have been a terrible shock for the lieutenant whose mistake had caused the losses. I thought of the mother and her children, saved by the bravery of two sailors; of Job, whose life has been so important to Beth and me; and, in amongst all the horror, of the goodwill of those who would put their own lives at risk to save others. This comforted me, and though I knew I would never forget the pain of Captain Campbell's tragic death, it was tempered by the saving of Job from the violent seas. I knew Beth would meet up with him one day in the future and I was thankful for that. When I remembered all that Job, or 'Joe', as Beth preferred to call him, had done for us, I felt a huge rush of love for the young lad.

## CHAPTER 16

*Eyebright (Euphrasia officinalis). Helps restore the sight decayed through age. If the herb was as much used as it is neglected, it would half spoil the spectacle maker's trade. Astrology: Under the sign of the Lion and Sol claims dominion over it.*

*Culpeper's Colour Herbal*

We were home at last and so happy to be there. Mr. and Mrs. Jenkins and Wini all rushed out of the front door as the carriage rolled up and Bartholomew very gingerly handed me down. I walked to the breakfast room and sat, feeling quite weak, but determined that no one would observe that. I was looking forward to seeing Eliza so I could catch up with the state of affairs of our mothers-to-be.

Bartholomew had grown to be quite respectful of Eliza. Initially he was rather dismissive of her as if she had been just a poor housewife helping me out, but over the past two years he had changed his attitude completely. I think he valued her commitment to me, and her fantastic memory - you never had to tell her anything twice - and despite being a tiny little woman she was very strong, both physically and mentally. I hadn't got much time for her mother but she at least helped by bringing up Eliza's little boy. As a family (her man worked in a local bakery) they were hard-working, decent people who deserved good things.

Mrs. Jenkins came in with a tray of tea and a cake made specially to celebrate our safe return. It made me cry; in fact, *everything* made me dissolve into tears at that time but these were happy tears of relief. Beth and Charlotte were so excited to be back, dancing boisterously round every room. I was so glad we hadn't yet told Charlotte that we were expecting a visit from the wonderful man who, we were going to explain, was her father, a man who had loved her from the day she was born despite seeing her for only two days. It broke my heart, and I couldn't even blame it all on the selfish bitch who was her mother. Shocked by my own nastiness, I reminded myself that her selfishness was our gain. I turned my thoughts aside and smiled affectionately at everyone. Mrs. Makepiece had arrived five minutes before, along with Miss Wardle and Grandpa. Another knock came at the front door and Bartholomew went out. I couldn't see who it was but I heard a man's voice before they disappeared into the surgery. Later, Bartholomew returned to our guests, carrying the little bell that was forever after to be known as

"Enid's bell". He gave it a shake, and everyone turned to him.

'Thank you all for coming to welcome Esther back,' he said. 'We sorely need her here to complete our happy family which is soon to welcome another little one. Now, I just wanted to tell you that the constable has called by to say that two of the men who attacked my family have been apprehended. The other one will, no doubt, be found soon. Men who enact such heinous crimes on a helpless pregnant woman with two small children will be hounded from decent society. There will be no hiding place for this man: he will be found and brought to justice - the gallows, if I have anything to do with it.'

Everyone started talking at once and I felt the energy drain away from me as I plunged back into the memory of the gig coming down on top of us, the pain and the awful noise Flossy made. I could feel nausea rising, with that awful sweat swamping me once more.

'Bartholomew,' I said, tugging at his sleeve, 'I need to lie down, I don't feel well. Can you help me up the stairs?'

He nodded, helping me to my feet. I kept up my smiling, though it felt a bit fixed, as I made my apologies for disappearing in the middle of such a gladsome reunion. I saw the look of worry on Mrs. Makepiece's face, so I said, 'Come and see me, tomorrow, and tell me all about our friend.'

'Aye, lass,' she replied, 'I will, that.'

I lay in the comfort of our bed, relieved to be there but with the sadness of recent events washing over me in waves. Every time I remembered how much I had to be thankful for, my spirits were dashed with sorrow for those I had lost over the years - my friend Captain Campbell and my pony Flossy being only the most recent of so many. I drifted into a half-sleep and a recurring dream in which I was struggling to rescue sailors from the raging seas. Flossy was with me, pulling on a rope tied to her saddle. Then the rope broke and she left me, galloping away into the distance. After that I would hear the sound of her screaming and then a shot. I would wake at that sound and find my cheeks and pillow again wet with tears.

I was aware of Bartholomew encouraging me to drink a sedative and of him wiping my face with a dampened cloth impregnated with my lavender solution and doing his best to soothe me. Eventually I fell asleep again and when I woke it was to a bright, sunlit room. The curtains had been drawn back, a cheerful fire lit and Mrs. Jenkins was busying herself with a breakfast tray. I felt rested and pulled myself up to a sitting position. The sharpened dig from my ribs was still there but dulling to something manageable. I was no longer frightened to breathe.

'The girls are very frisky this morning,' she said. 'I've asked Mr. Jenkins to wear them out in the garden before they come up to see you. I don't expect you are up to being bounced on yet.'

'No,' I laughed, 'but I will be glad to see them when they come back in. It looks such a nice day, so the longer they are outside, the better. The weather has been so cold and windy recently, they couldn't even go out on...' I was going to say 'Flossy', but the memory flooded back and I broke off as tears swelled beneath my eyelids and crept down my face.

'Ee, lass, you cry yourself out,' Mrs. Jenkins murmured as she moved round the bed, smoothing the eiderdown and straightening my pillows. 'Mr. Jenkins asked me to tell you when you're ready that Flossy has been buried at South Farm and he has cut a lock of her mane for you to keep. He is making a plaque to mark her grave.'

'Oh, please thank him for me! I've been so worried about what would happen to her. I couldn't bear it if she had been, well, you know, fed to the dogs at the hunt stables or something like that.'

'No, lass, there was no question of that. Mrs. Elwood was adamant that she be buried with due respect. The stable lads all turned out and one of them cleaned her bridle and it were buried with her.'

The picture this created in my mind reduced me to tears again but I reached out for my friend's hand before saying, 'Please sit down with me – I want to know how Mr. Jenkins is. He must have endured as much as Bartholomew down on that beach in such horrendous conditions.'

'Aye, but he is a tough old chap.' She settled herself on the edge of the chair by my pillow before she went on. 'He were very upset at what he saw, mind, and I don't think he will be forgettin' it in a hurry, like, but he were that glad to meet young Job and look after him awhiles. They had plenty of chat once the boy was dried out and he wantin' to talk so much about losing so many of his shipmates. The poor lad were deeply upset, he says.' She pulled a handkerchief from her apron and mopped her eyes. 'I have been hearing all about it ever since he got back, so as I can see it all now in my own head and it is playing on my mind, like.' She shook herself as if to dispel the unwelcome visions before turning her kindly face to me.

'Now, my dear, enough of the past. I am going to leave you to your breakfast, and if you wants anything more, you just ring that there Enid's bell.'

I laughed at the way she said it. 'Thank you, Mrs. Jenkins. I will get up after breakfast. If I need a hand to get dressed, I will be sure to ring the horrid bell. I never thought I would find a use for it!'

I managed to dress myself in the end and sat in a comfy chair alongside the fire. Both girls raced in to see me, with Wini in charge of them. Their lovely faces lifted my spirits, and after they had disappeared, Bartholomew came up from his surgery with a drop of my tea for us both.

'How are you feeling, my dear?'

'Much calmer. The girls don't let you get too despondent, do they? They are such happy little souls. I do sometimes wonder how Beth, who has seen so many terrible things, can still behave as if her short life has been wholly untroubled. Might it all surface later on?'

'Let us hope not. I don't think it will, because she did not understand the issues or what was happening at the time. But, yes, both girls lift everyone's spirits and I am glad you can laugh with them. You have been through such a lot, Essie, and if they can help you recover, then that is better than any medicine I can prescribe.'

'Bartholomew, I don't feel any sign of the baby coming yet. I'd have thought he would have been shaken out by now.'

'He is in the safest place and will come when he is good and ready. The longer the wait, the better for you, really, though I don't think your ribs were as badly fractured as I thought initially. You were so lucky, Esther, and I am hopeful you will recover quickly now from the physical effects of the accident.'

'I hope that the memory will dull too. I keep having these awful flashbacks. Do you think it wrong of me, Barty, to be so distressed by the loss of Flossy when people have lost their lives?' I asked. 'I feel guilty about it, on top of everything else.'

'The mind has its own way of dealing with injury,' Bartholomew said. 'I have long been convinced that it heals in much the same way as the body - you can't dictate as to what it should or shouldn't feel. Some memories might be suppressed until such time as you can deal with them; there is no right or wrong. The important thing is not to fret about it because your fretting will not affect the outcome. Now, I do believe Mrs. Makepiece was going to drop by this morning. She was very anxious about you and I expect Cecilia is wanting to know how you are too, so I am going to send Mr. Jenkins over with a message later on. He could take the girls with him, if you like.'

'Will they be safe?' I asked, as a stab of fear assailed me.

'If we leave it until after dinner, then I will accompany them all. How's that?'

'Thank you, yes. I will be a lot happier if you are with them. Is there any news about the missing man?' I couldn't bring myself to name him.

'No, no news yet. The other two have been sent to Horsham gaol.'

'And how is Mason? Was he hurt at all?'

'No. Everyone who came through the surf got battered and bruised but he had no significant hurt. He is terribly upset however about Captain Campbell and Charlotte. I am expecting him to call on us shortly when we must discuss the ramifications of the captain's circumstances. As a matter of interest, Mason has already been offered the captaincy of the *Lady Charlotte*, subject to his leg being sound.'

'But surely his leg won't allow him to move about the ship easily?'

'I think he will get around a lot easier when he is the captain. As you'll recall, it is the second-in-command who deals with all the men's squabbles and matters of discipline, which involves constant patrolling.'

I thought of Mason and said, 'I don't think the men are going to like serving under him. Jones will hate it.'

'I think you might be surprised. There are men on board who undertake everything for the captain. He leaves menial tasks to the stewards, cabin boys, his second and the mate - and whilst Mason is unlikely to change in character, the men's focus will be on the new second-in-command. Now, I have a patient due and a full morning ahead, so I will see you at dinner. Will you come down?'

'Yes, I think I must get moving.'

'Why don't you invite Mrs. Makepiece to stay with us for dinner and perhaps for the afternoon? I am sure she will be happy to oblige.'

∞

Mrs. Makepiece duly arrived mid-morning and brought me some early flowering primroses which had been growing in a sheltered spot in her little garden. They were a lovely golden yellow and looked pretty in the tiny cloam jug which Mrs. Jenkins found for them. Once we were alone, we got straight down to the subject of Beatrice.

'How is she?' I asked.

'I am not sure how to describe her state of mind,' Mrs. Makepiece replied uncertainly. 'At times I think her content and almost placid but then I hear her crying in the night. It is upsetting that this poor lass has endured so much unhappiness. But does she cry for what she'd found in her lover or for the cruelty she received at the hands of her husband – or, more likely, perhaps, for an uncertain future with no means of support? Neither do I feel she can have had a happy childhood with that mother of hers. I am not sure that we can resolve all her troubles. I just don't know, Esther, and I don't feel I can ask her anything. After all, I have only known her a short while and I am her landlady, not her confidante.'

'Perhaps we should just be there for her, without trying to bring forth any more than she wishes to tell us? I think she said that she was not ready to explain yet. All we can do is give her sanctuary until such time as she can cope with her own problems. Don't forget that she is Bartholomew's niece and he will not see her cast out - I know he is very taken with her. How is the pregnancy developing?'

'That doesn't help. She is very sick in the morning. Have you anything you can give her, Esther? I am worried that I will have a caller who will hear her retching. How would I explain?'

'As you know, Bartholomew doesn't want me to treat her with my herbs. The injuries to her back were a case in point - but perhaps you know how the creams worked now, as it was you applying them? Before we get to that, though, I have got some peppermint that could be given as a tea. It is such a common treatment for sickness that you could say you already had some in store yourself, if he were to ask you. Just a small cup last thing at night and first thing in the morning, with perhaps a dry biscuit, might be of help.'

'Well, it's an old-fashioned receipt but none the worse for that,' replied Mrs Makepiece. 'I'll try it on her tonight. And as to them there creams, I can vouch that the salve you made has worked best. I use it sparingly, as you said, but there is not much left.'

'And Bartholomew's cream?' I queried.

'That worked too, but not as well, and it has a nasty feel to it, as well as a musty smell. Beatrice says she don't like it but she won't tell her uncle that!'

I felt a moment's satisfaction that my salve had resulted in a good outcome before going on to say, 'Have you had any ideas yet about why Beatrice is in Lewes, a story we can use if someone gets to hear or see her?'

'No, but I thought you might have.'

I reflected briefly and then said, 'What if we were to say that she had come to visit a cousin who has been unavoidably delayed on the continent? Then she came to you, as an old friend of her mother's - which you are, in a sense. The cousin could perhaps live in Brighton, with her house remaining closed up until she returns.'

'And the pregnancy?'

'Unexpected, and so new that her husband has not yet been acquainted of the happy event.'

'And what if Enid hears of it?'

'No one knows Beatrice has any connection to Enid, so why would she hear about it?'

'Should we use her real name?'

'Perhaps we should avoid it, if possible. She could be, say, "Bertha" – just Bertha, without mentioning a surname, or that she is Scottish.'

'But she has a Scottish accent. Two Scottish women, newly arrived in the same small town, will point to connections.'

'Oh dear,' I said, beginning to feel a little weary, 'this is rather difficult, isn't it? Let me think about it. We seem to be getting too complicated.'

'Don't you fret about it. We will do as you say and hope no one hears her speak. She is very content to stay in the house and can take a turn in my little garden behind when I know she won't be overlooked by my neighbours. I think we might have to start sewing a few bits of clothing to disguise her shape.'

'She is a good seamstress,' I said, 'if her hemming is anything to go by.'

We sat gossiping together about other matters before going downstairs to eat with Bartholomew and the girls. It was the first time in a long while that I'd felt normal and more in control of my emotions.

## CHAPTER 17

*Fever-Few (Tanacetum parthenium).* Venus
has commended this herb to succour her sisters,
women, and to be a general strengthener of
their wombs, and to remedy such infirmities as
a careless midwife has there caused. Astrology:
Venus commands this herb.

Culpeper's Colour Herbal

I am feeling an intense desire to busy myself around the
house. My energy has revived and I know that this is often a
preliminary to giving birth: I think of it as "nesting". Christmas has come and gone with a family celebration for the
girls to share. Mr. Jenkins brought in armfuls of holly and
mistletoe early in the morning of Christmas Eve and the
girls clustered round to help him festoon the drawing and
dining rooms with the fresh boughs all dotted with red and
white berries. He had also made a ball from ivy and moss
and suggested to them that they hang a few nuts and some
sweetmeats on it. Beth managed to find some primroses in
the garden which she wove in amongst the damp greenery
and we then placed the ball in a glass bowl balanced on a bed
of evergreen leaves. The girls took such pleasure in making

this simple and pretty centrepiece for our table. On Christmas day Bartholomew walked with them to St. Michael's Church but I stayed at home and spent an hour dressing the dining room table with the ball in pride of place, making it ready for our roasted goose.

Bartholomew and I gave the girls a little dolly each. I had sewn some clothing for them: Beth's has a jacket and skirt made up of a pretty blue cotton with a piece of lace for the collar while Charlotte's is grey and gold with some tiny white embroidered flowers taking the place of buttons. They were overjoyed and later spent hours dressing and undressing them. Mr. Jenkins had kindly made a wooden crib wide enough for both dolls and Mrs. Jenkins had provided some small soft blankets.

It is just a few days now until the new year and new beginnings. I have resolved to put sad and painful memories behind me and to welcome the beginning of 1802 with a lighter heart and a rapidly recovering body.

∞

I am in the first stage of labour but I haven't got time to even think about it as all my good resolutions have been displaced by acute anxiety, with worrying thoughts going round and round in my head: the safety of Beatrice and Cecilia in their coming travail, as well as the security of

Beth and Charlotte; thoughts of Charlotte remind me of Captain Campbell and his fearful end; and, finally, there is my attacker Abe who has so far evaded justice. I struggle to focus on my baby and fall to wondering when will I be able to take up the reins of my life again. Will I even survive the birth when so many women don't? Fortunately, none of my mothers have died but some of their babies haven't made their way into full life. Why should I think my baby will be any different?

Eliza sees that I am distressed and goes downstairs to make some of my tea. As she pours a cup for me, she talks calmly in her unflappable way. I sip and smell the familiar herbs as she wipes my face with some fresh cold water and gradually my spirit lifts as her gentle but determined voice soothes and overcomes my agitation. I endeavour to listen and begin to shed my forebodings, realising that I need to immerse myself completely in this process of birthing and let it just happen around me. After all, I have so much support, with Eliza beside me for the first stage, and Bartholomew working with her for the second and third to achieve what we all wish for, a healthy child.

Many local women have their friends and neighbours present at their travail, known as 'the gossips'. I understand the need, and if any of my mothers-to-be want company, I do my best to accommodate everyone, provided they don't interfere with my work. Sensible women are a help, but not all are of that persuasion - many bring along their bottles of gin to help with the task in hand. There is so much waiting during the early stages, it can be encouraging to have friends to keep up the mother's spirits and they allow Eliza or myself the chance of a few minutes' relaxation until we are needed to actually deliver the baby.

At the birth of our child, though, there will only be Eliza, Bartholomew and Mrs. Makepiece. I haven't asked Cecilia - she has her own pregnancy to deal with as well as the care of Freddie and Felicia. I know she will understand. In any case, I am not sure if the class that she comes from has this habit of inviting other people to share in the birth! I would say not, but I must remember to ask her.

I hope that by tomorrow I will have a robust child to love and care for, and that I will be in good health myself; alas, I know all too well the hazards of giving birth. I thank God that I have Bartholomew with me, but it wouldn't hurt to say a prayer: I beseech my protector Saint Anne, mother of Mary, to help me in my hour of need.

# PART TWO
# January 1803

## CHAPTER 18

# One Year later

*It is hard to know whether a woman hath
conceived twins, only their belly is not even,
but divided with seam and wrinkles, and the
weight is commonly greater.*

*A Directory for Midwives. Nicholas Culpeper*

It is the twins' first birthday and the house is full of excitement. In a sense I feel it is my birthday too, as the birth of our twin boys brought a change to our domestic life that was akin to the strike of a weather event of enormous magnitude - an earthquake, perhaps! I think now and will always think of my life as 'before the boys' and 'after the boys'. Some days I don't know whether I am coming or going and Bartholomew tries so very hard to maintain his ordered life but fails dismally, so that by the time we sit down to our supper we are both exhausted. I have taken to writing a diary, in part for my own sanity, though it mainly consists of lists or a calendar of events for our four children and Bartholomew.

On the morning of the boys' birthing, we were of course expecting just the one baby but as the labour continued Bartholomew realised suddenly that there were two. It was the faint heartbeat of the second-born, William, that Bartholomew had heard occasionally over the months, saying it sounded more like an echo than a baby's heart. William was very small and terribly bruised from the confinement whereas Benjy was robust and clearly the one who had done all the kicking and punching. Within days, and following the application of one of my trusted herbs, colewort, the bruising had faded, and young William was putting on weight and making himself heard with great gusto. Myself? I thought my life complete and I was happy beyond measure to be the mother of two boys. Looking back, I wondered why I had not anticipated that I was expecting twins but they were not a common event and I had never been called upon to deliver twin babies. It was Bartholomew's opinion that William's diminutive size and position had effectively masked his presence.

As the boys made their appearance, Mrs. Makepiece took Benjamin and Eliza was handed William, while Bartholomew managed the final remnants of birth before pronouncing that all was well and that we had two healthy sons, though I noticed that he spent some time inspecting the afterbirth. A message was immediately sent to Cecilia and John Elwood who visited in their carriage later that day, bringing their two youngsters to welcome our sons.

I have yet to return to full-time midwifery but I think Eliza and I together make a formidable team now. We have also sought other ladies who are willing to help with the initial stages of labour in case we need to attend another birth. Recently we seem to have had so many night-time births that it has been difficult for me to attend, so our band of new helpers who are all mothers themselves, take the pressure off in the early stages.

I had promised myself a wet nurse after the first year of feeding and I have found a young woman who fits our needs. Her name is Clara. She has a little girl of two months and plenty of milk to fill hungry mouths during the day while I continue feeding during the night until such time as my milk dries up. I had not realised quite how wonderful it was to feed our babies in this natural way. After the death of her mother, poor Beth had to make do with a wet nurse after those initial drops of goat's milk and honey; but suckling a baby occasioned such delight in me, I was quite smitten with pleasure and joy as well as feelings of overpowering love. A year of feeding has given the lads a healthy and satisfying start but now I need to build myself up to full working strength again. Consequently, I have become a part-time feeding mother with a view to the boys being fully weaned in the next four months or so.

I stayed abed for a few days after the birth. It was a luxury that few mothers have but I was so very tired and more than a little battered and bruised. My sore ribs had added to the pain of birth but the wound in my side had at least healed enough not to reopen.

In the quiet moments when the boys sleep and the girls play, I have been able to look back over the year from the moment of the twins' arrival to today, *our* first birthday. It has been a busy time, including the secret pregnancy of Bertha (we'd all agreed that it was best for Beatrice to keep this name) and the subsequent birth of a scrap of a girl who was tiny but healthy. We had managed between us all to keep her secret despite one or two close shaves. Both Bertha's husband and lover were none the wiser about this child but she was greatly loved and named Grace after Mrs. Makepiece who was thrilled by the honour. Bertha asked me if I too would give my name to the baby, but I said it might be better not to. If there were any enquiries made in the future as to who knew what, where and when, the name Esther would be a giveaway.

Enid has returned to Scotland for the time being, as we understand from the locals who confide in Mrs. Jenkins, to attend to her property and re-let at more favourable rates. She told an acquaintance that she thought to find a property for herself in the nearest Scottish town, to be funded by the letting of her two cottages. I think the whole of Lewes breathed a sigh of relief when she left; she had not added to society here and her sour demeanour had turned most against her. I don't think she ever found out that her daughter was in the town, let alone that she was pregnant with Enid's first grandchild. All communication between them had ended. Bartholomew had negotiated long and hard for an allowance for Bertha as well as the return of the jewellery and clothing. I gathered, though I never heard the details, that Bertha's injuries were part of the leverage used by him to protect and provide for his niece. The funds he was able to raise supplied enough money for her to rent a small cottage and raise the child herself, and we made sure that this young woman and her baby were seen to be under our protection. There was no divorce, so she was still the wife of a sitting MP but we let it be known that they were 'separated'. If her husband ever reappears, which seems unlikely, he is probably not going to be interested in having a daughter: it was a son he had wanted, not a daughter, and particularly not one with a question mark over her paternity.

As Bertha is well-educated, it is hoped that she will find some work in one of the new schools opening up in the town, or indeed by looking after the many children we seem to have acquired between Cecilia, Eliza and myself. Cecilia and John had another baby boy about a month after I gave birth and his first birthday will be another great celebration. They have named him John Joseph. Getting a child through its first year is always a challenge, even for comfortably-off families. Disease is no respecter of status, and it isn't always the small and puny that die. Being terribly contagious, scarlatina sometimes took all the young from a family in a matter of weeks; I live in fear of seeing the strawberry tongue which sometimes marks the victims.

Lewes has suffered another smallpox outbreak and some residents were locked into their lanes with armed guards at either end to prevent them from mixing with the population at large. Regrettably there were some deaths, but the contagion did not spread far on this occasion. The malignant sore throat is also a concern but no one we know is blighted by its reach. Disease is always a worry in the town, particularly as so many have limited means to feed their children with nourishing food. Light bread has found its way into the shops again despite the action of some vigilant housewives who gave the bakers short shrift. The free soup supply continues, with many of the farmers and locals helping to provide fresh vegetables when there is a surplus. Not everyone welcomes the soup kitchen, though, thinking that it encourages laziness, but fortunately Lewes is a benevolent as well as a spirited town and most people are upstanding. There are still too many alehouses, however, taking money from those who have least; and there is also a marked intolerance of some religious sects which occasions violence and discord, even within families.

Last November's celebration of Bonfire Night was quieter than it had been in earlier years. When I first saw the bonfire event, as an outsider, I was dumbfounded by the atmosphere of menace which was intended as a direct threat to the town officials who had tried on occasions to prevent it taking place. I had quickly realised that for the townsfolk it was an important reminder to those same officials that they didn't always get everything their own way, and that the annual observance was enshrined in an act of parliament by the King whose government was saved from the attempt by Guido Fawkes to blow up the Houses of Parliament. In Lewes it was also an act of remembrance for the seventeen Protestant martyrs who had been burned at the stake in the

High Street during Bloody Mary's reign. Long may Lewes bonfire continue. It wasn't popular with everyone but I loved it.

∽

Recently I received a note via Charley in London from Job, saying that he was satisfied with his way of life at sea. The mate had become his close friend after both survived drowning in the terrible accident in Seaford Bay; they looked out for each other when some crew members got a bit mutinous. Job asked after Beth and promised to return to Lewes at some point in the future to see her.

I wrote back hoping that his friend the mate would read my letter to him, giving all our news and also some relating to his family at Coad Farm. I reminded him that there would always be a welcome for him here and, as Billy-alone and Cilla were now wed, they would put him up if he should want to stay a few days. I thought he would be uncomfortable staying with us. When I told Bartholomew about this, he laughed but also suggested that I could hardly call Billy 'alone' any more, particularly as Cilla was expecting, but I am afraid I can't lose the habit. Beth was thrilled to hear that 'Joe' had been in touch and talked about it for days.

Two of my attackers were imprisoned but Abe has disappeared, and I do my best to keep him from my mind, as I do with the Coads. I have heard that Farmer Coad still keeps a tight grip on the farm, but his two sons are living there with their women. No more attempts have been made by other smugglers to disrupt my life and I hope that the nastiness and brutality has now gone away. Billy, however, is not of this mind, and regularly warns me to remain watchful.

## CHAPTER 19

*Of the choice of the nurse. The blood that nourisheth the child in the womb is turned into milk to nourish him after he is born because he can eat no solid meat. And because from weakness or a disease the mother sometimes cannot suckle her child, she must have a nurse of good habit of body and red complexion, which is the sign of the best temper; and let her not differ much from the temper of the mother unless it be for the better. Let her be between twenty and thirty, well bred and peaceable, not angry, melancholy or foolish; not letcherous, or a drunkard. Let her breasts be well fashioned with good nipples, that the child may take them with pleasure. Let her keep a good diet, and abstain from hard wine and copulation, and passions; these chiefly trouble the milk, and bring diseases upon the child.*

*A Directory for Midwives. Nicholas Culpeper*

On one of my many trips to Cliffe in the spring, I was forced to stand waiting while a goods wagon was being loaded with grain when some rude fellows pushed past me and I felt myself jostled. It was unnerving as I nearly fell, my limpy leg slipping out of balance; but I was no lily-livered creature who could be pushed around so I accosted the man nearest me. I tapped him hard on the shoulder, saying, 'How dare you push me aside? Have you no manners?' He turned and stared at me before snorting with laughter.

'I dunno who youse think you is, woman. I remember youse when you were a kitchen skivvy for me ma. 'Ere, Flo, guess who we got 'ere? That uppity gel I told you of. 'Er who took me pa's by-blow and kept 'er.'

A blowsy-looking woman looked hard at me before saying to him, 'We should get the brat back. I need some 'elp in the 'ouse. Why don't ya?'

I felt a wave of heat creep up me as I faced them down. 'You'll not succeed in that, I tell you.'

'Why's you gone all red, then?' he said. 'You scared we will? Blood's thicker 'an water, ain't it, Flo?'

'You got 'er rattled, boyo,' said the woman. 'We'll get the old man to start off the process, like. You just wait, you uppity bitch. We's got your measure, you just wait.' She laughed loudly as she saw my discomfort, tossing back her long straggly black hair.

'Now, now, break it up. What's goin' on 'ere?' A customs officer pushed between us. 'You having problems,

Mrs. Grieve? Move on, you lot. You've no business here, move on now.'

They looked back at me as they walked further down into Cliffe before one of them (I don't know which of the brothers he was) spat on the ground, drew his finger across his throat and gave another raucous belly laugh.

The Coads had the ability to turn me into quivering jelly: the bones in my legs felt as if they were dissolving. I leaned against the side of the cart as I caught my breath and recovered myself. 'Thank you, Officer,' I said, 'I will be fine in a moment.'

'Do you want someone to walk with you? Are you going the same way as those ruffians?'

'Yes, I have a young mother in travail. I would be grateful if one of your men could see me to her door. She is not far, a few minutes away.'

The officer had already removed his cap which he waved in the air and shouted, 'Bert, come escort Mrs. Grieve down t'Cliffe, will yer?' He turned back to me, saying, 'I suspect they will be long gone by the time you have to leave but if I can be of any further assistance, just ask here at the office. I recall you helping me sister when she were givin' birth to my nephew. We are indebted to you, Ma'am.'

I nodded, shook his hand and thanked him for his timely assistance before Bert appeared at my side and took my bag into his big capable hands. I felt myself relax and took a deep breath as we walked into Cliffe and turned off to a row of dingy little cottages parallel to the river. This was not a place that the sun shone on for long; the ground was damp and green underfoot. I found the cottage and knocked hard on the door which was flung open instantly by a young woman who shouted out, 'It's all right, Molly, the midwife be 'ere. You'll be all right now.'

She grabbed my bag from Bert, saying, 'Cor, am I glad to see you, Missus. Me sister is in a right ol' state.'

My mother-to-be Molly was surrounded by her gossips and while I appreciated their kindly presence, there were too many for the small, dark room. Molly was crouching on a low platform with a thin pallet mattress which smelled like it was stuffed with mouldy straw - cheaper than hay, I supposed. After a quick examination I was able to calm her and explain that she was in the second stage of labour but we had a way to go yet. I watched the women all about her and chose the most sensible-looking to undertake tasks that would help; the others I asked to leave for the time being but to be ready to return if we needed help. Eventually, after a lot of giggling and ribald encouragement, there were just two others and myself: one to watch the mother and one to make gruel, serve small ale (the water from Cliffe was not good) and anything else Molly expressed a wish for, but their hardest task would be to support their friend.

I had brought some herbs with me: lemon balm, verbena, mint and marjoram all tightly enclosed in a linen pad. I had hoped to wipe it over any furniture or the bed frame to press the oils out and thus refresh the room. But there was no suitable wooden furniture. Instead, I filled a pot with lavender flowers and some dried but still sweetly scented rose petals. I had run out of violets but had remaining some fragrant geranium leaves to add to the mixture. I placed it next to Molly so that she could dip in and crush the herbs to release their fragrance and revitalise her spirit. I had also brought some of my tea to help calm her if she became agitated. Such items always had their place in my bag in addition to the instruments I might need for the birth or emergencies.

Bartholomew had told me recently that women in country districts fared well in terms of live births. He explained that this was because there was less interference from physicians who were paid handsomely for their services but who frequently had little or no experience of childbirth. I was amazed to hear that but then remembered my unfortunate encounter with the locum who had taken over when Bartholomew went on his travels. He thought he knew everything when in fact his skills were not only inadequate but downright dangerous, with all his inappropriate bleedings and what I would term 'quackery'!

Until very recently, Eliza and I had not charged for our services because most of our mothers were too poor to pay. However, we had received requests from other more well-found women in the town who had heard of our good reputation; we decided that we would charge them a standard fee, which would give Eliza some income and would enable us to continue free treatment for the poorest. Bartholomew had suggested this arrangement and all was working well. Any money left over was being saved in the hope that we could find suitable premises for lying-in facilities. I didn't take a wage for myself.

Molly, however, was clearly unable to pay for her delivery. Her house was small and damp and only had the most basic of comforts. She was well under twenty, possibly as young as seventeen, but had two children already. Sarah, one of the gossips, had taken them for a walk around the town. I wasn't expecting any great difficulties, but it didn't turn out like that. I had to ask Molly's sister to run and find Eliza as I needed help with what turned out to be a difficult and lengthy birth with the mother becoming distressed and flagging. Eventually, with all of us encouraging her, we were able to bring a live child into the world, but he was very poorly and didn't survive the hour. I cradled the poor little scrap as he struggled to breathe before handing him to his mother; after some painful minutes, he took his last shuddering gasps and then was no more. Poor Molly was exhausted, clearly bewildered and in need of the comfort of her friends and neighbours around her. She clutched the dead baby to her breast while we cleaned her up and tidied around. Finally, with the help of our two gossips, we carefully washed, dressed and laid the boy out. Molly's other two little ones came in to view their brother.

We took our leave with great sorrow; we could hear the mother keening as we walked away. I wondered whether the dampness of her home had caused the child's weakness but there could have been so many other factors that we would likely never know. I said to Eliza as we walked over the bridge: 'We have been fortunate not to have many deliveries like that. It is tragic after all those months of carrying a child, feeling him quicken inside you and enduring the agony of delivery, only for him to die as he finally reaches the world.'

Eliza replied, 'It always surprises me that these poor women are able to give birth at all and their children pull through when they live in such bad conditions and look so very hungry.'

I told her what Bartholomew had said about physicians and childbirth, and about my experiences of his locum before adding that because these women trusted us, I felt very badly when we couldn't bring things to a happy conclusion. She commented that at least most of our babies had survived so far and we had never had a woman's death on our hands.

I thought back to my first husband Wilf's former girlfriend: how she had died alone and uncared for in the workhouse, her baby still within her. It was a painful memory. I think Eliza and I returned to our homes with sadness for Molly in our minds and hearts, yet we were thankful too that our experiences were largely productive and successful.

My final task on Molly's behalf was to tell Bartholomew that a baby had died. He nodded and wrote it up in his daybook before squeezing my hand in sympathy.

## CHAPTER 20

*Of the Diet and Government of Infants: Of
the conditions of good Milk: It must be neither
too thick, nor too thin, for too thick cannot be
concocted, and the thin agues crudities. If it
be dropt upon the nail or a grass and falls not
easily off as water; if it stick too fast, it is too
thick. Let the colour be white, the more it differs
from that the worse it is. Let it be sweet, not
sour, salt or bitter, or sharp. Let it neither smell
burnt or sour, for then it will easily corrupt the
stomach of the child.*

*A Directory for Midwives. Nicholas Culpeper*

One morning I was surprised to be called by Mrs. Jenkins
to a visitor whom she had seated in the kitchen. I was
even more surprised to find that the visitor was Charley,
my young London friend who worked for the shipping
agent of the *Lady Charlotte*. I had learned long ago that
all in that close-knit shipping community were known to
each other and that what happened on one ship was soon
known by all the others.

'Charley, how lovely, and what a surprise to see you here!' I exclaimed. 'Are you having an outing with your pa or is there news from Mason that we need to know about? I hope he is enjoying being captain of the *Lady Charlotte?*'

'He is that, and doing a good job, too, so we hear, but it's not exactly what I've come about, Ma'am. What I means to say is me and pa thought to give you warning as Missus Campbell has been sniffin' round the office.'

'You used to call me, Esther, Charley - please, let's continue on first-name terms. Why would she be coming to the office? Surely she has no connection with the *Lady Charlotte* now?'

'She been askin' questions about the captain's will and what it contained, and me pa worries that if she finds out that he left a tidy package to his daughter, she will be after the money.'

'No! I can't believe that,' I said. On reflection, however, I could well believe it.

''Tis the truth, Esther. Me pa said to warn you that young Charlotte is her ticket to an easy life and that the people she hangs about with are no good.'

'Has the office told her anything? Surely it is confidential what a man leaves in his will?'

'Someone must 'ave said summat, but she don't know it all, and like I said, she is fishin' for answers.'

'As I remember, she was not included in the captain's will. He left everything to Charlotte, and he died well over a year ago. Why is she hanging about now?'

'He made a new will when he got back from the voyage you was on. He must have known 'is wife was a wrong 'un where Charlotte was concerned. The new will had a bit in it that said if anything were to happen to him, he wanted the people who took her in *willingly and with good intentions*, as did you and Doctor Grieve, to have a sum of money to feed and clothe her. Me pa reckons she will be after that, and if she claims Charlotte back, she will try and get the use of all the money.'

'How do you know all this, Charley?' I asked, wishing that Bartholomew was here.

'Pa asked Sir Magnus. You remember him, the gent who comes to Lewes Assizes? He spoke to the office and they told him the details of the will, as they supervised it all. As I said, Captain Campbell wrote a new will after your voyage. I think Sir Magnus be likely to come and see you when he comes down at some point.'

'Charley, I can't thank you enough for all you and your pa have done. Without your kindness we would have known none of this and Charlotte would have been at risk. I have no faith that her mother cares for her at all, but she does care for money. Have you seen her yourself?'

'Aye, I saw her with some cove who was the worse for wear - drunk, like - and she didn't look too good. She were at the Morpeth Arms which be one of the pubs that houses felons in their cellars before they is put on the hulks. It is right on the river and some says as it is haunted. I wouldn't go there meself,' he assured me earnestly.

Mrs Jenkins was open-mouthed with astonishment at all she'd heard of our conversation and I asked her to give Charley the cake she had just made so that he and his pa could have it overnight and on their journey back to London tomorrow. She nodded vigorously and went off to find a cloth to tie it in.

'In the meantime, Charley, would you like to meet young Charlotte and Beth and, of course, our two boys? I promise you that we will take extra care with Charlotte and won't let her mother near her. I will contact Sir Magnus once I have spoken to Doctor Grieve.'

'Aye, I would,' he replied, 'I'd be made up to meet the childer.'

I took him along to what was once the breakfast room but now a playroom for the children and left him for a few minutes with them scrambling all over him while I went to Bartholomew's study to see where he was. I couldn't find him, but as Charley and his pa were lodged overnight in the town, perhaps he could talk to them later in the evening. Luckily, the coach was not to continue onwards to Brighthelmstone as there were no bookings beyond Lewes. The return trip tomorrow would leave early, about five of the clock.

Of course, we knew that Charlotte had inherited her father's estate, but we had no idea how much money that involved. We had agreed with Mason that we would continue with her care until or if there was a better solution. We hoped that Charlotte would stay with us indefinitely and perhaps to adopt her, though the money for her care had never been mentioned and was in any case of no consequence to us. The details had not yet been finalised: we were still waiting on official paperwork from the shipping agent's lawyers who were treating her as a child abandoned by her mother. No money had yet been released and Charlotte's inheritance was, we thought, protected by the courts. Charley's news about Sir Magnus taking an interest was good news indeed. I wondered if we had been lax in not keeping in closer contact with the lawyers. Charley and his pa's intervention would enable us to guard Charlotte from harm though it seemed terrible to categorise her mother as a harmful person. Forewarned is forearmed, as the saying goes, and I would be pleased to meet up with Sir Magnus again soon.

After Captain Campbell died, Mason had been able to tell us a little about the captain's family who were elderly and unable to care for a little one; and about his arrangements for his daughter, should something happen to him, but not in any great detail as it was all too raw then. Mason, it seemed, had informed the captain about his wife's behaviour and her subtle cruelty towards Charlotte by leaving her in the care of wet nurses or servants while she sought to make a name for herself in Brighton, and how later on she had literally dumped the child on him. Interestingly, it transpired that the captain and Mrs. Campbell were not actually married. Theirs was an arrangement in which the captain clearly never quite trusted her enough to give her his name in law.

When I remember how she made a fool of him on the boat, screaming, raging and throwing crockery at his head, I realised that perhaps in death he had got his own back. He had obviously realised that she was an unsuitable woman to trust with either his daughter or his money. She had implied to me that the captain might not be Charlotte's father, but I never took any notice of that comment and had only told Bartholomew of it; no one else knew, nor would I ever mention it again. If 'Mrs Campbell' entered our lives once more and the subject came up, I would deny all knowledge, and do my best to make sure that Charlotte had all the legal protection of a beloved child.

## CHAPTER 21

*Angelica (Angelica archangelica). Our physicians...blasphemously call Pansies, or Heart's Ease, an herb for the Trinity, because it is of three colours; and a certain ointment, an ointment of the Apostles, because it consists of twelve ingredients. Alas! I am sorry for their folly and grieved at their blasphemy. God send them wisdom the rest of their age, for they have their share of ignorance already. Some call this an herb of the Holy Ghost; others more moderate called it Angelica, because of its angelical virtues. A herb of the Sun in Leo.*

Culpeper's Colour Herbal

An unusual package arrived for Bartholomew who disappeared into his office without sharing the contents with me. I had noticed however that it was overwritten with a close and cramped hand and had an elaborate seal. Later, when he went out, I stole into his surgery to see if I could find out what it was and who it was from but couldn't locate it. He probably knew I would do that and took it with him!

There is nothing like a mystery-letter to whet your appetite and set off all sorts of imaginary hopes or worries, and I thought about little else throughout the morning. At lunchtime I dropped a few hints and when they bore no fruit, I asked him a direct question, but he was not forthcoming and in fact teased me about being inquisitive. Bartholomew could be very provoking at times.

Later that evening he suggested that we all go to spend some time with Cecilia and John the following Saturday. It was quite an upheaval to get all six of us out at once but we managed it in the end. The weather had turned out fine and Cecilia and I were even able to spend an hour or two together enjoying a quiet chat. Cilla was in charge of the children, except for the youngest, and despite her pregnancy was throwing herself into games of Hide-and-Seek and the ever-popular Peep. Sometimes Freddie got fed up with all the bossy girls around him and escaped with his toy horses and some wooden soldiers that one of the estate workers carved for him. He was a loving child and always came to me for a cuddle. My two boys were very keen to play with him and his toys but they still needed a daytime nap which the older children had now outgrown.

I said to Cecilia, 'Bartholomew has received a myste-rious package and he hasn't told me what it's all about. In fact, he seems amused by my efforts to get him to tell me! I think he wanted to visit today in order to discuss it with John. Has he said anything to you?'

'No, he hasn't, but John did say that they had important matters to talk about. I wonder what it can be?'

'Well, I suppose he will let on, doubtless later rather than sooner! But I really want to know. I have a feeling it is important.'

As there was nothing further to be discovered, we turned to other things.

'How are Billy and Cilla getting on in their new cottage?' I asked. 'The baby must be quickening by now. I miss seeing Billy around so much, though.'

'They are both very well and Cilla still manages the kitchen work without complaint though we have a pot boy for the heavier work now. Needless to say, he is a friend of Billy's. Is there anyone that boy doesn't know?'

'If he doesn't know them, he knows their servants - and once you know the servants, you pretty well know everyone and everything.'

'I know that Mrs. Fisher may not be the easiest person to get on with,' reflected Cecilia, 'but time has sorted out her temperamental differences with Cilla and I can see that our kitchen is a happy place now, as all the staff congregate there. In fact, the children love to go down there too, probably because they know where the biscuits are kept. When John was a boy, the servant's quarters were out of bounds. And when I was a child, I didn't even know there was a kitchen. I have so much wanted to raise my children differently from my own upbringing that I sometimes wonder if my lack of discipline with them is a good or a bad thing.'

'I don't think it is discipline you are lacking at all. Your little ones are happy and polite. What more can you ask for? Have you thought any more by the way about Bertha taking on the teaching role, now I can't manage it?'

Cecilia and Bertha were now good friends despite my initial clumsy attempts to foist an unknown and pregnant woman onto the Elwoods. It had all come about after the boys were born, when Cecilia had invited both Mrs. Makepiece and me to afternoon tea and casually suggested that we bring Bertha with us, despite her still being with child and having no husband to support her. She had tactfully offered to send her carriage for us which would give Bertha privacy as well as the chance for an outing. At the time I was extremely grateful that my friend had extended the hand of friendship to one who could well become notorious if her secrets were found out. Since Grace's birth, the two of them had met up on many occasions and no questions were asked nor Bertha's status commented upon. I know that Bartholomew was more than grateful that the Elwoods had 'noticed' Bertha.

'Yes, I am going to put it to her in the short term and see how we all get on. The children love her and providing she can cope with Grace, your little ones, Eliza's and mine, it should work. If it is too much for her, we can spread the days around so that the youngest all work and play while Freddy and Beth do their sums and writing together as the eldest, already knowing the basics. I mentioned Eliza, but have you asked her yet if she wants to join with us?'

'I mentioned it in passing but she thinks her mother has objections. She is a bit strange - I think there may be jealousies at play.'

'No matter, but you will have to get a bigger trap, Esther, to get them all here.'

'I know, we have already spoken about it, and I am going to get a new pony for myself as well. It is about time that I moved on from Flossy. I still miss her so, but needs must. Mr. Jenkins will bring Beth and Charlotte along with Bertha and Grace. The boys will stay with me for a while yet.'

'John said to tell you that we have several young but steady ponies in the stables. Go and speak to the lads and see what you think. I think it is important not to compare but start afresh - after all, you have different needs now and a lot more experience. Flossy was perfect for you at one time of your life but things have changed now.'

Later we returned to the subject of schooling and Cecilia said, 'You are no longer worried about security?'

'It has crossed my mind, but I think the threat passed when Abe vanished. No one has seen him since,' I said.

'I have said it before, Esther, but you must maintain vigilance in everything you do,' she said, fixing her gaze on me. 'Please remember that. How are you managing your work as well as the care of the boys, now they are getting so big and into everything? Will you have to get help?'

'Wini and Mrs. Jenkins are very involved in looking after them and the wet nurse Clara is a great help. She fits in with everyone and her little girl is adorable too,' I said thoughtfully. 'Between us all it works, but I am not sure for how much longer.'

Suddenly there was a great clamour outside as the older children rushed by and up the stairs towards the nursery. When the nursery door slammed shut behind them, all the clatter abated and we were able to hear ourselves speak again.

'Cecilia, do you, like me, ever look back to when we first met and when we went to St. Anne's to leave our tokens and pray for our hearts' desires? Do you wonder at how different our lives are now in such a short space of time? There have been so many difficult times and so much worry and fear, but somehow, we have come through it all. I am thinking of going to St. Anne's for a Sunday service soon, just to say thank you.'

'Can you not say thank you at St. Michael's where the boys were baptised?'

'Well, I have, but I feel drawn to go back to St. Anne's. That day is so strong in my memory, I feel I must. Is it peculiar to feel like this? Especially as I have no great truck with organised religion - but if I can get beyond the priests, vicars and all the rules, I find I have belief which has grown since the boys were born. I honestly think that St. Anne has been looking after me. We went there when we realised that she was the patron saint of mothers, in or out of wedlock – I am sure she doesn't care if women are married or not. As the mother of Mary, she must have had such strong belief in her daughter who was unmarried yet destined to become the mother of Jesus.'

'I never thought I would hear you speak like this,' said Cecilia, with a smile. 'I am so pleased because I have always had belief, with or without organisation. It gives me comfort when I remember the dark days and when I feel unsure what to do, I pray.'

'It still worries me that there are so many different churches or groups here in Lewes and that some of the behaviour of their members seems far from Christian to me, but even so, I think if I go to St. Anne's church, I will be nearer her.'

'I will come with you. Do we have to go on a Sunday, though? Can't we just go, as we did before, on a normal day?'

'Yes, let's do that. I'll let you know once I've made arrangements for the children, or maybe when Bertha is in charge and Mrs. Jenkins can look after the boys. I am beginning to think that we will have to have a daily girl just to look after the children. Do you think we could do schooling at our house, as well, perhaps on alternate days?'

'Yes, of course. Let me speak to Bertha, and you check on Eliza?'

By the time we were ready to leave I was aware of a feeling of great peace and comfort, having at last made the decision to visit my special saint and protector in her own shrine.

## CHAPTER 22

*Hawthorn (Crataegus monogyna). The*
*gatekeeper: Hawthorn's frothy creamy-white*
*blossoms followed by plentiful red berries in*
*the autumn, give rich food for wildlife and*
*healing tonics for human hearts. A lusty tree,*
*Hawthorn's maypoles and garlands energise*
*Beltane festivities and country weddings.*
*May's thorns offer protection and the*
*pentagrams on each fruit invoke the healthy*
*balance of earth, air, fire, water and spirit.*

Yvonne McDermott of Forest Moons

The mysterious package turned out to have come from one of Bartholomew's former medical colleagues who had roped him into sailing on one of the ships accompanying Nelson's *Theseus* before Bartholomew and I met up again in Gibraltar. It included a detailed account of a celebrated battle two years ago which had been won by Nelson through superior firepower, clever tactics and, in the final days, diplomacy.

So, instead of holing themselves up in John's office to discuss serious affairs of state, it seemed that

Bartholomew and John Elwood had actually been re-enacting the Battle of Copenhagen! I did not understand how the reconstruction of an earlier naval encounter could be met with so much excitement but clearly in our husbands' hearts and minds they had as good as been there on that day in the Baltic. Their correspondent had certainly sent enough detail for them to think they were.

When Cecilia went into John's office later, she had found his desk cleared of all its usual piles of ledgers and papers to make way for lots of little sticks which represented positions of ships - demonstrating who fired on whom – with used fire spills to stand in for burnt-out boats. John later told Cecilia that this tactic of burning boats was apparently better than the Danish fleet and merchant ships falling into the hands of the French. The other members of the alliance were stuck behind winter ice so the battle had to be fought before the ice melted. Cecilia wrote to me that evening describing what the package contained and what our husbands had been engaged in. Later Barty showed me all the documents, drawings and observations of his friend who had been on Nelson's ship. I had to admit it was all very interesting and it amused me to hear that during this battle, Nelson apparently *chose* to look through his telescope with his blind eye and thereby *not* see the signal to retreat from his commander, saying to his flag captain: 'You know, Foley,

I have only one eye and I have the right to be blind some-times. I really do not see the signal.'

This spectacular piece of disobedience from Vice Admiral Horatio Nelson to the orders of his command-er-in-chief Admiral Hyde Parker apparently saved the day for the British Naval Fleet and earned Nelson the new title of Viscount Nelson. His action won the battle for Britain against a powerful Russian alliance: The League of Armed Neutrality which included Denmark-Norway, Sweden, Prussia and Russia. Nelson believed such a league was in French interests and thus presented a seri-ous threat to Britain's naval supremacy.

Once the battle was won, Admiral Hyde Parker was instructed to hand command over to Nelson and recalled to London. I felt a little sorry for him, despite it being over two years ago; he must have been hopping mad when his subordinate disobeyed him and took the rest of the ships with him into the fray, so that once again this daring man Horatio Nelson became the hero of the battle.

Unfortunately, despite my enjoyment that day of the account of the battle and my abiding admiration for Lord Nelson, a sting in the tail was lying in wait for me. Just two weeks later, the great man himself sent an invitation to Bartholomew to meet in London immediately for dis-cussion of a naval preferment for my husband. I was dev-astated. I knew that Bartholomew had acquitted himself well in the skirmish Nelson had fought at Santa Cruz and that he had subsequently undertaken some covert operations for the British Fleet and government. That was the reason he'd been in Gibraltar and able to secure my release from the transport ship! Of course, I knew he had to go, but not before I had argued, cried, and tried to make him feel guilty for leaving the children and myself.

'Esther, I can't tell you why, but I am needed.'

'But why?' I persisted. 'Why can't you tell me what you are needed for? If I understood, I might bear it better.'

'Because I have been told not to by His Majesty's government.'

'Surely you do not think I am going to gossip?' But Bartholomew just shook his head and walked away.

The next morning, we all made a great effort to see him off to the initial meeting with cheery faces and bright smiles. In my heart, I knew that he was thrilled by this exciting development, by being able to work closely with a valiant man like Nelson, and, more importantly, by the prospect of once again being back in the thick of things. Life would not be the same again for goodness knows how long. I fervently hoped the discussions would fail, that he would not go to sea again, that he would return and be content with our domesticity. I also knew that my hopes were baseless.

Before he left finally to take up his post in London, he called me into the surgery and showed me a hidden compartment in the wall behind a portrait of his father. Inside was his last will and testament as well as details of bank accounts and investments. He referred me to a local solicitor and to the bank located just between the Star and the market tower for my daily needs. He also gave me a letter to be opened only if he should die. I tried not to cry but these instructions all pointed one way only and I was fighting not to go down that path in my head, let alone my body which shuddered of its own accord whenever I thought of it.

I decided that we needed more help in the house. Bartholomew's absence made quite a difference to our lives and I also had to deal with things that he would normally have done himself, leaving me with even less time for the children. I asked Clara, our wet nurse, if she would move in with us and take on more general care of all the children. She didn't seem to think she could but promised to let me know the following day. I hoped she would consider my offer fully as it was a good step up for her. Bartholomew had made arrangements for his patients to be seen by one of the other Lewes physicians. Taking on a locum again was not to his taste, particularly after the shambles left by Dr. Crabbe.

The physician chosen was a youngish man of about thirty-four years of age who had an apothecary to help him with basic dispensing. I had never met Dr. Chappell and didn't expect to have any contact with him, which suited me well, but he began to call at the house repeatedly to ask for access to Bartholomew's notes. I got the feeling that he was just being meddlesome because when I produced the notes, he barely even glanced at them. He seemed more interested in my work and kept turning any conversation we might have towards my own experience, my patients and how much I charged for a straightforward delivery. I had no reason to refuse to answer his questions; if Bartholomew trusted him, then so must I.

Correspondence from London was a little sparse and I became quite low in spirit that I was left behind to cope with four children, my own practice of midwifery and all the domestic arrangements with our staff. Thankfully, Clara had decided she could work every day and, when it suited her, she would stay overnight. Everyone worked together, and with Mrs. Jenkins in charge when I was busy, the house ran smoothly enough.

I didn't know the nature of the work that Bartholomew was actually doing as he still hadn't told me, but I hoped that at least it would remain land-based. I had these sorts of thoughts throughout the day and I worried constantly about him, but at least he didn't appear to have gone to sea as yet.

I was expecting a visit from Sir Magnus to discuss our plans to care for Charlotte on a more formal footing. We had corresponded with him since Charley's visit and I was hoping that the matter was nearing conclusion. The captain's will had been detailed as to the care of Charlotte, specifying that if his 'wife' Mrs. Campbell undertook her care continuously and with kindness, then she would receive an amount of money to cover Charlotte's needs plus an extra sum that would be administered by Mr. Mason. She would have no access to the principal sum nor to a property to be held in trust until Charlotte's eighteenth birthday. In her own right, Mrs. Campbell would receive nothing.

Sir Magnus had taken statements from Mason and myself as to Mrs. Campbell's behaviour whilst Charlotte was a baby. He had also taken away the letter she had written to me in order to make the case that Charlotte had been previously abandoned, should Mrs. Campbell try to take the child back into her care and thereby gain access to some of the money if not all.

Based on the authority of Captain Campbell's will, Sir Magnus had also put our care of her into a wardship, a term and status that unfortunately had no legal teeth. In law, Mrs. Campbell could feasibly claim Charlotte back, so Sir Magnus's approach was to tie up the money and property so tightly that she would have no financial advantage in claiming her back. This applied also to Bartholomew and myself, but it was not an issue for us.

Sir Magnus had arrived in Lewes on one of his regular visits and planned to visit me that night. He was occupied during the day with his court work, and I was looking forward to having my evening meal with him. Beth and Charlotte were to stay up a little later so that they could be introduced.

When the bell rang, both girls hurried down, excited to meet Sir Magnus, and then ran off to play for a while before bedtime. The boys were already fast asleep. Mrs. Jenkins showed him into the drawing room where we settled down to talk about Charlotte and indirectly about Beth too. I was shocked to discover that the law was on the side of the parent who could still make a claim and get the child back, no matter the nature of the evidence against them. In Beth's case, she had some protection in place based on the court case whereby her grandfather had assigned her to me for care, with the judge agreeing to that. The court case had indicated that the surviving parent Farmer Coad was unfit to look after her. However, Sir Magnus warned that should the Coads decide to take her back, there was always a chance that they could succeed. In Charlotte's case, the same applied with Mrs. Campbell.

'I have tied up the good captain's intent in his last will and testament,' he said, 'so that Mrs. Campbell would not want to claim Charlotte as she would gain nothing financially. She clearly abandoned her daughter, so the proviso Captain Campbell made has not been kept. In other words, she is unfit to have the care of the child.'

I nodded, grateful to have his opinion and also to know that the administrators of Captain Campbell's last will and testament were Mason and another man connected to the shipping agent who would do their best to ensure that Charlotte would stay safe in our care. We had also appointed Mason as godfather and Cecilia as godmother when she was baptised.

'Sir Magnus, I always worry that Farmer Coad will seek to get Beth returned to his custody – but, in the event of his death, would his sons have the same rights, or would her grandpa's rights be stronger?'

'I think we should just carry on,' he replied, 'and hope that none of these unsavoury adults, nor any relations, will attempt to seize the children. If I were you, Esther, I would behave with confidence and tell no one about any of the legal possibilities. Very few people go to law: the costs can be ruinous and there is no way of knowing the outcome. You already have a judge's permission to raise

Beth. Mrs. Campbell has clearly defaulted on her obligations by dumping Charlotte on Mason and you and, as I said earlier, she would gain no financial benefit in getting her back. My advice to you is, least said soonest mended. I would also suggest that you maintain your vigilance against kidnap.'

I groaned. I had been feeling a little more secure recently but clearly mistakenly so if Sir Magnus was right.

'Thank you for your work on our behalf, Sir Magnus,' I said. 'Let's hope that neither Mrs. Campbell nor Farmer Coad attempt to take back Charlotte or Beth. To have two children at risk from different parents is horrendous.'

Our talk in the drawing room had been so concentrated that when Mrs. Jenkins came in to advise us that supper was served in the dining room, it broke the tension and we were then able to enjoy a very convivial meal together. Sir Magnus was good company, an entertaining as well as handsome man whose education and distinction shone from every pore. He was clean-shaven that night, with a fragrant scent of cedar following in his wake. For his visit to me, he had changed from his black court clothing and was wearing a bright blue silk neckerchief at his throat and a soft, tailored cream shirt which set off the colour beautifully; his attire completed by a cutaway brown jacket with the prettiest of buttons. His hair was full and tied behind with a brown velvet ribbon clip and I could see that a dressing had been used to keep his hair smooth. I thought him to be of an approximate age to Barty but looked rather less worn than my dear husband who in these last few years had had a lot to contend with.

Sir Magnus promised to seek out my husband when he went back to London at the end of the week and to stay in touch with both of us. By the time he left, I felt a great deal calmer and resolved to be circumspect with my knowledge about wardships and such like.

∞

Sir Magnus was as good as his word and called upon Bartholomew in London to chivvy him up about writing home. I am grateful to him for reminding my husband that I too was doing important work in looking after all the little ones alongside my midwifery tasks. I received notes from both of them the following week. Magnus said that he had found Bartholomew well but overwhelmed by all the paperwork he had been given by the Royal Navy. He reminded me of the substance of our conversation and told me to contact him at his chambers if I was in any difficulty. I was greatly reassured by his letter and thankful that he took an interest in me and mine; I had realised that his interest in me was personal and I was greatly flattered. When I told Cecilia all about him and described him as 'very personable', her eyebrows shot up and we both ended up giggling. I hadn't flirted with him - I don't really know how to flirt – and our conversation was too serious for levity, but it was nice to be admired. I never forgot that in most people's eyes I was seen as unattractive with my pox scars and limpy leg, so it left a warm feeling when someone so debonair paid me attention. It lifted my spirits at a time when I was lonely and saddened by the absence of my husband.

In Bartholomew's letter, he apologised for not staying in touch regularly. He explained that the work he was doing was secret and very soon I would hear the reason why, but that he obviously couldn't put it in a letter in case it was intercepted!

Intercepted! Who on earth would want to intercept a letter between a man and his wife? It wasn't as if he was vital to the running of the Navy or the country. I couldn't quite believe it and dismissed the comment as his attempt at joking, something he does not do very often. I wrote and told him my opinion of his joke.

I had to eat my words however when it transpired that the fourteen-month peace accord between the British and the French was about to be abandoned by the British. My words didn't taste good then and I wrote to Bartholomew to apologise for not believing him. I still had no knowledge of what he was doing but it seemed to be a job in the diplomatic service with special responsibility to the Royal Navy. I was reassured that he was in no danger, which was a great relief to me; clearly, he was playing an important role as they had requested his help through both his erstwhile colleague and Viscount Nelson himself.

When he replied, with an amused acceptance of my apology but still insisting that secrecy be maintained, he explained in detail that the British Government, under Addington, had sued for peace two years ago, but the French had got the better deal. In what was called the Treaty of Amiens of 1802, there was an agreement for various land swaps – the French gaining here, the English there. Barty listed all the countries that were involved but I am afraid it went over my head, other than feeling sorry for the inhabitants of those countries who on one day were governed by one nation and the next day by another.

Bartholomew wrote that this deal was never much more than a long truce. The French had taken the opportunity to reorganise themselves and both sides used the time to recuperate. The treaty will shortly be abandoned by the British, hence the secrecy, with neither country having fulfilled all their obligations. He finished with these words: 'The French are masters of the land but the British are masters of the sea!'

## CHAPTER 23

*Sorrel (Rumex).* Unclear which of the four
sorrels listed by Culpeper (Common, Mountain,
Sheep or Wood) were used by Martha Ballard to
bathe and heal.

Culpeper's Colour Herbal & A Midwife's Tale 1785-1812

Billy-alone called by. We were all so pleased to see him
and wanting to know how Cilla was. I hadn't been to
check on her for a few weeks and was very happy to hear
that she was blooming and that the baby had quickened. I
looked at this fresh-faced young man and was proud that
he had turned into such a wonderful, caring fellow after
a bad start in the workhouse with an overseer who tormented him. I remembered what a scamp he was when
first we met and how he had tried so hard to help and
protect me through all our troubles. I had turned him
into an honorary brother! He loved to come and play with
my own scamps and I knew he would always be there for
my two boys, setting them a fine example for the future.
The girls loved him too and clambered all over him whenever he stopped by.

I took the opportunity to tell Billy that we mustn't lose our vigilance over potential kidnap of the girls. I didn't need to explain why. He understood the dangers far more than I did. Hadn't he been telling me repeatedly that we were at risk of one sort or another?

'I called round, Esther, to tell you that the horse you settled on is about ready for you and she be a sprightly mare but with a nice nature. What you gonna call her?' he asked.

'I don't know. I think I must ride her and see what suits her character. Have the boys in the yard got a pet name for her?'

'Aye, they call her Peg. The master said "Pegasus" was the name of a winged horse in olden times. She were all white too, like this one, and fast of foot. Not that our Peg has wings,' he added.

I laughed. 'Well, that sounds as good a name as any, I'll try it. I will come over with Mr. Jenkins next week and ride her out, and I can check on Cilla at the same time, if that suits you both.'

'Aye, all well 'n' good, I'll tell her to expect you. We got a parcel of lambs born and more to come, so the little 'uns could go and see them with Master Freddie. He likes nothing better than bein' outside. Miss Felicia, she prefers to be indoors with her mother.'

'We'll make a day of it, then. Will you ask Cecilia if Tuesday week is good for her?'

'Aye, I'll do that. If you don't hear from me, take it that all is good with her.' He paused for a moment before going on to say, 'Esther, I also wanted to tell you that Charlie Dobbs is teaching me to ring the town bell - only when I ain't busy, like, and if Farmer Elwood can spare me.'

'I didn't know we had a town bell. Where is it?'

'In the Market tower, above the lock-ups. You must 'ave 'eard it when you were in the cells! It rings the opening and closing of the market as well as all the other times.'

'Oh yes, I heard it, all right. It got on my nerves - I was so beside myself that I would end up on a charge for murder. What made you want to do bell-ringing, then?'

'I don't want you to think I'm daft, Esther, but it's really old. King Harry, 'im with all the wives, it were cast when he were king, and there's a badge on it of his. Anyway, some cove called Cromwell, sold it from the big Priory, as was demolished. Then it were in the old broken church near here that got taken down, and it ended up in the new market tower, hundreds of years after it were made. I was there a while back and I climbed up to have a look. Charley Dobbs, 'im as rings it regular, like, says it has words writ round it. He says it do say, "I be named

Gabriel". Most of the townsfolk calls it "Old Gabriel" now. I thought it were really beautiful, Esther, and a bit sad and lonely, with no church to belong to, just stuck up there all by itself and nobody knowing much about it.'

'I think it's a lovely idea, Billy. You must tell me when you are ringing. I will be sure to listen. How wonderful to think of it! Do you know who Gabriel was, Billy?'

'Na, didn't know'd he were anyone partic'lar.'

'Gabriel was an angel, one of the archangels. He appeared to Mary to tell her that she would have a son and she was to call him Jesus. The thing is, Billy, she was preparing to marry Joseph, so she had never been with a man.'

'Did her husband not mind, then, 'avin' a son not his?'

'No. Gabriel told Mary and Joseph that she was to bear the son of God but was not to be afraid. He was Mary's guardian angel, I think.'

'I wish I'd 'ad a guardian angel, Esther.'

'Perhaps you have, Billy. You managed to escape the workhouse and that awful man who tormented you. Mr. and Mrs. Elwood like and treat you well, with a proper wage and a cottage of your own. Cilla loves you and soon you will have a baby. Not many people escape the workhouse and go on to a life like yours, Billy. I think you might well have a guardian angel!'

'Well, when you put it like that, I sees what you mean, but all those things only 'appened after I met you, Esther. Maybe it is you who be my guardian angel.' He grinned and got to his feet. 'Anyway, I must away. It's been good to see you and I'll tell Cilla and Mrs. Elwood about next Tuesday.'

'Thank you, Billy, it has been lovely to have you visit. I wish we saw more of you.'

I thought more about the bell after Billy left and wondered why it had been named Gabriel in the first place. The monks of the Priory would likely have favoured an archangel for their protection. But now the bell was hanging here in the centre of town, what would his purpose be?

As I mulled over this and the words of the angel banishing fear, a thought came into my mind unbidden: *as Gabriel had come to Mary, perhaps he was now in our midst as guardian of women in their travail?* I don't know where this thought came from, but it felt like someone was telling me it was so, directly answering my question. I sensed the hairs at the back of my neck stand up. From now on, when I went out into the garden, I would be able to hear Old Gabriel at his work, tolling the market hours, the town celebrations and the calls to office, and feel him casting his influence wide.

Later that day I went into town to see one of our new-ish mothers who had sent a message to say that feeding her baby had become difficult and asking if I could call by.

Mrs. Carver was a youngish woman, probably about twenty-one, and this was her first baby. The birth itself had been uneventful and I had left both mother and baby contented. Before I went home, Mr. Carver had come out and paid me for the delivery and care I had given his wife. I gathered that he worked in the brewing trade and was making his way in the town with some success. I liked them both very much and sincerely hoped that nothing was seriously wrong.

I was shown up into the bedroom and found Mrs. Carver in considerable distress as her breasts were tight and uncomfortable; consequently, the little one was having difficulty in latching on. I could see the pain in her weary eyes and furrowed brow. The agony of taut, swollen breasts was horrible: I'd had some personal experience with the uneven feeding of my twins which caused lumps that had to be pressed firmly and massaged to stimulate the flow and release any blockage. Mrs. Carver's condition was a great deal worse than I had endured and there was no likelihood of being able to press and ease the lumps out.

'Oh my, this is a sorry thing to happen to you, my dear,' I said. 'I am going to go back home now and quickly prepare a poultice of sorrel which will hopefully bring some relief. I will be back within the hour. In the meantime, gently bathe your breasts with tepid water, if you can bear it. It might take the heat out of them and make you more comfortable.'

Before I left, I asked the young maidservant to boil the water and put it to cool covered with a spotlessly clean cloth. (I checked that the cloth and water vessel were actually clean before I left.)

I hurried home and made a good quantity of the receipt. It was a remedy I had found useful in the past and was recommended to me by my mother, God rest her. I hoped that the condition Mrs. Carver was suffering wasn't too far advanced for it to work. I had noticed with some alarm a raised, angry patch under the left breast.

By the time I returned, the poor woman was almost fainting with the pain. I applied the poultice as gently as I could and then sat with her for some hours in the hope that it would calm the condition. Eventually, I had to accept that there was no improvement; the raised inflammation was angrier still and I could see that I had to do something drastic immediately.

I explained to my patient that I would have to take a knife to her breast to release the matter inside which looked to be the seat of the problem. I had never performed this procedure before but Bartholomew had, explaining to me that it was sometimes a matter of life and death. If the putrefaction spread, then the mother could be lost.

I didn't have time to worry about it. I knew that there was nothing else I could do, so I took up a sterilised scalpel and pressed it to the swollen and angry lump on the left breast. Immediately I could smell that the content was putrid and pressed a small bowl beneath the wound as the matter was released. As soon as the poison cleared, I laid my patient down and partially on her side as I swilled the area with tepid but previously boiled water. I did this for some time until I was satisfied that I could neither see nor smell pus. I then used my sorrel preparation to bathe and help with healing the wound. The other breast was also taut, but I couldn't see any sign of inflammation, so I continued with the earlier sorrel poultice treatment hoping that we had turned the corner.

I had been with Mrs. Carver for most of the day and had sent a message home to Mrs. Jenkins to say that I was unavoidably detained. After the young maidservant had delivered it, she was to go on to Eliza's home and ask her to come as soon as possible.

Eliza was such a support and took over from me as I cleaned the area of any remnants of the corruption. Both breasts were now looking more normal, with the right one showing some puckering around the nipple as the sorrel did its work, albeit very slowly - a measure perhaps of just how bad Mrs Carver must have been feeling. Together, Eliza and I agreed that the wound was now clean. I tried to bring the edges of the wound together and soaked a pad in self-heal and sanicle where previously I had used the sorrel solution to put over and then bind in place with a bandage, which was not easy. The young woman was very brave throughout and I had great respect for her forbearance.

Mrs Carver was exhausted and merely nodded as I explained that both Eliza and I would return early in the morning to check the wound and re-dress it. If, in the meantime, any further swelling developed, then she should send for me immediately. She was an intelligent lass and had understood what I was doing and why, but her husband was not quite so calm about it. I explained as patiently as I could, but I don't think he took in my rationale at all, even when I used the example of lancing a boil which I thought he might readily understand. I hoped he would leave his wife to recover quietly.

We arranged with the maid to feed the baby with a thin, sweetened milky gruel which Eliza had prepared from what she found in the kitchen, whilst his mother was having her treatment, but I hoped that the right breast would be fit for feeding him by the morrow. If the wound on the left healed cleanly, then she might soon be able to feed properly again, with care.

Wood sorrel is a powerful herb which must be used with caution - my mother described it as 'most useful'. I had some fresh plants in our garden underneath a hedge where there was plenty of moisture. I also kept some dried in my store cupboard, being not only useful for dealing with putrefaction of the blood but also containing other health-giving properties.

When we visited Mrs. Carver next morning, I could see that the wound was clean, lacking any putrid smell and not weeping. I was extremely pleased. The right breast was no longer taut and, as I removed the poultice, I suggested that once the breast was bathed again with good tepid water, she might try to feed young Joseph. Ideally, one wants to feed babies evenly from each breast, but a day or two's grace for the left side might be wise. I was aware that I might have to stitch the sides of the wound together, but not quite yet. I would persist with self-heal and sanicle. Mary, the maid, said that Joseph had taken the gruel after a few attempts and seemed to accept it. We were all incredibly happy at the outcome and Mrs. Carver could not thank us enough. The strain in her face had dropped away, leaving her skin smooth and calm. I re-dressed the wound with a fresh solution and prepared to go home, promising to return early the next morning. Just as we were about to leave, there was a commotion outside the door which was abruptly thrown open by young Dr. Chappell with a nervous-looking Mr. Carver hovering behind him.

The physician addressed me angrily: 'Mrs. Grieve, how dare you interfere with my patients? You have no right to be here, Madam, especially with no recognised qualifications to your name, I must ask you to leave and do not return. Step away. I must insist you do so.'

For a few moments I was struck dumb by his show of temper and then again by his rudeness but as Eliza started to slide anxiously out of the door, I turned on him with an anger equal to his own.

'I am a qualified midwife, Doctor Chappell. If I have no bits of paper to show, it is because they don't exist. I have been trained in all aspects of midwifery by my husband, Doctor Grieve, who, I might remind you, is a senior physician and the town coroner. I was invited here by Mrs. Carver who was in great distress, and the condition she suffered from has been alleviated by my skill. My skill!' I repeated. 'How dare you speak to me in that hectoring tone?'

He was quite taken aback, so I continued: 'Your presence was *not* sought by Mr. & Mrs. Carver for the delivery of their son, and the condition I met with yesterday came within a midwife's remit. I am proud to say that Mrs.

Carver looks to be healing nicely from what was a very nasty, putrid inflammation which impeded her attempts to feed her boy and which if left longer could have killed her.'

I saw him swallow (and noticed Mr. Carver edging away at the same time) before he tried to make up his ground with a sharp riposte.

'I accept you have been trained by your husband, but Mr. Carver is *my* patient and not your husband's, therefore you have no place here. Kindly do not attempt to interfere with my patients again.'

I wasn't having that, so I replied, 'As I said, I was invited here to attend *Mrs.* Carver. You were *not*, so I am not intruding on your position. Or is it perhaps the loss of income that worries you?'

At that moment the lady in question spoke up quietly but firmly and we both stopped our posturing to listen to her.

'Why did you call him out?' she said to her husband. 'I told you I wanted nought to do with him in my travail. Mrs. Grieve knows what she be doing, and that young doctor shouldn't shout at her so. If I call on my midwife, then I am entitled to do so, no matter what my husband nor anyone else thinks.' She fixed her eye on the doctor as she said this before lying back on her pillow, a pink spot in either cheek, and waved us all away.

I returned to see Mrs. Carver on three occasions and re-dressed her wound. Privately, I was so thankful that I had made the right decision and executed it properly. Young Joseph was enjoying his milk again and it was flowing smoothly. I did offer some advice learnt during my own confinement in that if she felt her breasts were becoming even slightly lumpy, then she should place a bowl of hot water beneath each breast thus encouraging the milk to flow.

Several days later I was called upon by Mr. Carver who produced some coin for Eliza and myself. He said, 'My wife thanks you for your great kindness and skill.' He followed this by mumbling awkwardly, 'We are both extremely grateful.'

∞

One morning in early June, I walked down to visit Mrs. Makepiece, taking Clara with me to help with the children. Walking from the castle to Keere Street normally took just a few minutes but when the boys were with us it seemed to take hours. They were both walking tentatively and often dropping onto their bottoms when they decided enough was enough. In the end we carried them. Charlotte and Beth skipped happily in and out of the other townsfolk who were trying to make their way in the opposite direction. It was all good-natured and cheerful until I saw a familiar face near where the West Gate used to be. For a moment I thought it was Abe and my heart missed a beat, but when I turned to look back, the man had disappeared, probably up the nearby passage. Did I imagine it?

Mrs. Makepiece had been a bit down at heart since Bertha had moved out to make a home for herself and Grace in a cottage near the White Lion. The purpose of our visit was to cheer her up and I hoped Grandpa would be there too, as he so often was. Again, I couldn't help wondering what his wife thought of all his visits to another woman's house.

The girls tore down the steep hill holding hands and shrieking with laughter. They banged on the door with their little fists and ran inside as soon as it was opened to them. I said, 'We weren't sure you would be in on this lovely day. How are you?'

'All the better for seeing you, lass, and the little 'uns, too.' She took William from me and gave him a fierce cuddle and a kiss before swapping for Benjy. The children were so loved and happy in their carefree world. I sat myself down and took both girls onto my lap while Grandpa and Mrs. Makepiece cuddled a boy apiece.

'Clara,' I said, 'why don't you go and get those bits of shopping we talked about and come back for me in an

'Money. They think they should be earning the money that families are happy to pay. I knew that's what that physician was about and, apparently, it is happening all over the place. They don't mind the midwife doing the long hard initial stages of birth but then they want to swoop in and take the glory, or, more importantly, the money.'

'I thought you didna' charge, Esther?'

'We don't as a rule because our mothers can't afford a reputable physician most of the time. But we are seeing more and more better-found families coming to us because of our reputation. We charge them a small fee which goes towards paying Eliza and saving for a cottage for those women who can't deliver at home for one reason or another. When Bartholomew comes home, I will make sure he puts that young man in his place. He was very rude to me.'

Mrs. Makepiece laughed once more and said, 'It be all over town what you said to him. I don't reckon he will want to cross *you* again soon.'

It was good to see my friends again and Mrs. Makepiece looked much more cheerful by the time we left. We also invited them both, as a couple, for a midday meal with us a few days later.

## CHAPTER 24

*Germander (Teucrium chamaedrys). It is
commended by some as a specific for the gout.
Astrology: Germander is a herb of warm thin
parts, under Mars.*

Culpeper's Colour Herbal.

Bartholomew has been and gone again. We'd all had a joyous reunion and the children were thrilled to see their papa again. He was looking well but tired and had clearly missed us all; he said that he was finding the diplomatic work on behalf of the Navy tedious. I think he had imagined being involved in some adventures, if not actual medical support for the fighting men; but the reality was knocking heads together in a government that was backward in coming forward with adequate cash and provisions to improve the King's Navy.

'Viscount Nelson has the best of it,' he had grumbled, 'everyone hanging on his word here, there and everywhere, only too eager to put his requests into action, whereas most of the merchant service is undermanned and scrabbling round for provisions and competent sailors. The transportation ships are like a battleground between factions - who can undercut who - and I've been trying to find reputable physicians to man the ships. Fortunately, I am listened to because it has become known - I don't know how - that I have inside knowledge of the dodges, necessities and medical shortfall on these ships. Believe me, I have not passed on your story in any detail, Esther, but even so it appears to be known far and wide. As a result, it seems that as your husband, I am revered for it! I know this is totally undeserved.'

Bartholomew looked a little embarrassed by this but when I just smiled, he returned to his main theme: 'You know, I am in two minds about Viscount Nelson. He is conducting a scandalous affair with Emma Hamilton and they openly have a daughter, Horatia, with Lady Hamilton's husband privy to it. I feel for his poor wife Fanny who I am told has done nothing but promote her husband's interests and is entirely blameless in this affair, not that *that* seems to count.'

'I thought you liked him?' I asked. 'It was Nelson who summoned you to London, after all.'

'I did, or I *do*, of course I do. But this matter is a little too blatant for my liking. Everyone is talking about it.'

I changed the subject then. I'm afraid my memories of Bartholomew originally asking me to be his mistress rather than his wife were never far below the surface. I didn't think to remind him of that shameful interlude.

I was surprised to hear his tale of how my experiences had become so widely known but we both eventually assumed that the Gibraltar garrison staff had propelled my story to every ship and naval dockyard in the land. In my heart I was regretful that my unhappy situation on the transport ship was one of the reasons that Bartholomew had been called to serve the government, leaving all of us at home to suffer his absence.

Whilst he was with us, I told him all about Billy and the town bell, and how I had experienced a strange feeling of conviction when wondering if Gabriel might be there to guard the women of the town whilst in the agonies of travail.

'As you know, I am not subject to the insights that you experience, Esther,' he said, pausing to reflect for a moment as I glanced at him to see if he was being sarcastic. 'There is something I could tell you, though, that might seem to have a connection with this. It's thought Old Gabriel was cast during the reign of Henry VIII for the old Priory of St Pancras where the bell was first hung. The original founders, centuries earlier, were William de Warenne and his wife Gundrada. She died in childbirth and was buried in the chapter house of the Priory in 1080 or thereabouts. So, Esther, your 'strange feeling' has a ring of truth, as it were. Perhaps Old Gabriel took on this role thereafter in honour of his founders? A little too mystical for me, however, and I am not sure I could bring myself to believe it, but there you are.'

If he had left it there, I would have been delighted at his interest but then he went on to say that the reality would need to be 'tested' against live births in a similar town with similar disease patterns and poverty levels. I smiled and walked away, throwing over my shoulder the remark, 'Your comments are invaluable, as always, Doctor Grieve.'

Some weeks after Bartholomew returned to his work, still not having decided whether to keep or relinquish his position of coroner in Lewes, I too was called upon for my services by an agent of the government. In this instance I was to receive a visit from a gentleman waging war on the smugglers. His official position was given as Senior Officer of His Majesty's Excise in London.

I was notified by post that one Nathanial Judge would be pleased to call upon me, at my convenience, to discuss matters of great import to the governance of the country. I couldn't imagine how I could be of any service to such an important fellow but I agreed to the request that he visit me on the morning of the twenty-second of August at a quarter past ten of the clock and subsequently arranged that the children would all be at South Farm for lessons and play. It was with some apprehension therefore that I rose from my chair when Mrs. Jenkins showed Mr. Judge into the drawing room.

I was astonished to see that he was a youngish man, and one of fashion too. His clothing, though dark of colour and made of fine wool, showed touches of flamboyance in a patterned waistcoat revealed by a smart cutaway coat; his breeches were tight-fitting and I noticed an elegant leg encased within soft leather boots adorned with decorative silver buckles. Used as I was to our country-town apparel, Mr. Nathanial Judge was most definitely a cut above and a gentleman. My knowledge of the local customs men, who were often to be seen down at the Cliffe, was of a ruddy-faced crew, toughened from long exposure to the elements, but although Mr. Judge's demeanour was manly, with neatly trimmed whiskers, he clearly spent a lot of time indoors. I also noticed that he did not wear a wig, like so many others who had instantly dropped this fashion once the government put a tax on it! I had never liked wigs anyway - I thought they harboured lice and even fleas.

Mrs. Jenkins took his hat and gloves, leaving me to address my guest. I nodded to let her know that refreshments were needed and within minutes she reappeared with a pot of steaming coffee and some shortbread. I busied myself with pouring as I gathered my wits, thrown into some disarray by this unexpectedly handsome visitor. Whilst I'd had no preconceived opinion as to the appearance of this official, I was thrown off balance to find a gentleman at my table, and a very comely one at that.

'Mr. Judge, I am at a loss to know how I can be of help to you,' I began, handing him his cup of coffee with a slightly shaky hand. 'Your clerk notified me that you would explain all and I am looking forward to hearing what you have to say. But perhaps you expected my husband to be here?'

'No, Mrs. Grieve,' he said with a smile, 'it is you that we wish to talk to and, if I may say so, it is a great pleasure to meet you. I have been made aware of your history and I must say that you are greatly admired for your skills, fortitude and courage.'

'I'm sorry, I don't understand. Admired by whom?'

'The body of government, Mrs. Grieve, but, more importantly, by the men of justice who are asking for your assistance in seizing certain individuals, common fellows, who have stolen a large cache of goods rightly belonging to the government.'

'Smugglers?'

'Precisely, smugglers. Not the riff-raff that bring in the odd case of brandy, some silks or baccy. No, it is a group that has become too powerful and are believed to operate in this district with impunity. I can tell you, Mrs. Grieve, that your aunt's disappearance to the colonies left a vacuum and the men who stepped in to fill it are a wholly different breed. They are perpetrators of the worst kinds of crime and we have had our eye on them for some time.'

'Well, I still don't understand why you think I can help?'

'I would be grateful if you could tell me everything that you remember, particularly places, during your dealings with the original group of smugglers led by your aunt. The new lot are using the same networks and many of the same people, but the men at the top who come to Sussex from Kent, are the ones we are after. Recently, they stole a consignment of goods - money, jewels and confidential documents - and because of the high value, we believe they are holding on to it in order to achieve a better payoff by means of blackmail and the usual smuggling device of avoiding taxes on certain items. We urgently need to find that parcel of goods. Will you help us, Mrs. Grieve?'

He took a sip of his coffee before continuing: 'The transportation of high-value goods is a closely-guarded secret, particularly with regard to the Bank of England, so may I just say that in this instance normal directions and arrangements en route to London were reconfigured in order to collect important documents from a certain gentleman who occasionally resides in Brighthelmstone. When valuable goods are transported overland, particularly if they have previously come by sea - which in this case they had - they are loaded into a large and strong vehicle which looks like an ordinary coach of some size, so as to not draw attention, but is, in fact, far from ordinary. Those who are not 'in the know', so to speak, would just see a vehicle with a number of passengers who represent all walks of life. In reality, these passengers are armed guards in disguise.

'Our coach detoured from its favoured route from Portsmouth to London in order to collect these items of value from Brighthelmstone. As it continued its onward journey, the coach was ambushed and robbed by violent means and a number of our guards were taken hostage. Fortunately, of those left for dead, one of them was able to describe the assailants before he expired. We do not know if our abducted guards are alive or dead, nor where they are if they indeed survived. We suspect that the movements of the coach and its cargo were disclosed, alas, by a dishonest guard to a band of smugglers, the Kent men. The ambush took place at Ashcombe near the village of Kingston. The perpetrators were then able to head, via a country track over the downs, to an area where they could hide their haul. They abandoned the coach and horses in favour of a dray wagon of their own which was more suitable for the terrain.'

'Good gracious, what a dreadful tale,' I said. 'Well, I will do all I can to help. But I have to make clear that my life has been and still is seriously afflicted by smugglers - the original Sussex gang, that is. My children are always under threat from them and their families, as am I. The last thing I need is to bring further troubles to my door.'

'I understand and will keep that in mind throughout,' Mr. Judge said, shifting in his seat to lean towards me. 'You and your family's safety throughout will be my priority, I can assure you of that. If we can start at the beginning of your involvement with the gang, Mrs. Grieve, and if you can remember names as well as places, that would help.'

Mr. Judge (I wondered if that was his real name) sat with me for the remainder of the day. I told him everything that had happened and everyone I had met. He became quite animated when I described the area around Southease and asked in what manner of building I was confined after the shooting of my cousin when I first became involved with them.

'It was an old barn,' I said, 'but, unusually, it had a cellar. I can't think what more I can say.'

'How long did it take you to get there from Southease itself? I understand you were blindfolded, but did you have any awareness of time?'

I thought back and reawakened memories I had long tried to suppress.

'I was riding pillion with my cousin Sam. The horses were walking carefully, not trotting. I imagined it was a narrow path because I felt the vegetation brush against me. We were near the river, which was on my left – I knew that because there were waterfowl nearby and I heard a coot. I could also hear the reeds whispering – it's such an eerie sound. I think we were about ten minutes or so from Southease. It was a dry day but I could smell the river mud.'

'If we look at a map I have here, Mrs. Grieve, could you pinpoint where you might have been?'

The map was drawn neatly and clearly by someone who had only a rough idea of the terrain. After studying it for some time and forcing my mind back to the period when I had been fetched up from the cellar, I was able to see where I could have been. There had been woodland to my right; I remembered that because I had later seen Job Coad there with his pack horse, ready to take goods inland. In fact, there must have been a large clearing because a lot of horses and some donkeys were tied up. There was also a track other than the one we'd come along - my injured cousin was taken down it on a cart. I remembered too that we were on a made-up track for a short while before joining the public way between Lewes and Newhaven.

'The barn, you said it was old. What made you think that? Would you recognise it again?'

'It smelled old and some of the slats I had to walk on were rotten. It was very musty - yet, though we were near the river, it didn't smell damp. I don't know, I could be quite wrong. My blindfold wasn't on when I had to go into the scrub to relieve myself.' I could feel myself flush as I explained this necessity. 'And before we went back to Southease, it wasn't on for a while, so yes, I would recognise it, I think.'

'This young lad you talk about, Billy - tell me about him?'

I explained how Billy had followed me around and taken care of me; how he had helped me find out all about the Kempes; and then how he had helped to rescue me from them. I laughed as I said, 'Billy knows everyone and their servants. If you want information, he is the one who will have it.'

'Would he talk to me?' asked Mr Judge.

'I think so, if he thinks it will help me and mine. He is my dearest friend. I look on him as a protective brother even though he is much younger than me. But I wouldn't want him put in any danger.'

'And the boy Joe, or Job, who is himself a Coad?'

'He has escaped his family and is on a merchant vessel. I'm afraid he could be anywhere now, but my husband or even our gardener Mr. Jenkins likely will know which boat he is on.'

'If he is on a boat then we can find him,' he replied, taking notes as he spoke. 'Would he talk to me, as well?'

'Again, I think so, if I ask him to, but I would have to pass a letter of explanation to his friend here in Lewes to send on to him.'

A thought came to me, then, long buried: 'What about the priest, or vicar - whatever he was - in Southease?' I asked. 'Why don't you look for him? He was privy to all their actions and terrified of the Kempes - he was prepared to marry me to my cousin Sam against my will under threat of violence from them.'

'There, Esther, I knew it would be enlightening to talk to you! We were unaware of a cleric being involved with them.'

'He might be dead.'

'And he might not.'

'I would suggest that you go to South Farm,' I said, 'and ask Farmer Elwood if you can talk to Billy and perhaps ask to look at the estate maps. They are detailed about all the properties and show neighbouring estates, too.'

'I will do that. Would you think me presumptuous if I called you Esther? And, of course, please call me Nathanial. I wonder if you would kindly accompany me to South Farm, say, tomorrow, if you are free?'

I nodded and said, 'I will send a note to John Elwood when the children are brought back this afternoon.'

Agreeing to meet at the farm tomorrow, we parted company, but not before I suggested that he should dress in more country-like clothing. He told me that he had come prepared! We agreed between us that he would say he was a visiting gentleman farmer. Although fearful, at the same time I couldn't help feeling excited at the prospect of running some of my old enemies to ground. I hadn't mentioned Abe to Mr. Judge, though I should have - it was a mistake that I would come to regret. I had a feeling that Bartholomew would disapprove of me involving myself in this escapade, but he wasn't there to comment.

∽

The following day I took the children with me to South Farm and once they were all engrossed in their activities, I sat down with Cecilia and later John Elwood to explain about the gentleman who had visited me yesterday and why he was coming to see them soon after our midday meal. We all agreed that he would be introduced as a farmer who was asking to view John's sheep-breeding methods and discuss the introduction of sturdier and leaner breeds to improve his flock. I hadn't had time to tell Cecilia about my impressions of Nathanial, so I was really looking forward to seeing how she reacted to this rather unusual young man.

We sent for Billy who was out on the downland pastures and asked him if he was prepared to help. As I expected, he was wholeheartedly agreeable to having a discussion with Nathanial. I explained that we would need to protect ourselves from being associated with HM Excise and thereby give the local smugglers another reason to hate me, in particular, but all the rest of us too. As we knew, no one escaped their vengeance.

Nathanial arrived, looking very much the gentleman farmer, dressed in a sturdy frock coat with nankeen breeches. As we followed him into John's office, Cecilia caught my eye and mouthed at me: 'So handsome!' John took out the maps of his estate, and by comparing the relevant one to the document Nathanial had shown me yesterday, it was clear that the estate map showed in much more detail the properties and outbuildings. As well as being a useful map, it was a thing of beauty in itself.

I pointed out where I thought I had been held captive and John immediately said that the area of land was not his but that of his neighbour Lady Arbuthnot who was not often in residence. Billy chimed in with the information that she had a bailiff who lived near the main house.

'Do you know him, Billy?' I asked.

'No, them as down there keep themselves very much to themselves. The bloke who manages the place is a surly old chap - I wouldn't mind betting he be one of the local smugglers himself. No one goes there much 'cos 'er ladyship is never there.'

'Do you know if the barn might be there, back away from the river and hidden?'

'I ain't noticed a barn but it's possible. Perhaps we can go down-river and, as we know where to look now, we might see it. Otherwise, we would have to sneak over the fence from our side and hope no one is around or looking out. But if you don't know where your lot of stuff is, Mr. Judge, it might be a bit of a long shot!'

'Perhaps it might be better to try looking from the river first,' said Nathanial, 'if you are sure you will recognise where the spot is?'

'Well, I know where Farmer Elwood's land ends because it is used for cattle, so it can't be far from there.'

'Are the cattle there now?' I asked John. 'I'm wondering if one of them could accidentally get through the fence, and then perhaps you and Billy could go down to have a look with an excuse to go on Lady Arbuthnot's land?'

'That might be a better plan,' said John Elwood. 'If someone goes down the river and keeps staring into the vegetation - and there is a lookout - they could be easily noticed.'

John jumped to his feet, ever the man of action. 'Come on, Billy, get some tools and we will go now and have a look round.' After instructing Billy to fetch a pony and a sack of useful gear, they prepared to leave.

'What about us?' I asked?

'You stay here with Mr. Judge,' John said firmly.

I noticed that Farmer Elwood had not used Nathanial's Christian name despite being asked to do so. I wondered if he had seen Cecilia's admiring look.

John went on: 'It is better that Mr. Judge is not seen away from the house, especially since there are no sheep down there for him to visit and thus establish his credentials. We all know that there are smugglers and their accomplices everywhere, and anything out of the ordinary will be noticed. Billy, don't breathe a word about this, not even to the stable lads. If you take Peg, Esther's new mare, we will at least have a reason for riding her out. Nero is hitched outside the kitchen door. I will meet you there in ten minutes, boy.'

'It goes against the grain to have others do my work for me,' said Nathanial, looking troubled, 'but I can see that at this moment it is for the best.'

I said in a whisper to Cecilia, after they had gone, 'Did you see how much John and Billy wanted to be off and doing? They had the same look on their faces as Bartholomew does when there is a bit of excitement in the air. How long do you think they will be?'

'I don't know, but the maps are drawn to scale. We could work it out and then add some on for letting a cow loose.'

I decided against it. 'I think I might have to be getting back to Lewes with the children now. Nathanial, do you want to follow me? And then perhaps Billy could come and update us when he gets back? If you stay here, you might be hanging around for hours, which gives even more opportunity for suspicion.'

∽

Billy called on me during the evening when the children were all in bed. Mr Jenkins took a message to Nathanial at the Star and he joined us shortly after. I asked Mrs. Jenkins to provide some light refreshments in the drawing room.

'Well, Billy, what happened?' I asked.

'We got down there without being seen and pulled some fencing loose. The cows were over it in no time and were soon grazing the other side of the fence, so we gave them a bit of time to get further in and then went after them.'

'Did you find the barn?' I asked eagerly.

'Aye, there be a building, and there is a lot of scat grass and trampled ground. There was no one about so while Farmer Elwood went off, pretending he was looking for the estate man - and then if he found him, to keep him away - I snuck off and looked a bit closer. The door was padlocked, and it was a new padlock, but I could see inside and there was nothing there, it were empty. I reckon if there be anything stored in that barn, it is hidden underground, where they kept you, Esther. I don't reckon they are leaving a lookout because it is so well hidden - and even if anyone were to come across the barn and get a bit curious, they wouldn't know it had a cellar, like.'

'Were either of you seen?' said Nathanial.

'No, don't reckon we were. We rounded up the cows after and got them back beyond the fence and put it all back together again. We were in and out in no time at all. The cows didn't do no damage so I reckon no one would be any the wiser that we were ever there.'

'I am much obliged to you all for helping us out. I will arrange for some of my men to come - they are already in the area - and we will raid the place as soon as possible. There will be no connection to any of you, so no danger of repercussions.' Turning to me, Nathanial said, 'Esther, will you tell Farmer Elwood that my men will come down the river at dusk tomorrow? All we will need you to do is mark on the map where the barn is.'

Billy said, 'Trouble is, I don't reckon you will spot it from the river, and even if you do, it be too dangerous getting through the reeds between the river and dry land. There are paths there but only visible to those that made them. Your men could easily get sucked into the mud and you'd never get out. Also, seeing a load of strangers getting into a boat would invite questions.'

'Can't you go the way Farmer Elwood took?' I asked.

Nathanial hesitated. 'I was hoping to avoid any connection to any of you, including Farmer Elwood', he said quietly. 'But I will call on him tomorrow morning and see what is to be done. In the meantime, Billy, Esther, thank you for all your help and advice.'

'What will you do about the men who stole it all? If you just get the goods back, then they are still free to carry on,' I said, thinking that I would still be at risk and all this had been for nothing as far as I was concerned.

'First and foremost, we need to get our valuables back. Also, the documentation that goes with goods. It is critical that we retrieve that, as the smugglers might not yet realise exactly what they have got in their hands, in which case I need to get to it before they do.'

'And then what?' I asked.

'As soon as the cache is in our hands, we will surround the place and keep our men hidden there to wait for them. They will come, sooner or later, and we will take them, dead or alive.'

'That will take a lot of men,' said Billy doubtfully. 'One lot to find the stuff and carry it off, then another lot to hide in wait. The local smugglers can easily muster thirty men, and even if they don't all come looking, there might still be enough of them to catch you out.'

'I have access to soldiers from Seaford Barracks,' Nathanial replied, 'so manpower is not an issue. But timing is. We need to get this underway for tomorrow night otherwise they might move the goods before we get to them. The only thing in our favour is that the stuff the smugglers stole is heavy: it's bullion, gold bullion. Not their usual chuck-on-the-back-of-a-horse plunder.'

'Well, if you can't take it off by boat,' said Billy, 'how are you going to get all this heavy gold away?'

'I don't know yet. I will have to talk with Farmer Elwood about transporting it up to the road instead. But once I've got it safely there, I don't need to keep it secret. I am the law. I can have a cart surrounded by armed men to get it to Lewes and then we will put it in your town lock-up, again with an armed guard, until it can be safely delivered to where it belongs, the Bank of England in London. And the missing documentation will be on my person. It will not leave me under any circumstances.

'In terms of your safety,' Nathanial went on, 'as I said earlier, I don't want to add to your dangers. We know where the Kent faction is based, near the coast. We will conduct a raid there, too. By the time this is all finished, I want both the Kent and Sussex gangs reduced to nothing - with any luck that might be upwards of eighty men.'

'But you don't actually know yet,' I said, 'that the barn near Southease is the right place.'

'If it isn't, we will all melt away into the night and I will have to admit defeat. However, I am confident that we have found our quarry and the lair. I can't tell you more than that without compromising our knowledge.'

'Have you got an informer, then?' I asked, but he just shrugged and said no more.

As it happened, I was due to take the children to South Farm for their lessons the following day, so I heard what was to happen that night, with Farmer Elwood's co-operation. The plan was to pass Southease in the cart and get it as near to the entrance to Lady Arbuthnot's land as possible. Farmer Elwood thought it could be manoeuvred down the slope near to where the cows were let loose yesterday. Unless there were lookouts hiding in the trees, it would be completely hidden from the road and anyone on her land. The only worry was that the weight of the cargo would make it difficult to get the cart back up again. But if this plan didn't seem practicable, the alternative would be to take the bailiff prisoner first and then direct the unladen cart straight down her lady-ship's driveway to the point nearest the barn and return with it the same way.

At nightfall, a troop of soldiers would join them from Seaford and surround the area. They would be hidden in the vicinity of the barn and on Farmer Elwood's ground as well. At a given signal, Nathanial and a few hand-picked agents would force the lock of the barn and prise open the trapdoor to see if the stolen goods were hidden below. If they were, and he seemed confident they would be, the entire hoard would be taken up, carried to the waiting cart and then pulled up to the trackway leading to Southease. Nathanial would take the important doc-uments to keep on his person, then accompany the men with the cart to the market tower in Lewes where the sto-len goods would be locked into one of the cells.

If the smugglers got wind of all this movement, Nathanial hoped they would make their way to the barn to check the stash and then be taken by the soldiers. If they didn't get wind of it, then the soldiers would stay in place until they eventually turned up. Clearly, he was hoping that they would realise something was up soon after the stash had been safely commandeered.

Neither Billy nor Farmer Elwood would be involved once they had pointed out where to leave the public track and how to get the cart down as near to the barn as possible.

We went home later in the day, taking the opportunity to wish the officer good fortune in recovering England's gold and the mysterious documents. I couldn't help wondering who it was that would be embarrassed if they were to be discovered by the wrong people.

Before I left, I said to Billy, 'You won't go on this venture, will you? I know it might be exciting, but you have a wife now and soon a child who will be needing you.'

'Of course not, Esther, don't you worry none, I'm not gonna go. And Mrs. Elwood won't let her husband out of the house, no matter what he says.'

Somehow, I didn't believe him.

## CHAPTER 25

*Garlic (**Allium Sativum**). This was anciently accounted the poor man's treacle, it being a remedy for all diseases and hurts except those which itself breeds. Astrology: Mars owns this plant.*

*Culpeper's Colour Herbal*

Unsurprisingly, I spent the entire night worrying about what was going on: whether Nathanial had succeeded in getting his stolen goods back and in capturing the smugglers too, or a good number of them, at least. I barely slept a wink and when the dawn came, I rose quickly and breakfasted with the Jenkinses. I asked Mrs. Jenkins to warn Clara that I would be out for the morning and would leave the children in her care. Mr. Jenkins prepared the gig for me and I left the house for South Farm as early as I possibly could. As I got down to Southover, I was surprised to suddenly catch sight of Nathanial himself in the distance, and then shocked to realise that he was talking to a young man who was no stranger to me. I pulled over and watched. Neither of them was aware of me and after a few moments they disappeared down an alleyway at the side of a public house. The young man was Abe. Smarter, cleaner, but undoubtedly Abe. I wondered if he was the informer and felt sick as a sudden and unwelcome warmth crept over me. My hands were unsteady on the reins and I had to grip hard to control myself.

If Nathanial was already back here in Lewes, did that mean the scheme had succeeded? Perhaps I should turn Brown Betty around and go up to the market tower to find out. Yes, I would do that. I returned home and asked Mr. Jenkins to keep her ready while I went off as fast as my legs would carry me without actually running. I had just reached the Star when my arm was seized and I was pulled into the entrance where I turned quickly on my assailant. It was Nathanial.

'Why were you talking with that man?' I cried. 'He tried to kill me and the girls. He very nearly succeeded. I was badly hurt, and they killed Flossy, my pony, too.' I burst into tears. 'I agreed to help you, Nathanial! We have all put ourselves at risk for you and now I see you in cahoots with that wicked creature. He should be in jail with the other two, or better still facing the hangman.'

Nathanial pulled me into a corner inside the hotel. 'God above, Esther, keep your voice down. I am sorry,' he said, speaking low, 'and I may not like it, but in this desperate trade, I have to deal with a lot of unsavoury characters. I didn't know about your history with Abe. He is a low-life scoundrel who is willing to sell his fellow-smugglers down the river for a reward.'

He called over to a waiter, 'Some coffee for us, please, and a tot of brandy,' as he edged me towards a small table where he pushed me down into an armchair, then drew up another alongside me. He paused before saying, 'Esther, my friend, try to be calm. Here, dry your eyes. You don't want Lewes people seeing you and wondering what on earth is going on.' He produced a large handkerchief and attempted to wipe the tears from my face.

I knocked his hand away. 'I am not your friend! How do I know that anything you've said is true?'

'I will show you I am exactly who I said I was, in a minute. In the meantime, compose yourself and drink this.' He handed the brandy to me. 'Then we will have some coffee here like any businessman conducting his affairs with an important lady of the town.'

'My business is midwifery. I don't think we would have much to say on that subject!' I declared, but I drank the brandy and glanced around to see if anyone had noticed my outburst. There were a few people at the reception counter more concerned with paying their bills than watching me.

'That's better,' he said. 'Now I will tell you what happened last night and then you can decide whether I am genuine or not.'

He pulled his chair round so that his back was to the room and spoke quietly, so quietly I had to lean nearer to hear what he had to say.

'We took John Elwood's tree-haulage dray – that is, six of my officers and me - and just after nightfall made our way to the place Billy showed us to pull off the track. John had supplied two of his heaviest Sussex horses so we were confident they would be able to pull the load once we had got it safely away from the barn, and we had plenty of manpower if we needed it.

'A group of thirty soldiers made their way down Lady Arbuthnot's drive, with two going ahead to take the bailiff into custody. He and his wife were surprised, so it was not difficult to seize and restrain them. The captain left them in the cottage with their captors and instructions to search the place and 'encourage' them to talk, which they did, like singing canaries. The remainder of the soldiers dispersed through the trees with a watch on the river in case the smugglers returned that way. We took the cart down the track and steered it close to the barn. Then we left Billy and John to unhitch the horses, turn the cart round and hitch them up again, so they were facing in the right direction for the getaway.'

'Did you *have* to take Billy and John?' I interrupted angrily. 'You said yourself they were not to be involved, and they promised me they wouldn't go'.

Nathanial looked fraught for a moment. 'Look, I know this is dismaying to you, Esther,' he sighed, 'but there was no stopping them. And in all honesty, I have to admit that they were of vital service to us in the haulage of that heavy load. The way they managed and coaxed the best out of their horses was something none of us could have achieved.'

Then there was nothing else I could do but subside into an exasperated silence.

'Shall I go on?' Nathanial said gently. I nodded.

'My men and I then broke into the barn at the back. We didn't want to disturb the padlock if, for example, there should turn out to be nothing there.'

'And was there?'

'Oh yes, there was indeed. I conducted a brief search and found the documents and the bullion. We worked as quickly as possible to remove all of the hoard. It wasn't easy as everything had to be taken up a ladder but with a winch, ropes and sheer elbow-grease, we managed it in the end, and with the soldiers' help we got it all on to the cart. The horses pulled and after a lot of guiding and encouragement from Billy and John, we eventually got the cart back up to the track. We tidied up behind us, put back the slats of wood we had removed and rebuilt the fence where the cows had very co-operatively disguised the trampled grass. The bailiff and his wife were sent to Seaford barracks with two soldiers, while others were kept back to guard the cart as we made our way to Lewes market tower, where the cache is now, under lock and key, with some of my men and four armed soldiers. But Esther, a good number of soldiers are still secreted in the woods to see if the smugglers come to investigate. I would expect they already know that there is something of value in the tower and they might want to check their hiding place. We have scouts watching, ready to alert the soldiers.'

I gasped. 'A total success, then?'

'In one sense, yes, but we had hoped to pick up some of the smugglers before now. We will continue to watch the area of the barn, ready to pounce as soon as they show up. Unfortunately, one of the cases from the cache was missing. It contained jewellery, and I imagine the smugglers saw that as easily transportable so kept it aside from the main cache.

'Now, Esther,' he said, taking my hands in his, 'I want you to carry on your life with as little change as possible. Do not draw attention to yourself - we don't want these people to know who was involved. I could provide an armed guard for your household if you want but it might occasion the sort of gossip we would prefer to avoid.'

'No, as long as you keep Abe under your guard,' I said quickly. 'If he knows that I was involved, he will double-cross you and talk to the smugglers just to get back at me. My death would have more value to him than whatever money you have promised.'

'Abe is not under guard. I wasn't aware until you appeared this morning that there was a problem with him. I will try and round him up. Have you any idea of his haunts?'

'No,' I said, 'but possibly the Castle. It's a public house just up the High Street, not a very nice place, and the type of people who use it are usually on the wrong side of the law. If you walked in there yourself, the place would empty and any cover you have would be completely lost. I would watch it and if he is there, take him when he leaves. He is wanted anyway for the crime against us, so I am surprised he has come back. He is not very bright - perhaps he thinks he has let enough time pass by and everyone has forgotten him. Also, some of his brothers and sisters are in the workhouse, so he might be there.'

'What about this family, the Coads - could he be with them?'

'I don't see why, other than that they also have a grudge against me. The Coads are heavily involved with the smugglers, as are lots of locals, but they are down-right evil. Others just want a few pennies extra, with some brandy and baccy. I suppose Abe *might* hide out at

Coad Farm, though, because it is out of the way, upriver in Hamsey.'

'I think you should go home now, Esther, and stay there. If I have any news, I will send you a note, or visit, if your safety is not compromised by me. No one in Lewes except Abe has any idea that I have a connection with the goods in the market tower; to all intents and purposes I am a gentleman farmer. I need to keep it that way, and Billy and John understand that. Go home, Esther.'

I nodded and left him still sitting there in the public lounge but not before I saw a man signal to him, wanting a word. As I walked back towards home, I felt real anxiety that Abe was nearby and watching my every movement; it was as if my skin was prickling and heating up. I was so thankful to turn into our garden that a huge sense of relief flooded over me to be home.

I spent the rest of the day uneasily, with half of me thinking that I should have taken up the offer of protection and my logical side arguing back that I was adding two plus two and coming up with five. The smugglers could have no idea that I was connected to last night's operation and Abe didn't know of it. The only danger I was in was from him but in the same way as before, and I was well protected within my own household. If I were Abe, I would be lying low. Informers were not treated well: his own father had been murdered because he spoke out on my behalf against the smugglers.

Fortunately, I had a visit from Bertha later in the day and her news put my fears aside, for a while at least. Bertha is a striking woman with a lot of presence, so I was surprised to see her looking dispirited and not as well-groomed as she normally was.

'Esther,' she said, coming straight to the point, 'my husband has tracked me down. I don't know how he found out where I was, but he turned up on the doorstep last night. He saw Grace.'

'God above!' I said, pulling her quickly into the drawing room. I seated her in an armchair, took Grace from her arms and then sat opposite with the child on my knees. 'It must have been an awful shock for you. What did he want? Surely he isn't still determined on ruining you?'

'At first, I thought that was exactly what he was planning,' said Bertha, her face pale and drawn, 'but after he'd come in and finished grumbling about all the trouble he'd had to locate me, he sat down and we managed to have a reasonable conversation. He asked me if Grace was his child.'

'What did you say?'

'I said it was very possible as she has his colouring whereas my "friend" was light of hair and fair-skinned.

Then he asked if he could pick her up and from that moment, with her in his arms, he softened.'

'But what does he want?'

'He has met someone new and would like to remarry, which is only possible if I die.'

'Can you not divorce?'

'Yes, we could. It is possible under Scottish law, but it is something far beyond the likes of us. The cost is prohibitive and the social damage to a member of parliament is incalculable. As to myself, I would be completely ostracised. I have said I would not make any difficulties if he wanted to begin a new, discreet relationship. We are both going our different ways and there is no need as yet for a lawful separation. If George feels he must get a Scottish divorce in the end, I will not oppose it, though it would be degrading for both of us. There is something more though, Esther. Can I ask for your total secrecy on what I am about to tell you?'

'Of course, I give you my word.'

'George asked if I would consider him selling me on to another man!'

I don't think I have ever been so shocked in my life as I was on hearing this appalling idea. I couldn't find any words as my breath was completely taken away.

'Can he do that?' I eventually gasped.

'He says he can. Apparently, it still happens, and couples – so he says - agree this between themselves in order to break their marriage vows. The thing is, though, the wife has to agree.'

'I cannot believe this, Bertha!' I cried out. 'I have never, ever heard of such a thing.'

She was looking down, her eyes not meeting mine, as she mumbled her response.

'If I agreed, then some sort of auction would take place and a man, one who might be my lover, would buy me and my children, if that's what had been agreed, or any other man who paid the highest price.'

'An auction! For heaven's sake, is that legal? I can't believe that it is,' I repeated.

'George says so and he asked if I would consider it.'

'And *would* you consider it? I mean, you talk about being ostracised for being divorced, but what would a *sale* result in? You would be allowing yourself to be treated as no better than a slave. It is preposterous and utterly degrading.'

She looked up at me before saying emphatically, 'No, I would not agree to it. I think he was hoping that I would do *anything* to be with my "friend". But I wouldn't, and that was what I told him.'

'Do you think he was really serious?'

'For a moment, yes, I think he really was. But then he backed down and laughed it off. I think seeing Grace and recognising that she might be his child might have had something to do with his change of mind.'

'Well, if that is that is the case, perhaps you should ask for an extra settlement, for Grace,' I said. 'I would in your shoes. It is horrifying to think that a man, and a member of parliament as well, would stoop so low.'

'Would you?' Bertha thought for a moment. 'It would complicate things, though, and I can just about manage as I am. Uncle Barty's sale of my jewellery brings in enough interest for me to live quietly whilst Grace is so young.'

She looked so forlorn and alone as she sat there that I couldn't help asking whether her friend kept in touch with her.

She looked out of the window and I saw the trace of a smile.

'Yes, we do communicate, and if I were divorced, then perhaps we might have a future together. But if I continued to live here in England, where it is even more difficult to arrange matters legally, I would end up as an outcast here as well as in Scotland. Being separated is much more acceptable to the wider world.'

'Shall I write to Bartholomew and tell him? Not about the selling bit,' I added hastily. 'He had a lot to do with town and is a wanted man still. You must have been see-ing things, my dear.'

'He didn't look so scruffy and was clean-shaven. If it was him, that is.'

'I think you must just keep your wits about you and if you see this man again, go and get the constable straight away.'

'Yes,' I nodded. 'I was probably just seeing things, as you put it. I do still take precautions with my routines and there is always someone with me. I won't worry about it.'

'How is Bartholomew getting on?' she asked, chang-ing the subject for me.

'Very well. I hear regularly from him now and he is hoping to come back for a week later this month. I should get a fuller picture then about his role in the Navy. Also, he must decide whether to relinquish his role as coroner. The chap who is keeping his seat warm is very affable, but he comes in from Horsham and it is a bit too far away. I think he hopes Bartholomew will give up the role and then he could move his family here and settle permanently.'

'And what about that young physician?' asked Mrs. Makepiece, laughing. 'I heard you gave him what for.'

'I haven't seen him since, and I hope not to again. Bartholomew says that the medical profession is trying to drive midwives out of their traditional role.'

'Why would they be doin' that?' asked Grandpa.

hour?' She smiled agreeably and left us all to gossip and help cheer up our friend. 'I haven't seen Miss Wardle for some time. Is she well?' I asked.

'Oh, aye, she is that, and very taken with a new litter of piglets. She treats them like her children.'

'Is Polly still with her? And Billy, does he still visit to see Gertrude, the old sow?'

'He does that, and Polly leaves him to it when she can get away with it. But she knows how to manage them all, better than she manages her own mother.'

'Are you missing Bertha and Grace?' I queried gently. 'You could always ask them to live with you permanently.'

I noticed that Grandpa was keeping his eyes on the floor and looking a bit uncomfortable or embarrassed. Perhaps that was the reason Mrs. Makepiece preferred to live alone.

'Oh, they visit often enough, when she is not teaching all these children you have between you and Mrs. Elwood. Is it working out well?'

'Yes, it is, especially when we swap days and places to suit us all.'

I paused for a moment before then saying, carefully, 'I thought I saw Abe up near where the old West Gate was just now. I hope I was mistaken.'

'I don't think he would dare come back after what happened to you and the girls. He was vilified around the

George when you were in hiding and pregnant, and it took some time for them to come to an agreement about your jewels and clothing. I could ask him if you should make a claim for Grace's future if, as you said, she is of George's colouring and thus very possibly his daughter. In fact, I seem to remember you suggesting that not long after you arrived in Lewes.'

'Yes, please, and I will write too. Uncle Bartholomew is very dear to me, as are you, Esther. You have enabled me to see how families should be. I had no idea from my mother's example and later George's. I could have gone through life never knowing true happiness or realising that give and take is permissible between couples and their families, but most of all what love is. I don't know if you understand how important that has been to me?'

'I do understand, Bertha,' I replied, 'and I am glad you have found some peace in all this. But I am so sorry you can't find someone to share your life with.'

'I am afraid it doesn't work like that. It would be easy for George to take a companion, but society would not allow that for me. Do you know, Esther, I wouldn't be surprised if it was my mother who'd told someone here that I might be in Lewes. You know how people talk. And perhaps, over time, someone made the connection – two women with Scottish accents, the right kind of age difference, both suddenly turning up in the town. Perhaps, once Grace was born, one of my mother's so-called friends felt it her duty to inform my husband.'

I persuaded Bertha to stay for a light supper with me. Beth and Charlotte both adored little Grace and their presence would keep my own anxieties at bay. Mr. Jenkins would walk them home safely later.

Half-way through supper, and when we were certain the children were not listening, Bertha said the most surprising thing: 'George apologised to me. Can you believe that?'

'Well, what exactly was he apologising for?' I replied. 'He didn't appear to be the sort of man who would know what an apology was.'

'For beating me! He said that Bartholomew had made him feel ashamed and over time he has come to see how cruel he *might* have been, though he would like to think of himself as "misguided" rather than cruel. He says he has changed.'

'I rather wonder about violent men who claim to have changed, particularly after trying to get you to agree to being sold off at a public auction like a farm animal,' I said. 'But can you forgive him?'

'Don't ask me that, Esther. I don't know. Perhaps, in time.'

After Bertha and Grace had gone home and the children were all tucked up in bed, I sat down at

Bartholomew's desk and wrote to tell him all that had happened. It was a long letter and I must own up to glossing over some of the details of Nathanial's smuggling operation. I didn't mention George's request of his wife - I knew he would be horrified. My conversation with Bertha had brought home to me how much I missed Bartholomew, his companionship as well as his love. I hoped he would return soon.

## CHAPTER 26

*Flax (Linum Usitatissimum). It is of great*
*use against inflammations, tumours and*
*imposthumes. Mercury owns this useful plant.*

Culpeper's Colour Herbal

Several days later Billy was knocking on the door before
any of us were up and I knew as soon as I saw his face that
Cilla must be in labour. He had arrived on my new horse
Peg and as I climbed up behind him, I could feel just how
tense he was, so I tried to calm him down as we rode towards South Farm.

'It's too early, Esther,' he said, over his shoulder. 'I
thought we had another couple of weeks yet.'

'Dates can easily be confused, Billy. I am quite sure
that Cilla is full term or as near as dammit. Let's not
worry about a few days here or there. Is she at home or
at the farm?'

'She be at the farm. She was going to help Mrs. Fisher
with some peeling. I took her into your old room and lit
a fire - it were so cold in there at first. She's a bit worried,
like. So am I,' he said, his voice wavering, 'but her ma is
coming over to help, like.'

'You wouldn't be normal if you weren't worried, Billy, but I will do my very best to help Cilla bring a lovely child into the world. Now, let's put this pony to a fast trot and see how she does. I am really looking forward to taking her home for good.'

Cilla was a healthy young woman and her travail was surprisingly quick for a first baby, consequently her pain was undoubtedly greater; but less than eight hours later, we had a fine young boy in our arms who was to be named Noah. Both she and Billy were exhausted - she from the physical strain and he from sheer agitation: he had been dodging in and out of the kitchens all day. They were so very happy, it made me want to cry. The whole household came downstairs to visit and I was glad to see what a popular couple they were. Cilla's parents were even more delighted, laughing and joshing Billy for being so flurried. I knew that they had lost a number of their own children to one thing or another, so they undoubtedly understood how precious this little baby boy was to their only surviving daughter.

Bertha had been teaching the children in Lewes, so I took the opportunity to take Peg home with me. Fred, whose leg had been broken when Abe attacked us, accompanied me. I asked him how it was now; I knew it had been difficult to get his leg fully straightened.

'It be good. I was right glad Doctor Grieve were there to tend it, otherwise I reckon I'd be a cripple. There is a bonesetter nearby, I heard, but I'd rather have Doctor Grieve any day. Missus Elwood was good to me, too, and I didn't have to work full time while it healed - I just cleaned tack and stuff like that.

'Now, Peg, here,' he went on, reaching over to give her neck a pat, 'she is quite mettlesome, not as gentle as Flossy, but she is always pleased to see yer, especially if you give her some apple. She do love apples. I think you will grow to love her once she 'as learned your ways, Miss Esther.'

'My ways are quite simple, Fred, so I don't think it will take long for us to get to know each other. She is a beautiful animal and I love her white coat.'

'She do have a little dark grey on her belly but you can't see it. She has got good blood in her and I know Farmer Elwood is proud she turned out so well. Her dam is real quality.'

When I got home, I found a note from Nathanial on the table in the hallway. I broke the seal. After the greeting he had written:

*I am pleased to inform you that we apprehended twenty smugglers in the early hours of this morning. They were all local men which means we have more to do in catching the men at the top of this group. They are all in the Market Tower and we will move them as soon as possible. We are actively pursuing the*

*Kent faction and hope for positive news on this within days. I regret there is no news of Abe. I daresay he will turn up when he wants his pay-out.*

I had mixed feelings about this and hoped the men would be moved very soon. My own experience of being jailed in the market tower had not impressed me with its security. Usually, the only people held there were minor offenders and some of them were probably glad of the free shelter. It was different when the assizes were on but, alas, they were not in session just then.

∞

Just two days later, I received a welcome letter from Bartholomew, saying he was on his way home. He professed himself to be alarmed by my recent account of the operation here, going on to say that as he knew from experience I wasn't able to distance myself from these black-hearted men, he thought he had better come back in order to protect me from myself!

I laughed as I read this. I expect he imagined I had been in the raiding party myself with a pistol at my hip and handcuffs in my reticule. The thought that with any luck he would be on the afternoon coach today made me happy, and I knew Mr. and Mrs. Jenkins would be pleased too. I had noticed traces of anxiety in their faces recently.

Billy came by to tell me that Cilla and the baby were doing well, and that he was in Lewes to run a few errands for Cecilia.

'I be going to have a look at the prisoners in the market tower. I'll say I am doing the bell-ringing, then they will have to let me in. I heard they be going to be moved today.'

I was alarmed by this. 'Don't let the smugglers see you, Billy! You don't want to be associated with this in any way.'

'Of course, I won't. I have a key to the stairwell, so I should be able to look down on them through the cracks in the floor.'

He came back a little later to tell me that there were a lot of soldiers in the town and they all looked 'edgy'. The smugglers were being moved late morning to Horsham with a heavily-guarded escort of armed men. They were to be carried in a large flat-bottomed cart with their hands tied to the side rails. 'It'll be quite a sight,' he said regretfully, not having managed to get in to see them.

I spent the morning with the children, then tidied up in readiness for Bartholomew's return. I planned to go and meet him at the Star, where the coach was due to arrive at half past three of the clock. The sun was shining, we were all safe, and I was so looking forward to him coming home to us. During the afternoon I checked with

Mrs. Jenkins to see if her husband could walk with me to meet the coach, but she said he had gone on an errand.

'Well, it's only a five-minute walk,' I said, 'so perhaps I'll meet him on his way back and then we can go on together.' I saw a shadow of disquiet flit cross Mrs Jenkins's face.

'Don't worry, I'll be fine,' I reassured her. 'There are so many people about mid-afternoon and Billy said there were lots of soldiers on guard.'

Mrs. Jenkins looked none too convinced, but I was so keen to see Bartholomew that when the time came I hurried out before she could detain me with sensible words.

∞

The coach wasn't in yet when I arrived at the hotel and, surprisingly, I hadn't seen any soldiers at all. I took my place outside, listening intently for the sound of horses' hooves and the heavy carriage trundling along the High Street but there was no sign of them, so I thought I would have a quick look in at the market tower while I was waiting since it was but a few short steps away. I had just reached the big double doors and was about to mount the steps, when I felt a sharp thud in my side. Shocked, I pitched forwards as a rough hand grabbed at my arm.

I turned my head to see Abe right next to me, so close I could feel his rancid breath on my cheek. I looked down to see a knife pressed against my lower ribs, the same spot where I had been pierced before. I gasped, unable to speak as my throat closed in pain and fear.

He muttered in my ear, 'Don't you say a word. I was wondering 'ow to get into the market tower, with all that lovely gold. But when I sees you trotting along, not a care in the world, I knew you was sent to me by my ol' ma. She wanted you dead and now I got yer.'

I tried to shout but nothing came out, my throat was dry and my tongue seemed to be stuck to the roof of my mouth. I felt faint as a further, sharper jab came in my ribs.

Abe leaned on one of the doors and surprisingly it yielded; it hadn't been shut properly. He dragged me inside, still managing to keep the knife sharp at my side. I felt him kick the door shut and the latch click home.

Where were all the soldiers, I wondered? Had all of them gone off with the smugglers? As my eyes adjusted to the dimmer light, I saw there were only two men there: the town constables. One of them put his hand up as if to prevent us coming in any further but when he saw the knife pressed into me, he dropped his arm and called out to the other, 'Oi, Harry, we got visitors.' He couldn't take his eyes off me.

He shouted again, 'Harry, come 'ere quick,' before turning to Abe, saying, 'Look, mate, drop the knife, will yer, what do you want? The smugglers is all gone and the stuff is too heavy to carry. Let Missus Grieve go, will yer?'

'No,' he said belligerently. 'Where's the keys to the cell where the stash is? Quick, or I will kill 'er now in front of you.'

Harry had come up behind his colleague and also clearly recognised me. The first constable unhooked a big bunch of keys from his belt and dropped them on the floor, his hand was shaking so much.

'Pick 'em up', Abe shouted. 'Don't mess me about, go and unlock both cells, quick, or I'll stick this in you too.'

They both nodded and rushed to do as they were bid, then I was pushed into an empty cell and locked in with them.

Abe said, 'Don't think you are safe, Missus. You will be filleted before this day is out, mark my words.'

Despite his words I breathed a sigh of relief that I still had some time left on this earth, all the while clutching my side where the knife had drawn blood. I tried not to think of my boys, the girls and Bartholomew; if I did, I knew I would not cope. It was easier for me to puzzle over what on earth had been in Nathanial's mind to leave the tower unguarded like this. The constables were unarmed and clearly not up to the job of guarding the loot; even the main door was open, when it should have been kept locked. Surely Nathanial couldn't have thought it safe here just because the cache was too heavy to move easily?

The first constable, called Rob by his mate, said, 'What's you planning, then, young fella? You got some front coming in 'ere when the town be full of soldiers?'

'But it ain't, is it?' Abe sneered. 'They all be gone - off with the prisoners, I shouldn't wonder. And if you keep gobbing, you won't live to tell the tale, neither.'

No one spoke after that. I watched Abe closely. He was clearly expecting someone; he had unlatched the main door and repeatedly opened it a crack, looked out and slammed it shut again. He wasn't good at doing things quietly. I remembered thinking before that he was none too bright.

I don't know how long we waited. I sat down on a stool and kept as still as I was able even though my side was paining me. We all had our eyes glued to the door. Frankly, I was terrified but wasn't going to show it in front of these men though I was beginning to feel nauseous and hoped I wouldn't spew. I made myself breathe slowly.

If Bartholomew arrived on the afternoon coach, he would soon realise I was missing and come looking for me. Everyone knew that the market tower was at the centre of all the recent happenings and Mrs. Jenkins knew I was going to meet him at the Star just nearby. I prayed that the coach wasn't too late and that my husband was actually on it. The sooner it arrived, the sooner I would be missed.

Abe was fidgeting all around the cell where the cache of stolen goods was lying under a heavy tarpaulin which still reeked of tar. He couldn't resist having a look and when he wasn't by the door, he was untying the ropes that bound the pile. We too were straining to see what was there, and when he finally got a rope off and threw back the cover, I for one was disappointed to see just boxes. I had no idea what gold bullion would look like and, clearly, Abe didn't, either. He looked dejected.

He came to our cell and said, in an oddly conversational tone, 'You got a claw hammer or crowbar in here?'

Harry shook his head but replied in the same manner: 'We got a small hammer, not a claw one, over in the cupboard behind that door.'

I listened to him in shock. Why would he volunteer information like that, stupid man?

Abe disappeared for a few minutes, then came back and started smashing into the nearest wooden box. Just then there came a thundering noise outside. He dropped the hammer and ran to open the door.

I looked on with fear in my heart as a rabble of men crowded in and bolted the door behind them. I couldn't believe what I was seeing. Had Nathanial's plans all come to naught? Where was he? God forbid he was hurt, left for dead in a ditch somewhere.

When the men saw us, they pulled neckerchiefs up over their faces, though I didn't recognise any of them. Immediately they began to haul the boxes out of the cell, but not before one of them continued what Abe had been doing. Satisfied, he nodded to the men to proceed and they dragged the boxes towards the rear of the building. Some of them were clearly weighty and they took them first. My companions in the cell were stunned into silence; just a moment before they had been whispering between themselves. I think we all three thought our time was up.

A stocky man with thick black greasy hair was organising the ten or so men. He instructed them to put the heaviest boxes into the centre of a wagon they had out the back - there was a small lane up the side of the market tower and they were using that exit to steal back the hoard. Within minutes they would make their getaway - it was that fast - and I was breathless with the cheek of it: steal it, lose it, reclaim it and make off with it, all under the noses of the authorities and with the booty supposedly under lock and key with an armed guard. Unbelievable. I had heard of smugglers taking back their haul from the excise men but nothing like on this scale.

Abe was dodging here and there and generally getting in the way when the dark man suddenly spun round, pulled out a huge knife and thrust it into his stomach. I turned away and retched as he bled all over the stone floor, falling to his knees before collapsing, already unconscious. I knew he would die very quickly from such a catastrophic wound. I had seen violence before, but this was completely callous.

Dear God, I hoped we weren't going to suffer the same fate. I pushed my shoulders into the bars at the back of the cell trying to appear too insignificant to bother with. My breathing came ragged and thin as I found myself more frightened of this surly man than I had ever been of Abe. My companions were as white as the walls that surrounded us, both staring in horror at the congealing blood on the floor.

'Teach you to double-deal with us, you little runt,' the killer said as he kicked Abe and spat on him casually before walking towards the rear door. We three remained as still and quiet as statues. A niggling thought found its way through my fear: how did this fellow know Abe was a turncoat?

Within minutes all the men had scarpered. I heard horses clattering off and the wheels of a wagon squeaking, with horses clearly straining to pull the load uphill. The man walked calmly over to our cell and unlocked it. I shrank back, my heart hammering against my ribs, as he said to me, 'You, you're coming too, out.'

Neither of my companions made any attempt to stop him taking me, not even issuing a word of rebuke as I passed them, stumbling, my leg having gone to sleep. He relocked the cell and I was pulled outside after him. Out the back, another man was holding a huge horse. He gave the smuggler a leg up, then seized hold of me and flung me up behind him. The horse was so broad that I had to cling to him while struggling to get my legs astride with my skirt all rucked up around my knees. I could feel another trickle of blood seeping down my skin where Abe had stuck the tip of his knife in me.

Following some hard riding with me hanging onto his belt, we were on our way out of the town. Though I was just about managing to hold on, I was terrified and perilously close to falling off. We must have been near the river, but the ground was firm as the man urged his horse on. I shut my eyes against the wind and his horrible greasy hair whipping my face. I couldn't grasp what was happening: one minute I was standing outside the hotel, the next locked up in the market tower, and now abducted after witnessing a brutal murder.

Eventually, as the horse began to slow, I straightened up and tried to look over the man's shoulder but had no view as he was wider as well as taller than me. Looking around sideways, I thought we might be in Chailey.

We came into a clearing in lightly-shaded wood-land and waited for the great lumbering wagon that was bringing the cache of gold. Clearly, we had got there by a different, faster route. When it arrived, the poor horses were breathing hard and foaming at the bit, and I could see immediately how the men were planning to transport the cache. Waiting for them were two smaller carts with a couple of men alongside each. Next to the carts was the freight they had evidently carried: steaming piles of manure which had just been tipped onto the ground.

We were at some sort of woodland crossing. To the left was a continuation of light scrub and immature trees, but in front of us the terrain quickly became dense and the track much wider. There was a third pathway still, narrow and heavily grown with ferns at either side. One of the carts was turned towards it. As soon as the wagon arrived, it was stripped of some of the boxes which were then hauled onto the smaller carts. We rode around and between them as my captor - obviously the gang leader - instructed the men how they were to be loaded, with the heavier boxes in the centre equally distant from front, sides and back. Although I could not hear much when he leaned down to whisper in the ears of the carters, I gathered he was passing on detailed directions, as if they did not know the way; this confirmed my suspicion that these were Kent men. Once enough of the stolen goods had been divided between the wagon and two carts, the foul-smelling manure was flung on top and the boxes thereby hidden. The big wagon now looked much more comfortable for the tired horses to pull. The men who had raided the market tower moved alongside each cart as guards.

At a shout of 'Hold up!' from the leader, everyone stopped and looked at him. He raised his arm, pointing, and the first of the smaller carts pulled slowly away on the scrub track to the left of where we were standing. When it had disappeared into the woodland, he looked to the second cart and nodded to the carter to move out down the other narrow path. This trackway was a lot less used and the guards rode in front and behind.

Finally, we moved off ourselves along the widest central track to accompany the heavy wagon, now with a much-reduced load but for the addition of the horse dung covering what remained of the bullion. As we headed towards the dense forest in front of us, there were four guards in front, with us following behind. My rider, who had answered to the name 'Mathias', seemed even more tense than before, constantly peering around us, his eyes flicking everywhere. I had heard him mention Sheffield forest when we were in the clearing and guessed that we were headed for the area where Martha and Chalky had once lived.

We had been moving steadily for about half an hour when we heard in the distance the thud of fast-moving horses coming down the trackway towards us. The carter kept going as the load looked innocent enough for any traveller to meet without arousing suspicion. However, we and the other guards pulled off into the trees, keeping parallel but hidden. Mathias spoke softly to me.

'If you squark, it will be the last thing you ever do, understand?'

'Yes,' I muttered. I had no wish to put him to the test and I was hardly in a position to argue, anyway.

The two riders who came upon us were clearly known to the men. I thought I felt the leader relax when he saw who they were. The wagon came to a halt as Mathias moved out of cover, then he raised his leg over the horse's head in one fluid movement and leapt to the ground, leaving me stuck behind the saddle. The others also appeared out of the trees and a heated discussion began between them. I couldn't hear what was said but evidently it was urgent. When Mathias pulled himself back into the saddle, he turned away from the wagon, and with the two new riders accompanying us, he changed direction completely, leaving the wagon to go on as it was, still with its guard of four men.

The three horses rode hard and with as much speed as the ground and the darkening skies allowed. My only sense was that we were going uphill and that the terrain was altering from coppiced woodland to darker, dense shrubbery, with high, threatening trees.

I was so exhausted; I must have dozed somehow while still pressed hard against my rider's back and with my fingers clamped to his belt. I jolted awake much later to find myself in a different setting altogether.

My thoughts flashed back over what had happened as Mathias shook free of my grip and pushed me off the horse before he jumped down, casting a contemptuous glance back at me. There was not a trace of kindness in those eyes. I was cold and weary, frightened that I wouldn't come out of this predicament alive. I had been through so much; it couldn't all end now in some miserable camp in the High Weald after what seemed like hours of riding in the dark, not just in the clutches of a vicious smuggler but one whom I took to be the chief of the Kent gang himself. To him, I was just a hostage to fortune, a bartering tool. If not that, why would he keep me alive?

Mathias spoke: 'Make yourself useful - tend the fire, we need to eat. If you try and escape, we will hunt you down and kill you - and in ways that will take a long time for you to die.' I didn't doubt it after seeing him murder one of his cronies with not a second thought. The young man had died with a knife in the stomach. While I had no reason to care for the victim, I was sickened to see life ebb away as his blood pooled on the floor.

I was very sore from being bounced around on the back of such a huge horse. My legs felt like they wanted to give way, my knees bruised from clamping the animal's sides as I'd tried to stay on. But worst of all, my back felt distorted from crouching over the back of the saddle.

I collapsed to the ground, crawling round on my knees as I tended a fire sited just outside the entrance to a wide-mouthed cave. It went back deep inside the rock; I could feel the temperature drop and a cold draught creeping out of the dark interior. I couldn't see far inside but some men came out and after a lot of muttering I could hear one of them grumbling about having left their stash of gold in the forest. I watched as Mathias approached the fellow and then stopped directly in front of him, only inches from his face. I couldn't hear what he said but it was obviously threatening as the man dropped back, cringing.

I had heard the others call him 'Bob', and when I was unobserved, I studied this Bob's dissatisfied face and concluded that he was habitually disgruntled. His attitude was sullen and he had deep grooves from nose to mouth which turned down as a matter of course. His eyes were hidden beneath heavy lids and black bushy brows which joined up over his nose. His hair, however, was iron grey with patches of scalp visible between greasy thinning locks. He felt my eyes on him and when he turned abruptly to look at me, I shivered, sensing the malice hiding within him.

I kept my head down until I was given a dead rabbit and some sort of game bird along with a sharp knife and then made a scratch meal with some root vegetables that were also dropped in my lap. No one spoke to me and once they had taken food from the pot, as well as taking some into the cave, I was left with a little in the bottom which I scooped up in one hand. They all seemed to have their own bread or biscuit to mop up their dish. With no moon to be seen, it was very dark, and the men were all sat round the fire, talking in soft voices. I knew they were discussing the events of the day but after a while I gave up trying to understand them.

Eventually they all settled down to sleep and I was edged even further from the fire. I thought there must be at least six men, maybe with more inside the cave. No one offered me a blanket, so I too lay down and tried to nod off, hoping the temperature wouldn't drop too much.

I couldn't get to sleep, however, with the wound in my side throbbing and pains shooting down my leg, so I let my thoughts range freely over my family and friends. I hoped that Cilla and Billy were enjoying their little one and that my last patient Mrs. Carver was now in full health, with no more infections trying to take her. Bertha came into my mind too. How I hated that name! I wanted to call her Beatrice again, as she was christened. I wondered if she was happier after the partial reconciliation with her husband, even if it was just because he wanted a divorce that he couldn't afford. By asking a few casual questions of Mrs. Jenkins, I'd discovered that the business of selling wives was indeed conducted amongst the poorer classes of people. I mused that Beatrice was my niece by marriage and I was glad to have such a close association with her and Grace. Finally, and most painfully, I could see Bartholomew in my mind's eye alongside our youngsters. I knew that he would be doing everything to find me. I also knew that he would be devastated if I didn't return, but that he would always love and care for our babies and the girls and never let them forget me. I wiped away some tears.

I wondered if I should try and escape, but as I would have to clamber over several men, it would be madness to try. Even if I did manage it, I knew I would not get far after that punishing ride.

## CHAPTER 27

*Elm (Ulmus Minor).* The leaves thereof bruised
and applied heal green wounds. A cold and
Saturnine plant.

Culpeper's Colour Herbal

When I was kicked awake the next morning, it was barely dawn. It would take a high sun to pierce the tree canopy that surrounded three sides of the clearing with the rocks behind us. I felt awful, every bone in my body ached and my mouth was dry and sour. I backed into the cave and tried to tidy myself. I might be in the company of a band of thieves, but I had my own standards. I could hear snoring which seemed to be coming from deep within the cave: clearly there were men bedded down in there. I pinned my hair and stepped out of the darkness towards the fire. Lowering myself down carefully, I felt the cut in my side open again and a trickle of blood add to the stains on my blouse. I looked to the fire and with a bit of puff and some slivers of birch wood and dried leaves, I was able to coax it back to life. Clearly someone had banked it last night though I hadn't seen them do it, so perhaps I was asleep after all. I would have sworn on a bible that I never closed my eyes all night.

The leader Mathias didn't seem to be about. The atmosphere in the camp was a lot lighter and there appeared to be even more men around. I was even offered some bread and cheese which was very welcome. The fellow who gave it to me said in a jocular voice, 'So what be your name, then, Missus? Why did the boss take you? He already has a doxy.'

Some laughed, but I noticed an intense stare from one of the men. I moved out of his sight as he was making me feel uncomfortable. Later, as I sat as near to the fire as I could get, watching a pan of water come to the boil, the same man came up with extra wood, saying I had asked for it when I hadn't. I knew it was a ruse and I hoped he didn't have designs on me.

'What be your name, Missus?' He bent down close to me and spoke quietly, his back to the other men. I saw him staring at the pox marks on my face.

'What is it to you?' I muttered.

'You looks familiar and I know he got you in Lewes.' He squatted down next to me, ostensibly tending the fire. 'I think you might be Esther. Esther Coad that was, and you be a midwife of that town.'

My heart pounded, fear clawing at me. I neither confirmed nor denied before I whispered back, 'And who are *you*, then?'

'My name be Sam. You did save my wife when she gave birth to my youngest. My girl May told me what you done, how she came and begged that you attend my missus, and you did, out of the goodness of your heart, knowing that we could not pay you.'

I was wary but instinct prompted me to trust him. I replied, once I had checked that no one was watching us, 'May, from North Street. Aye, I remember your girls. They told me about you, how you had to leave Lewes after you got caught poaching. You joined what was left of the Hawkhurst Gang. They didn't tell me that, but I guessed when your wife said you had to go to Kent to find work. Also, I saw an owling lamp in your home, so I knew you were a smuggler.'

'You best forget all about that, my dear. Mathias, he is the grandson of the original Hawkhurst Gang leader, and after his grandpa's band of men got caught, he grew up with a chip on 'is shoulder. He is a mean bugger, so watch yourself.'

'Yes, I will. Sam, I was that grateful when you sent me a message to say that my Aunt Tilly had moved in with the Coads and was threatening me again. Not that it did me much good in the end. Can you help me get away?'

'No, lass, my life would not be worth livin'. A number of men have died because of you, remember? Don't tell him who you are. Your name is notorious amongst smugglers and he'd as soon kill you as look at you. I won't tell on ye, you have my word on it. You're lucky this lot are all from Kent, so no one 'as recognised you, 'cept me. Try not to limp, Esther - they knows of the Lewes woman who is crippled and has the finger of the pox on her. Someone might lay middle and both ends together, so to speak.'

He nodded and a slight smile crossed his face as he rose to his feet, giving me a token shove before moving away.

As I was thinking about this strange conversation, Mathias and one of the men we rode with yesterday charged into the clearing. Both horses were lathered, with nostrils flaring, and Mathias looked rattled as he shouted orders to everyone. The men scrambled for their weapons and horses. I tried to make myself very small, hoping they would ride out and leave me behind, but no such luck. Mathias nodded to one of the men not yet mounted who picked me up and slung me behind May's father. It was fortunate that Sam just happened to be the rider nearest to me. As we rode out of the camp, I saw that several men were left behind, one of them squinting at us through his one eye; he had a patch over the other.

We moved rapidly through the woodland on clearly defined paths and it seemed that we were headed back the way we had come, going south. As everyone was strung out along the path, it was difficult to see how many of us there were, but I thought there had been at least 20 round the fire this morning.

I tugged at Sam's jerkin and whispered, 'Where are we going?'

'Better you don't know, Missus, and better you don't talk to me. We'll both be safer that way.'

We rode tight together. I was much happier putting my arms around Sam rather than clinging to Mathias' belt - I would have preferred to crash to the ground rather than ride clamped to that man again.

It was almost midday by the time we were in recognisable Sussex woodland with its coppiced form and evidence of industry. It was much gentler terrain than where we had been, where the trees were dark, sinister and interwoven with huge, untended shrubbery. I was fairly certain we were back near the Sheffield Park area, probably where the cache was that we had initially accompanied.

When we eventually reined in, there was consternation and a volley of fierce oaths from the men as they leapt from their horses and searched the surrounding area. I listened closely to exchanges between Mathias and a man who had suddenly appeared from behind the trees.

I heard him say, 'We was followed from Lewes, it were the Excise. As soon as we made camp 'ere, they moved in mob-handed. Everyone was taken, and the wagon as well, it all be gone.' He looked anxious as he told his tale; perhaps he was nervous they might not believe him. I thought to myself, he would hardly have hung about if he had taken the stuff himself.

Nevertheless, Mathias looked suspicious. 'Why were you left behind, then?'

The man turned hostile. 'I was having a leak, wasn't I, and heard them coming, so I climbed up a tree. I been up there till I heard all you below. I didn't know if they had left someone behind to keep watch.'

Mathias looked at him sharply, then shrugged before turning back to the rest of the men. 'We been set up,' he said, through gritted teeth. 'We need to check where the rest of the haul is. They can't 'ave followed all of us and there's normally only four men patrol this area. We have two more carts and ten men to find. And I am the only one here who knew where they would be.'

The men were muttering to each other, angry at the loss of a third of their stash. One of the riders said to the man left behind, 'You said "mob-handed". How many were there?'

'There were soldiers, too, maybe ten or so. I couldn't see, I was too far away.' He clambered up to ride pillion with a scrawny fellow who had a port wine birthmark down one side of his face and neck. They slapped each other in recognition.

Mathias turned in his saddle, saying loudly, 'Stay close! If there is any trouble, scatter and return to Rye when you can. If any of you think to turn against us, then your families will pay the price, d'you understand me? If you can't get to the coast, then Blind Bill is holding the high rocks camp where the prisoners are. Razor, Peterkin, stand by me now.'

He took the named men aside and quietly disclosed the whereabouts of the two remaining sites. I wondered if we were going to split up but we didn't. Perhaps he was passing on all the details in case he was caught himself. My heart had leapt when I heard that the excise men were on our trail but I knew now why I hadn't been rescued yet. Both the authorities and Nathanial, if he was still in charge, had chosen to target the cache rather than recover me. Bartholomew would never have allowed that, so perhaps he wasn't home yet. As I thought all this through, it occurred to me that this area was most likely being watched right now. Nathanial wouldn't have been satisfied with only a partial recovery of his haul. He would want it all back, and then - only if it were convenient - he would try and recover me too. He clearly didn't know that Mathias had broken away from the wagon travelling from Lewes to Sheffield forest. Perhaps I could forgive him that.

I wondered, not for the first time, why Mathias had split away from the wagon before it reached its destination yesterday. The two riders who had intercepted us with a message, given only to him, had made him change his plans. But, I thought, if I had gone to all the trouble of stealing back the cache from the lockup, I would stick with it through thick and thin, particularly as the Excise had shown as much audacity as the smugglers in getting their goods back. The camp in Tunbridge Wells had at least twenty men in it. Why weren't they all guarding the significant hiding places? Billy had told me that no one really knew how many smugglers there were and that when they combined, it could add up to eighty men or more, which didn't include the little men who turned a blind eye or hid a load. He had also said that the Hawkhurst gang had suffered huge losses when they'd been caught years before, many taken after a raid on Poole Customs House, but there were always more men ready to join the smugglers, with money and drink making it worth their while. Perhaps the Tunbridge Wells group had only arrived there yesterday and were expecting to join up later with their fellow Sussex smugglers. I had thought that four guards per cart not many to guard a fortune in gold.

We were off again, but this time it wasn't the same sort of ride. We were picking our way carefully through narrow tracks and along unused byways. One of the men, Peterkin, was leading; several times we went near hamlets or farms but were always shielded by shrubs and trees. No one spoke. Finally, we came to yet another woodland, thick with vegetation and un-coppiced, where we were met by men materialising soundlessly from the dense growth. It took me a while to adjust my vision. We came upon one of the carts, still carrying its foul load, so I assumed it to be intact. Mathias indicated that the men remain mounted as he jumped down and talked to a heavily-bearded fellow who looked to be in his fifties.

When he came back to us, he said that half the group should go on with him and the remainder stay put in this dismal dark wood guarding the cart. He reckoned to return early the next day once he had established the situation of the one remaining cart and gave instructions for the men to spread out in case they were come upon. He also wanted the cart to be pushed deep into the shrubbery, with branches cut down and layered over it. He shouted a lot at the men for not making a better fist of hiding the goods. Perhaps they had never before experienced such a sustained attempt from excise men to retrieve stolen goods (or they were too used to greasing their palms) and had become lazy and complacent. There was a lot of grumbling in amongst the relief that this cache was still intact.

Once again, we were away, but this time I was given a horse of my own with a leading rein tied to Mathias. I was a bit disappointed by that as I had quite liked leaning on Sam; he was comfortable, and I felt safe with him. We hadn't gone far when Mathias stopped and listened. The man at the rear waved, indicating that everyone should move under cover; perhaps they had heard something that I didn't. Tied as I was to Mathias, I felt very vulnerable: I might be in the firing line if the military came upon us and started shooting. They wouldn't attempt to take prisoners. I was sure it would be a policy of shoot first, ask questions later.

It was deathly quiet. I couldn't even hear birdsong as we waited, motionless and out of sight. I thought we were headed into a trap. Then, suddenly, I glimpsed the smuggler called Bob who had caused trouble up at the high rocks camp moving stealthily along the trail we had taken. I was fairly sure he was amongst the number who were told to stay put, so why was he secretly following us?

Mathias let him get past us and watched as the man lost our tracks and then slid off his horse to study the ground. As soon as he was down, everyone broke cover and circled him. Mathias demanded to know what he was up to. The language was colourful but amongst all the swearing, I heard him say, 'You black-hearted bastard, you're the informer, aren't yer? It were you that led the Excise to the barn at Southease. All that moaning was just a cover!' He drew up alongside Bob and kicked him in the chest. 'Take his horse,' he said to Sam who had come up near me and did as he was instructed.

'What you got to say for yourself, yer weaselly no good lump of shit? Are there any more traitors, ey? Tell me now and I might not slit you from gullet to gizzard.'

Bob spoke up defiantly: 'I ain't got nuffink to say, 'cept why was you leading the men into a trap down at Sheffield yesterday and then left 'em to it? What was so important for you to abandon our stash?'

The rest of the men were sitting astride their mounts but every one of them was listening intently and there was distinct agitation at his words. Bob was not to be intimidated, though, despite his lowly position on the ground.

He raised his voice and pointed at me, saying, 'And her, why d'ya need an 'ostage if we were just fencing the loot on? Who was you expecting to bargain with?'

He looked at each of the men in the circle before turning back to Mathias.

'You know what?' Bob went on, 'I thinks *you* is the one who has squealed. You was the one who left the wagon and the men. Why did you do that, eh? Thanks to you, we've lost our stash and some good blokes is all heading for the gallows.'

I watched Mathias looking down on him with contempt in his eyes but not before I saw him blink and swallow in quick succession. As I was nearest him, I don't think anyone else would have seen that tell-tale moment. Could it be true, was the leader of the gang an informer? I was as stunned as the rest of the men.

'You thinks you're in charge,' Bob continued angrily, 'but I'm sayin' you ain't a patch on yer grandpa, with your high and mighty ways, your secrets and whisperin', and treating everyone like they is your lackeys. Ever since you took over, we 'ave 'ad nothing but trouble and next to no reward.'

'Anyone else think I is an informer?' Mathias rose in his saddle and shouted. He stared fixedly at each man in turn. 'Na, I didn't think so.'

'Well, come on then, why did you leave them?' Bob piped up again. 'Had a good reason, did ya? Tell us, then! What was this message that was so urgent you had to jump ship?'

No one moved a muscle, but they were all looking at Mathias, expectantly.

'I don't need to give reasons, maggot. I don't need to account for myself, 'specially on a job like this. This is the biggest haul we ever had. We're all gonna be coining it in, while turds like you whinge and moan, cause trouble and waste our time. I'm the leader, right, and I don't need to answer to a worm like you. This was *my* plan. *I* snatched the stash in the first place, *I* took it back again after some shit squealed, and *I* am the one who will make us all rich.' He leaned down towards Bob. 'Mark my words, though, I am gonna make you pay for this. I skewered that little runt Abe 'cos I thought he were the informer.'

'Now boss, let's not be hasty,' intervened one of the men. 'Bob, 'ere, 'as been with us a long time, and we all knows how he moans, none of us takes any notice of him. Give 'im back the horse and let's get on to the camp. We can give 'im a bit of a slap, later.'

I didn't know who the speaker was, but he seemed to command some respect from the rest of the men, as they all muttered in agreement. For a moment I thought Mathias was going to ignore him, but he backed down and indicated to Sam to give the reins back. As we continued towards the third site, I mulled over the conversation and thought that if I were Bob, I would be scared witless right now and maybe thinking of cutting and running. Mathias hadn't answered either of the questions and the one about me being a hostage was a good one. Put it all together and it must have cast some doubt in the men's eyes; they couldn't all be stupid.

Eventually, we arrived at the third camp - I heard someone mention Waspbourne Wood. The men and cart were where they should be, waiting for further instructions. Mathias got everyone scurrying round as we all dismounted and made preparations to spend the night. I was instructed to make a meal out of more rabbit and a couple of squirrels, I think, which had already been gutted and skinned, while one of the men threw some turnips and an onion into my lap. I needed some water and was sent to a small spring a few yards into some shadier woodland. I found the spring with its little runnel of clear fresh water but just as I was turning back, a hand was clamped over my mouth, my wrist grabbed and my arm twisted up behind me.

'Keep quiet and answer me. Who are you, what be your name?'

I recognised Bob's voice. Remembering what Sam had advised, I replied, as he released his foul-tasting fingers from my mouth, 'My name is Mrs. Jenkins. I am housekeeper at the castle.'

It was the first thing that came into my head but the bit about the castle was nonsense. The castle did not have a housekeeper. It was a ruin and a monument.

He replied, 'I knows the landlady, she used to ave a place in Kent. I didn't know she had an 'ousekeeper.' He seemed amused by the thought.

Realising he thought I meant the Castle alehouse, I said, 'She don't let many behind the bar. She wouldn't want tha' to know she could afford help, otherwise you might all refuse to pay top whack for tha' beer. She's a cunning ol' bird.'

Someone shouted, 'Where you got to, woman, where's the water?'

He let me go reluctantly. I took a few deep breaths and made my way back. Mathias was watching me as I shuffled about, and when he wasn't watching me, he was staring at Bob. I felt like I was sitting on a keg of gunpowder and it was all going to blow up on me at any moment.

∞

There was a lot of drinking that night, with a couple of jugs constantly doing the rounds. This left me even more nervous when it came to the men bedding down much later on. I was thankful that Sam had contrived a place next to me, after quietly directing me to sleep on the outer edge of the clearing, just as I had done in the high rocks camp. I clutched my skirts around me, thinking how chill it had become. September was already on us and you could smell the damp and cooling soil with its air of must and decay. I lay as still as a mouse convinced that something violent was going to happen. An owl hooted in the distance and the nearby answering call made me jump. Eventually the sound of snoring and deep breathing relaxed me into the thought that it might be safe to sleep, when I felt a tug at my arm. I opened my eyes and looked straight into Sam's face opposite mine on the ground. It looked white and ghostly in the fitful moonlight.

He whispered, so quietly I could barely understand him, 'Get away - I'll create a diversion. The men are all suspicious and it is likely to kick off. I will go and have a piss. If anyone is watching, they will be looking at me. Go as soon as I get beyond the fire.'

I nodded, too frightened to stay, but terrified of being caught if someone should look my way instead of at Sam. We could both end up with our throats cut.

When the moon went behind clouds, he got up quietly and made a point of heading well away from me before he stumbled loudly and swore as he lurched over a log at the far edge of the fire. He kicked it hard and sparks flew in every direction as he stamped around pretending to put the fire out, muttering and cursing.

As he kicked about, some of the men started awake, grumbling and swearing at him. I had time to think how brave his actions were; then, moving as stealthily as a fox, I slipped deep into the darker edges of the night, away from the glow of the fire. I got to the comfort of the bushes and felt the twigs reach for me as I crept silently round them, my ears straining for the least sound that I was missed at the camp. As soon as I thought I was out of earshot, I ran and ran. I kept wanting to stop and listen so I would know if anyone was following me but I forced myself to keep going. When I heard a sudden angry shout far away, I panicked, blundered through some dry broom and came to a halt, flustered that I had given my position away. I silently prayed that Sam was all right. I would have hated for him to be blamed if they'd discovered my absence.

I listened again for raised voices but could only hear my heart thumping before taking my courage in both hands and rushing on again through the woodland as fast as I was able. I was finding it more and more arduous to run whilst trying not to make a sound, especially with my sore leg bedevilling me. Out of breath finally, and with a stitch in my side where I could still feel the knife wound tugging, I had to stop and take shelter behind a huge oak tree. My chest was heaving as I tried to force gulps of air quietly into my lungs and I longed to just sink to the ground. Eventually, I felt calmer, and peered cautiously back around the tree trunk to check no one was coming after me. I gave a little sob of relief and turned to press on but just as I moved forward, I crashed into someone right in front of me, inches from my face. A hand slid all over my chest and neck, pushing me back against the tree before another covered my mouth and nose, and then I felt a man's hard body press into me. I thought my heart had stopped but with the very last remnants of spirit I had, I bit hard into thick fingers and jerked my knee up. I heard a grunt and knew I had hurt him, but he didn't release me, just tightened his fingers on my throat. There was a darkness at the edge of my vision and I knew I was falling into unconsciousness. It was all over.

## CHAPTER 28

*Pine Tree (Pinus Sylvestris) The kernels are
excellent restoratives. Astrology: It is a tree of
Mars.*

Culpeper's Colour Herbal

The wood was still dark when a loud noise woke me. For
a few moments, my heart raced, and I cowered at the
sound of shots firing very close to me, with images of
Flossy flashing before my eyes. There were soldiers everywhere, running and shouting. I was on the ground with a
blanket wrapped tightly round me and I struggled to free
myself. In my confusion I didn't know which side I belonged to, the smugglers or the soldiers. Who had tried
to kill me? Why was I back in the camp when I had run
such a long way to escape from it?

Within what seemed like only seconds of pandemo-
nium but must have been longer, everyone, including
me, was rounded up and marched off through the dark
woods. My mind felt hazy and I was unable to think
straight, but I know I thought to myself: 'I am a prisoner
now, one of the smugglers' women'. I kept stumbling
over roots and tufts of ferns, and at one point fell to my

knees. A soldier nearby yanked me up and dragged me on though the blackness. I could hear horses behind us and in front was one of the bullion carts, surrounded by armed men in the uniform of the Seaford regiment whom Nathanial had enlisted to his cause. The horses pulling the cart had been kept in their traces overnight in case a speedy getaway was needed by the smugglers. I had heard them discussing it. This had worked to the soldiers' advantage, as I later found out: they had managed to creep up without anyone noticing and take hold of the horses and cart before rousing the inebriated smugglers.

The woodland was vast and I had no idea where we were but when we finally stopped, I could see upwards through straight, lofty trees to a dark sky sprinkled with millions of pin-prick stars. The smell was of pine and the ground was deep in needles and cones. I was glad of my boots.

We must have walked for more than an hour, it seemed, before coming to the soldiers' camp. I was deeply wearied and still hurting from my enforced ride with Mathias while the wound below my ribs kept reminding me in piercing jabs that it was still there. As they went among us, more soldiers joined in to search the smugglers and direct them into small groups where they were then seated on the ground, backs together and tied hand to hand. I could also see a big pile of evil-looking weapons that had obviously been taken from them. I was approached by a young soldier who, without saying a word, took me by the arm and dragged me towards a group of officers gathered at some distance from the prisoners. At my stumbling approach, they fell apart; and there, sitting in the middle on a camp stool, was Nathanial. The look of relief on his face was gratifying as he sprang up and drew me into his arms with a great hug.

'Esther, thank God! We had hoped to pick you up before now. Are you hurt, has anyone abused you? My God, if you have been mistreated, I shall want to know by whom and take pleasure in thrashing him to within an inch of his life.' In no time, a stool was found for me, a blanket and a mug of something hot, maybe coffee, put into my hands.

The officers had walked away to a discreet distance, leaving us to talk, but a silence fell between us as I sipped at the warming liquid and gradually collected myself. Nathanial had resumed his seat and was leaning forward with hunched shoulders. It dawned upon me that his handsome face was looking unnaturally pinched and grey. Finally, he spoke, but what he said came as a complete revelation to me as I realised that his relief had given way to what seemed like long pent-up fury. Nathanial was distressingly angry with me, and I soon became acutely uncomfortable as he made me look at my actions through his eyes.

'What were you thinking of, Esther,' he erupted, 'going to the market tower like that? You *knew* I was conducting a surveillance operation with the intention of catching all the smugglers, both the Kent and the Sussex men. You nearly ruined the whole thing! I had to detail ten men just to follow and be ready to get you away if the smugglers decided to sacrifice you - a damnably real possibility, I hope you realise? Did you learn *nothing at all* from what happened to you before?'

I started to speak but he was having none of it; I just had to sit and listen as he held forth. I couldn't help but feel deeply sorry for my foolhardiness in going near the tower. He carried on relentlessly and I cringed under the blistering tone of his words.

'You greatly endangered my men and, what's more, potentially destroyed my career! We were all put at huge risk because of your meddling. *And*,' he went on, his face mottling red, 'did you have no thought for your husband and children - not to mention your friends - all desperately worried by your disappearance? I have to say, Esther, it almost beggars belief, the pain you have put your poor husband to.'

'I'm so sorry, Nathanial,' I stammered, tears clouding my vision, as I sought to explain and not break down. 'I was dragged at knifepoint into the market tower by Abe - I admit, I shouldn't even have contemplated going near it - and then I couldn't get away. I was locked up in a cell when that horrible man Mathias murdered Abe in front of us. I don't know why I was taken - they didn't know who I was. Well, no, one of them did, later on, a Sussex man, but he kept my secret.'

'So, he was endangered as well? Even if he was only a smuggler?'

I tried again to explain that I had gone to the Star to meet Bartholomew and that Abe had caught me outside the market tower; that I hadn't deliberately sought to get involved in the excise men's operation but just wanted to see what the bullion looked like, and had thought there would be lots of soldiers guarding it instead of just two unarmed constables. After repeated apologies and garbled explanations from me, Nathanial eventually began to calm down a little bit.

I started to tell him how one of the men had tried to kill me when I was running away, saying it must have been one of the smugglers because I had ended up back in their camp. He looked a bit shamefaced as he said, 'My scout was trying to rescue, not kill you.'

'Your *scout*? But he was throttling me.'

'He had to silence you after you kicked him in the groin. They took you with them to the smugglers' camp because he was unable to walk properly. One of the other soldiers put you over his shoulder and then dropped you on the ground when he got to the camp in Waspbourne Wood. He knew you would be safe because the soldiers were already in control.'

Once we had established who had hurt whom, he asked me to describe everything that had happened after I entered the market tower with Abe; but before I could, he explained that as promised they had tried to find Abe, both in the Castle alehouse and around town, but couldn't track him down. Nathanial added, 'If only we had got him then, the whole operation would have been so much easier. He should never have gone anywhere near the tower if he wanted to keep his life. I know you said he wasn't too quick on the uptake, Esther, but I think it was more than that. He didn't seem able to follow even the simplest instructions. He could have got clean away, and with money in his pocket for informing on the smugglers.'

I began my tale and tried to give names, places and descriptions, doing my best to make up for my earlier poor judgement. I think my story didn't disappoint and gradually Nathanial responded more positively to me. I didn't mention that I had thought he was more interested in getting the cache back than finding me. It was clearly another misunderstanding on my part to think that.

I continued: 'There is one of them who seems to moan a lot, but I'd found some of the leader's actions surprising, myself, and he did, too. His name is Bob. I can point him out to you. He was one of the Kent men, and I heard them say that they were joining up with the Sussex smugglers to guard the haul.'

Nathanial nodded, and I went on: 'Mathias, the leader, is the grandson of the original Hawkhurst Gang chief, the gang that was broken up years ago, apparently. What I can't understand is that he seemed quite sharp, yet he appeared to leave holes in the security of his plan. He abandoned the first wagon, the biggest one, and took me and two others up towards Tunbridge Wells, an area built on a sort of rocky outcrop. I couldn't understand why. He'd got some sort of message and then left the wagon to go on its way with just a guard of four men. There was no advantage to it that I could see - and then when we came back to find the cache the next day, it had gone. There was only one man left - he'd shinned up a tree, so as not to be taken by your men.'

'Can you describe this camp, the high rocks area? Are any men still there? If it is where I think it is, then it is just south of Tunbridge Wells, as you say. A bolt-hole of the Kent men, obviously.'

I nearly asked why he didn't know about it already since his men were supposed to be following me, but I thought better of that.

'Someone called Blind Bill was left behind with a couple of others. They seemed to be guarding some prisoners in a cave.' I could feel a rising excitement in Nathanial as I said this. 'After the first cache was taken, Mathias told everyone that if anything went wrong thereafter, to go to Rye or to the high rocks place. He also threatened their families if anyone turned. They all knew what he had done to Abe, what he was capable of. Nathanial, it was so gruesome, the stabbing. I think the two constables were as much in shock as I was.'

Nathanial shook his head and sighed. I knew he was thinking once more how foolish Abe had been. Perhaps he was regretting ever taking up his services in the first place.

'It occurred to me, Nathanial,' I ventured, 'that maybe Abe wasn't your only informant. For one silly moment, I wondered if Mathias himself was in cahoots with you. Bob certainly thought so - he nearly got himself gutted when he confronted Mathias with it. He is only a little man, but I thought it took real courage to square up to Mathias like that.' I watched Nathanial's face intently as I spoke but he didn't choose to reply and I could see no indication that I might be right.

At this point in our discussion, Nathanial broke off and went to speak to one of his officers. I guessed they were talking about the high rocks camp. As he had seemed not to know much about it, clearly his informant had not been entirely forthcoming. Shortly after, I saw a detachment of men mount their horses and leave the camp.

Nathanial then asked one of the soldiers to rustle up some food and arranged for some basic treatment for the wound in my side. Gradually the sky lightened, and the early sun shone its rays through the trees bringing much-needed light and warmth. As we ate, I asked Nathanial if something could be done about Sam. I explained how I'd come to know of him and how he had helped me on this and one other occasion. 'I would hate to see him caught up in this trap and come to harm,' I said. I did my best to impress this on Nathanial and even pretended some distress, in the hope that he would assist him in some way or at least not charge him as vigorously as some.

'The immediate problem, Esther,' said Nathanial, 'is that if you show preference to any of them, at a later date they will end up with their throats cut or a knife in the back, as happened to your friend Digger.'

'No one understands that more than me,' I said with some bitterness, 'but before the reckoning, surely you could find a way to let him escape?'

Nathanial looked a little taken aback by this and I knew I was pushing my luck. He gave the slightest of nods, however, so I was satisfied that I had done my best.

'I'll think about it,' he said. 'I can't make any promises. Sam chose that way of life, after all. No one forced him.'

'But he only joined the smugglers because he was caught poaching, Nathanial,' I replied. 'These are desperate times for many. He had to feed his family, and they are a lovely, caring and industrious family too.' But this was clearly going too far. Nathanial merely shrugged it off before getting to his feet.

'Now, Esther, we must get you away from here. Apart from Sam, no one seems to know who you are, thank God, and we want to keep it that way. A couple of my men are going to take you back to Lewes and to Bartholomew, who, incidentally, knows that you are safe, and I want you to get on with your life and never mention this to anyone. If someone comments on you having disappeared for a few days, have your excuses ready. I can't tell you all there is to report yet, but I can assure you that there will be no more Hawkhurst Gang and that the Lewes men are already in custody, or most of them at least. By the end of today we will have all our goods back and it will require just a bit of mopping up to bring the whole operation to a conclusion.' He gave a wry smile as if to hint at an understatement of huge proportions.

Well out of sight of the captured men, I was mounted on a very fine horse and readied myself to leave the camp with an escort of two soldiers. I looked down at Nathanial and felt a rush of emotion as I asked, 'Will I see you....' I saw his eyes widen as I corrected myself, blushing: 'Will *we* see you again, even if not for a while?'

'It is very possible, Esther,' he said, looking amused. 'Your husband's work has certain cross-overs with mine. I will look forward to meeting you and Bartholomew again, and perhaps John and Cecilia, too, as well as young Billy-alone. Despite all your meddling and getting in the way, I know I couldn't have succeeded here without you. I am truly grateful, as are the people I serve.'

I looked back as we left the camp and saw Nathanial raise his arm to me. I hoped that he succeeded in his efforts to rid the district of the smugglers, but I also hoped that Sam would be allowed to escape. I had guessed that would probably be the only method that Nathanial could employ to avoid his prosecution and perhaps the gallows.

## CHAPTER 29

*Hops (Humulus lupulus). A decoction of the
tops cleanses the blood, cures the venereal
disease and all kinds of scabs. Astrology: It is
under the dominion of Mars.*

Culpeper's Colour Herbal

It took a while for me to understand all that had happened after I was captured by Abe. Bartholomew seemed
to know everything, and once we were properly settled
again, I looked forward to talking it through with him.
But before that, most important of all was to re-unite
with the children as well as Cecilia, John and Billy. Then I
had to sleep. The whole 'adventure', as Mrs. Jenkins might
call it, had lasted little more than two days, but it felt like
a lifetime. I was exhausted and needed some peace and
quiet to rest my leg and let the wound in my side heal. I
was still very sore from all the riding. Nobody questioned
me about where I had been. I gathered that Nathanial
had warned them about the excise men's operation and
sworn them to secrecy. It had all happened so fast, it
seemed to be over before anyone really knew.

Later, when Bartholomew and I were able to discuss everything, I realised that the success of the whole operation seemed to have come about because of a stroke of good fortune. But perhaps that is unfair, because effectively it was down to Nathanial's diligence and surveillance of a very wide area. Bartholomew told me that only the day after Nathanial's raid on the barn near Southease, some excise officers had in fact captured and arrested Mathias and his two lieutenants as they rode towards the barn to check out their cache. The prisoners were taken to Lewes in great secrecy and with blankets over their heads before being ensconced in the cellars below the Star. I was stunned to realise that as I was having my forthright discussion over coffee with Nathanial at the Star, he already had his most important prisoners incarcerated and they were right below my feet!

Nathanial was not one to let the grass grow, Bartholomew said. It seems he lost no time in convincing Mathias and the other two captured men that they had no option other than to co-operate with him. I wondered if Nathanial had put them down in the cellars specifically to intimidate them. The basement was used nowadays by the Star to store their wine, beer and discarded furniture but it was also ill-famed locally as the place where the Lewes martyrs had been imprisoned before they were led to their dreadful fate of burning alive at the stake for their religious beliefs. Such a fearful place, with their chains still anchored to the old walls; the kind of prison that would leach all hope from you.

Bartholomew explained that after a lot of hard bargaining Nathanial had offered the three men their freedom along with tickets on ships to the New World. In exchange he demanded that Mathias should lead him to the missing case of jewellery; furthermore, he must return the abducted excise transport officers to Nathanial; and, finally, break faith with all of the smugglers in Kent and Sussex. If everyone was arrested (Nathanial was estimating a hundred or so men across the region) and all the goods and prisoners recovered, then Nathanial would keep his side of the bargain. If they did not comply, then following an accelerated trial they would shortly be headed for the gallows along with the men already caught - a goodly number, but far from all of them. According to Bartholomew, he gave them an hour to make up their minds.

Did I think he should trade with such wicked men? Not really, but I had come to realise that Nathanial was nothing if not pragmatic and that he'd had to strike the best deal possible to secure the return of the government's riches as well as to ensure the disruption of the entire smuggling industry across two counties for the foreseeable future. He would accept no half-measures, nor would the government. In addition, banishing three such hardened criminals to the other side of the world at little cost to the public purse was a practical benefit since smugglers had a habit of escaping from the most secure of prisons and frequently evaded justice through the duplicity of magistrates and lawmen. My Aunt Tilly was a case in point: she had done exactly that, bribing her way to freedom.

Clearly, time was of the essence if a plan was to be cobbled together that would achieve everyone's demands. Mathias and his two men had already been in custody for half a day, and if they were to be released to put the plan in place it had to be soon, before the other smugglers became suspicious.

Bartholomew needed writing materials to explain in detail how the scheme was to be carried out. Together we leaned over his desk as he plotted a blow-by-blow account of Nathanial's strategy. I was reminded of that time when he and John Elwood had, with great excitement, drawn up and re-enacted one of Nelson's famous battles on John's desk at the farm.

'So,' said Bartholomew, quill pen in hand, 'this is how it was to work.'

Mathias was to be given temporary freedom of movement to mount an operation to take back the bullion from the market tower and then resume his original plan for the stash, which had been to hide it in the forests until such time as he could get it to his contacts in London for exchange into ready money.

Bartholomew went to great lengths to explain that, once in the forests - to avoid the possible discovery of the entire haul - Mathias had previously planned for the stash to be broken up into three parts and then moved to different hiding-places. The beauty of Nathanial's new plan was to mirror the old one! After the cache had been split into three, the two lieutenants who had been captured with Mathias were to suddenly appear with a spurious 'urgent' message to get Mathias away from the first wagon, then on its way to the Sheffield forest area.

With Mathias out of the way, Nathanial would then bring in a large force of soldiers and excise men who would follow and capture the first wagon-load of bullion to which Mathias would have added the missing box of jewellery.

I didn't interrupt Bartholomew to remind him that I knew all about most of the arrangements because I had been there! I could see that he was enjoying the plotting of Nathanial's master plan to recover the cache and seize all the smugglers, so I kept quiet.

With his own safety net of soldiers following the gang and waiting to intercept everything and everyone, Nathanial was confident that Mathias would have no choice but to lead him to the goods dispersed about the various woodlands. In addition, Mathias had to lead the Kent men down to the Sussex woodlands, supposedly to help guard the valuables, as this was also part of the original plan. Once they arrived, then Nathanial would proceed to pick them off a group at a time.

Now I knew why it had been so easy for the gang to come into Lewes in the first place and steal the cache away again: Nathanial had facilitated it himself, not anticipating the likes of Abe or myself blundering in to hinder the arrangements.

'If you hadn't got in the way, Esther,' commented Bartholomew, 'it would have been a very smooth operation. But once again your inability to mind your own business nearly ruined everything and could have resulted in your own death.'

I chose to ignore that remark until I understood everything better. Instead, I said, 'Surely Mathias and the two lieutenants will be marked men when all this comes out?'

'They will be long gone overseas by then and, with the arrest of so many men, they are unlikely ever to be hunted down to the ends of the earth by anyone who has an axe to grind. If the others should be fortunate enough to evade the gallows and are imprisoned instead, it will be out of this area. Their trials will also be held elsewhere because the local judiciary has been known to release smugglers despite incriminating evidence of the strongest nature. Incidentally, Mathias and his two men will all get tickets to different destinations in the New World so they can't set up any gang together wherever they end up.'

'Why did Mathias take me with him?' I asked.

'He was hedging his bets. You were, as you guessed, taken as a hostage. Mathias is a clever man and he wanted a further prize as insurance, in case it all went bad. At that stage, he still had the jewellery from the cache, which he could also have withheld. The only part of the operation that wasn't nailed down was that Mathias had not yet told Nathanial where the abducted Ashcombe men were.'

'I knew where they were - in a cave,' I said. 'I told Nathanial and he sent soldiers up to the high rocks area.'

I could see it all clearly now because it fitted Bob's view of what was going on.

I said to Bartholomew, 'The only person who seemed suspicious was a smuggler called Bob. He tried hard to get the others to realise that there was something wrong. Did Nathanial stay in touch with you throughout?' I asked. 'You seem to know so much.'

'Yes, messengers were going to and fro. He was so worried about you, Esther, as were we all. He thought your life was on a knife-edge.'

'I knew you would be working to get me released, Bartholomew, but I was really frightened when that soldier appeared to be throttling me. That was the point when I really thought I was going to die.'

'I'm not surprised. If you hadn't put up such resistance, he would have just warned you to keep quiet. But not you, Esther, you always have to fight back.'

I didn't mention that the man had pressed himself against me and had taken the opportunity to feel me up. He deserved being bitten and kneed in the groin.

In my heart, I admired Nathanial for his vision and that he was willing to take such a big risk. Giving violent smugglers access to all the government bullion in order to conduct a complete retrieval operation was either a stroke of genius or a catastrophe in the making, and Mathias himself had not taken the bargain for granted. I'd seen him check the stash when he got into the tower, clearly just in case Nathanial had tried to double-cross him. They must have distrusted each other deeply but were bound by the end result: freedom for the three smugglers and recovery of everything for Nathanial.

Of course, he could have halted the operation altogether after regaining the cache from Southease and capturing Mathias and the group of Lewes men. Most people would have applauded him, saying he had done his job. But Nathanial's conscience couldn't have settled for that. He needed a clean sweep: all the smugglers, the missing Ashcombe men, the jewellery as well as the bullion. Only then could he be satisfied that his work was done. I said as much to Bartholomew, and we agreed that people like Nathanial were few and far between. Perhaps living so close to the wrong side of the law made them more daring, prepared to take risks that people like us would never contemplate nor be able to carry off.

There were so many facets to the tale that we returned to it again and again, usually when some little detail came back to nag at me. I kept wondering why Abe had gone to the tower. Had he just wanted to see the bullion or was he led into a trap so Mathias could pay him back for informing? Bob's position puzzled me, too: Mathias must surely have been looking for opportunities to get rid of him before the others started to believe his story. If they had taken Bob at his word, then Mathias would have been heading for the ruination of the scheme and his journey to the gallows assured. Why didn't he kill Bob, I wondered, when he had the chance? Unfortunately, the answers to questions like these would never be known, no matter how much they continued to plague me.

Once we had talked ourselves out, I suddenly realised that, as a result of Nathanial's daring, I would no longer have to live in dread of my own or my children's lives. It would take time to absorb that. I had lived with it for so long, I had forgotten what it was like to be free of such deep-seated fear.

## CHAPTER 30

*Sloe Bush (Prunus spinosa).* The Juice
expressed from the unripe fruit is a very good
remedy for fluxes of the bowels. Astrology: A
saturnine plant.

Culpeper's Colour Herbal

Bartholomew had decided not to return to his role in the
Navy; the excitement wasn't enough to keep him satisfied.
He soon settled back into his life as the town's foremost
physician and coroner and we were all greatly pleased, as
were his loyal patients. I didn't think young Dr. Chappell
was of the same mind, however: he went to some trouble
to avoid Bartholomew, which is not easy in a small town.
I wouldn't have been surprised if he had moved on; the
town gossips were still discussing the words we had had
before Mrs. Carver intervened, and whilst I wouldn't have
wanted to be the cause of his displacement, I didn't think
he would be allowed soon to forget his challenge to me.

The year had produced a generous harvest, and
with an Indian summer on top of that, life had felt better all round. The poorest of townspeople were at least

nourished by nature, at her best with hedgerow fruits, sloes and rosehips as well as nuts and, later on, mushrooms for the picking. There were a lot of windfalls to be had and I saw a deal of scrumping going on as I walked about town with the children and Clara, marvelling at my new sense of freedom. I had found time to harvest some late plants, not as many as I wanted, but I had good stores set by and had been looking forward to a settled spell when I could go into my little stillroom and do some bottling and drying of herbs. The day came at last when I could embark on the process and I had gone into my stillroom when there was a heavy knock on the back door. It came as a great shock to me to overhear that it was one of the Coads who had come visiting. Clearly, they were not amongst all the captured Lewes men. I flattened myself against the door in terror.

Mrs. Jenkins told him that I was not available, that he was not to come round again and sent him away with a flea in his ear. When she told me that it was Jacob Coad and that he had come to ask for my help, I was flummoxed and went weak at the knees. Bartholomew had also heard the commotion and insisted that we once again take more care with our safety, which was easier said than done when I had to take children out for their lessons. Because our trips to South Farm were as regular as before, it was not difficult for anyone of a mind to do so to work out our routines. Thus it was that on one crisp, late autumn day, Jacob Coad, sitting astride a scruffy pony, cantered up alongside me. I couldn't hope to get away, so I tried to calm my anxiety as I clicked Brown Betty forwards at a steady pace, without even looking at him. My mouth ran dry and my chest tightened in fear.

'I been trying to see you, Esther,' he said, as he matched my speed.

'So I heard. What do you want?' I hated to hear him sully my name.

'My woman, Flo, she be expecting, and it don't seem to be going right.'

Instinct took over and I couldn't help myself as I replied, 'In what way?'

'She do keep bleeding and her ma says that be wrong at this stage.'

'How far on is she?'

'She say 'bout seven months.'

'Then I suggest you call in one of the town's physicians. Perhaps Doctor Barnes? I understand he has some skill.'

'She wants you,' he said bleakly. I could hear that he was deeply uncomfortable at having to make this request of me.

'You must be mad if you think I am going back to Coad Farm after all you have done to hurt me and mine - and Job, too, your own brother.'

I turned and glared at him. He looked shamefaced as he acknowledged my furious words with a nod. I hadn't set eyes on either of the brothers since meeting them that time down at the Cliffe when one of them, probably Jacob but I am not entirely sure which, had pushed me aside.

'Would you come if she were somewhere else?' he said meekly. 'Her ma do live in Lewes. Flo is asking if you would kindly see it all as water under the bridge and help her.'

Would I ever be able to see Becca's suicide and all the other subsequent wrongs as 'water under the bridge'? No, I didn't think so, but this woman had nothing to do with those events and her child was an innocent. I needed to remember that, even though I wanted to run away from this persistent, ghastly man and hide.

He continued, sounding a little desperate, as if he didn't dare go home with a negative answer: 'She is a good lass, a bit mouthy at times, but since our ma died, she is the only one who cares about us. The old man is sour and he gets meaner every year. He expects her to work like a skivvy on the farm, cleaning, cooking and runnin' round after 'im.'

I pulled Brown Betty up. 'Where does her ma live?' I said, in a resigned voice, knowing that I couldn't turn away from a woman who was in trouble.

'Down t'Cliffe. She be a respectable woman, and it were 'er who suggested askin' you. One of 'er neighbours had a little 'un and it died. She were there and said you did everything you could and were kind to the mother.'

I didn't know what to do. My inner self said: *don't go, they have no right to ask you*. And yet what I said out loud was, 'If I agree, I will want an assistant with me and someone I know who will stand guard, just so you can't trick me. And afterwards, I never want to see you again nor be troubled by your threats to little Beth. Do you promise? And, another thing,' I added, 'you are not to hound young Job if he ever returns to Lewes. He loves his half-sister, and we will do everything we can to protect him.' I repeated: 'I want your promise on both these things.'

I could see him mulling this over before he said, 'Aye, I do that, and I speak for my brother Josiah, as well. We will leave you in peace, you and the little girl.'

'And Job.'

'Aye, and Job.'

'All right,' I said, barely trusting him but knowing that I couldn't turn away from a woman who was trying to keep an innocent baby alive, even if it came from the seed of the Coads.

∞

Bartholomew was out when I returned home, but I left him a note saying where I would be. I wrote that I would take Eliza and Billy with me; and that if I couldn't find Billy, I would go to the constable and explain.

Fortunately, Billy was at Miss Wardle's and agreed to accompany both of us, so later that day we set off for Cliffe and found the cottage. It was two hovels down from where we delivered the baby who had died within minutes of birth.

It was Flo herself who opened the door at my knock and she flushed deeply up to the roots of her hair before saying, 'Thank you, Missus, I be grateful, and I will make sure that Jacob and his brother never bother you again. They ain't bad lads, it be their old man who goads them on.'

I couldn't speak, I was so perturbed; especially as I recognised in her the woman who had laughed at me and threatened to take Beth. Eliza took over from me initially but then we both examined her. There was no apparent reason for what amounted to spotting, and after a number of questions and answers going between us, we agreed a plan of action which amounted to bed-rest, some fortifying eggs and stout, and less gadding about. She seemed healthy enough but if she was working at Coad Farm and looking after three men, perhaps it was all too much. Her mother certainly seemed to think so; she grumbled all the time about her girl being taken advantage of.

As we made ready to leave, and it wasn't a moment too soon, Flo volunteered the information that it was old man Coad who had pushed his wife down the stairs, with my Aunt Tilly egging him on.

I nodded, saying, 'I guessed as much. One day he will get his just deserts. I can't understand how his sons can live with him knowing what he did to their mother and all the others he has damaged over the years. My friend Becca died because of him,' I said, my breath coming short and leaving me gasping.

'They wants the farm, that is why they stays. I keep tellin' them to rat on him to the constable. They thinks they can keep the upper hand because of what they knows.'

I just shook my head and walked away. If we needed to help this woman give birth, then Eliza would have to do it. A surge of misery rose up and threatened to swamp me as I remembered Becca's forlorn body floating in the Ouse.

## CHAPTER 31

*Meadowsweet (Filipendula ulmaria). An*
*excellent medicine in fevers attended with*
*purgings. Astrology: Jupiter is regent of this*
*herb.*

Culpeper's Colour Herbal

Bartholomew was being mysterious again. He had received a lot of official letters recently, probably trying to entice him back to London, but he didn't seem inclined to go which was a relief for us. I was curious but knew he would tell me what was in these messages in his own time. In any case, he seemed much happier here. Our boys had grown so much and they had such a wonderful way with him that he seemed to have got younger despite being so busy. As to myself, when I looked in a glass, I didn't notice the pox marks anymore. I could see a few more wrinkles but I thought I looked much calmer and definitely had a fuller face. I was comfortable about my looks, though sometimes wished I too felt a bit younger - being busy suited me inside if not always on the outside.

We had been invited to Cecilia's for Christmas Day and everyone was extremely excited. We were to arrive during the afternoon for tea, in time for games for the children including Buffy Gruffy as well as Hide and Seek and Pin the Tail on the Donkey. Mrs. Fisher planned on making some little dainties for the children and I knew we would have trifle, one of her specialities, as well as mince pies, but without meat on this occasion. We didn't plan to stay overnight and as far as I knew Eliza and I had no imminent births to draw me away. Our next due was Flo, the woman who lived with Jacob Coad. The child would be a niece or nephew to Beth. I tried not to think about that.

Bartholomew suggested that we have a special New Year's Eve celebration, with all our close friends invited. We hadn't entertained before and I was quite anxious to ensure that it was a success. I asked Cilla and Billy if they would come and help Mrs. Jenkins prepare a substantial cold collation. We thought an evening without the children would be the most enjoyable and practical option, so I sent invitations with a fashionable nine of the clock arrival time which would allow all the youngsters to be put to bed and leave their parents free to have a night to themselves.

Mrs Jenkins, with advice from Bartholomew, drew up a menu. She would have extra help on the day as well as Wini who would arrange the dining room and the drawing room too for when the ladies wanted to retire after eating. Bartholomew thought we should start with a white soup, followed by salmon, and then cold meats: beef, ham, venison pasty, brawn, as well as egg and bacon pie with colcannon and bubble and squeak. I thought some lighter desserts were called for: jellies and syllabub with shortbreads, small custard tarts and Bartholomew's favourite of mince pies was added at the last minute. We would also have some good cheeses after the clocks had chimed in the new year. Mustard would be served with the cheese, another Bartholomew favourite. I hoped that this combination would appeal to the ladies as well as the gentlemen who seemed always to want plainer, more rugged food. All in all, we would number eleven at table.

Later, it came to me that we would also need a cloak-room for the ladies and fortunately there was a suitable room upstairs. I looked out a good mirror and moved in a small dressing table and a dainty chair. I decorated with some dried flowers from my collection and thought a small bowl of sweet-smelling herbs would also be attractive along with some tiny tablets of my lavender and rosemary soap on a dish near the water jug and bowl; I'd also found some matching squares of linen for drying hands. As it was all so very pretty and useful, I thought to leave the room as it was for future use.

Barty unlocked a cupboard that I had never even looked in before and took out some magnificent candelabra that belonged to his mother and to which Enid hadn't laid claim. There were also some beautiful platters and serving dishes in yet another locked cupboard in the library.

'When were these last used?' I asked. 'It is a shame to hide them away as they are so beautiful.'

'I believe when my sister left to go to Scotland. My mother was very mean towards the end and she always suspected the servants were stealing from her. It was all nonsense, of course, but it is the way a lot of old people go.

'I had forgotten them, myself,' Bartholomew went on, 'but Mrs. Jenkins asked if there were any suitable dishes about that she could use. Then I remembered the candelabra, as well. When we have a bit of time, we can go through all Mother's hiding places - there are probably lots of bits and pieces that you might like. Enid didn't take anything because her husband was so wealthy and they lived in such grand style, at least at the beginning of their marriage. She married for the status her husband offered and I don't believe there was any love, or even much affection involved, which is maybe why she strayed. She was also a good-looking woman in those days.'

'Really?' I said, in some disbelief. 'Well, Beatrice is very beautiful, particularly her eyes. But much of her beauty shows from the inside. Surely Enid never had that?'

'No, Enid was never kind, nor even vivacious, but she knew how to disguise her true nature.'

I asked the kitchen lad Pot to do a bit of cleaning and buffing of the silver and bought some new beeswax candles that would grace the dining table. Barty unlocked the case with all the cutlery, again dating from his mother's time. After all the pleasure and bustle of Christmas, we had a few days' grace before beginning a round of traditional New Year cleaning and polishing in readiness for the party.

As I helped Mrs. Jenkins practise and prepare some dishes in advance, the house began to smell wonderfully appetising from all the spices, crisp breads baked with herbs and different cuts of meat and game. We had ordered a magnificent salmon that would come up from Brighton on the day of the party. I had never celebrated New Year before; my lowly status in the past didn't allow me the wherewithal to entertain nor indeed the knowledge of how to, so it was all very exciting and I was enjoying the planning of such a joyous event in our own home.

Beatrice (no longer to be called Bertha, I'd decided) was invited, of course, and she gave me some ideas, telling me all about how things were done in Scotland where the new year, or 'Hogmanay', as she calls it, was celebrated in style. She described a tradition known as 'first-footing' where the first visitor to cross the threshold after midnight has to bring a lump of coal with them. Once inside, the first-footer would be led through the freshly cleaned home to place the coal on the fire, and then offer a toast to all who lived there before leaving by the back door, thus taking all the year's troubles and sorrows away with them. What an inspiring way to be rid of past sadness and worries! There was only one problem with this: Beatrice said that the stranger had to be tall and dark. I couldn't think of anyone who would fit the bill so I decided to forgo this ritual.

After talking to Beatrice, I suddenly realised that everyone would dress formally and flew into a panic, having nothing to wear except my wedding dress from when I married Wilf. I pulled it out of my chest but decided I couldn't wear it even though it had been cleaned after the horrors of that day: it brought back too many sickening memories. I found a pastel silk dress that Cecilia had given me some years ago and after making a few additions to the embroidery round the bodice, decided it would do very nicely. Beatrice offered an elegant wrap in a soft heather colour that she thought would suit me and there was a beautiful pin to fix it together, as well. I would also be able to wear the jewellery that Mrs. Makepiece gave me, again for my wedding with Wilf.

∞

When the big day came, Clara managed the children while I kept an eye on the kitchen. Everything was prepared in advance so efficiently by Mrs. Jenkins with Cilla's help that during the afternoon I even managed to have a little nap before going to the dining room to assist Wini in dressing the table. I gasped when I went in because it all looked so elegant and beautiful, wholly transformed from the usual chaos the children left in their wake. I noticed, however, that she had laid for twelve instead of the eleven of us who would be sitting down to supper. When I mentioned this to her, she said, 'Oh no, Doctor Grieve came in and told me to set the table for twelve.'

'Well, I don't know who this extra guest will be,' I said, after she kept insisting that the table was set for the right number of guests, and resolved to ask Bartholomew when we were upstairs getting dressed.

I lit the candles to see the effect and delighted in the mellow, buttery glow they cast on the polished wood before snuffing them out so they would look new and fresh when our guests arrived. It was all a far cry from the smoky rushlights Becca and I used to make at Coad Farm. I still couldn't waste candles: old habits die hard and beeswax was very expensive. Most people used tallow to light their way.

I took the children into the different rooms just before bedtime and was thrilled to see the excitement lighting up in Beth's eyes. After such difficult times, she had once again settled into being a happy little body, with no shadows troubling her. I put this down to her real mama's sunny disposition. When I thought back to all she had been put through - witnessing two violent deaths, kidnap, being thrown out of the gig when Abe tried to kill us all, then my slow return to health after that awful incident - I could only thank God that her natural inclination to cheerfulness and enjoyment had carried her through such dark moments. Bartholomew had later shielded the children from the knowledge that I had been taken as a hostage by the smugglers, telling them that I was just having a few days away with an old friend.

The only event that seemed to have had a noticeably detrimental effect on Beth was the loss of Flossy. Every time we visited South Farm and went out into the gardens, she insisted on visiting our friend. She would pick a little handful of daisies and buttercups or marigolds and lay them down next to the wooden plaque Mr. Jenkins had made to mark her grave, which was not too far from the kitchen gardens. Now and again, she would sidle up to me and whisper that she missed Flossy, and that though she loved Peg, it wasn't the same. It made me want to cry but I couldn't let her see that. I would just give her a cuddle and whisper that Flossy was happy where she was now and had other ponies to play with. I decided to have a brooch made with a small lock of Flossy's mane twisted inside; and when Beth was old enough to have such delicate jewellery, I would give it to her as a keepsake.

When I showed the little ones how pretty the dining room looked, the boys weren't at all interested and just wanted to be off sliding on the newly polished floors or down the stair bannister which had been wiped clean of all their grubby little finger-marks. It was a different matter with the girls who were mesmerised by the magical atmosphere the rooms had taken on. I remembered how Beth used to lick the furniture when we first came to work with Bartholomew, delighting in seeing an image of herself in the shiny wood and perhaps even enjoying the new taste of Mrs. Jenkins's beeswax polish.

Once all of them were settled down to sleep, Bartholomew and I retired to our bedroom and I dressed myself slowly and carefully. I put some salve on my lips and cheeks before putting my hair up with confident hands. I was quite pleased with the result and Barty came up behind me, saying, 'You look lovely, my dear, and I have a little New Year's gift for you.' He handed me a tiny jeweller's box, inside which were nestled the daintiest earrings I had ever seen.

'Oh Barty, they are exquisite. Can you help me fix them? My hands are all of a tremble,' I cried as I tried to take them out of their cushioning box.

'You deserve nothing less, Esther, but don't let those boys get hold of them or they will be lost in no time. We will put them in the safe after you have worn them.'

'What are the stones?' I drifted my forefinger over them, feeling the cut edges, and marvelling at the sparkle of white stones and the depths of the blood red ones.

'They are diamonds and rubies. The setting has been designed and made especially for you.'

I felt tears come to my eyes and, taken with emotion, I turned to bury my face in Barty's coat. When I pulled away and looked up at him, I said, 'I hope the coming year will be good to us. I am so looking forward to seeing our children grow and to you being here at home with us. I hated it when you were away. I missed you so much.' I looked up at him with his distinguished sideburns, dark tailcoat and white starched cravat. He looked so handsome that if I hadn't loved him before, I would have fallen in love with him all over again, then and there. But, of course, I had loved him constantly for a very long time now. I loved his fastidious ways and his impeccable manners, his dry humour and, most of all, for seeing the differences between us and not trying to change me.

'Yes, my love, I will be at home,' he said, kissing my forehead. 'I can't promise that I won't always be busy, but I know that we will be happy.'

When we went downstairs together to welcome our guests, I felt almost overwhelmed with pleasure to be amongst our good friends. What more could I ask for?

The answer came a few minutes later when Mr. Jenkins, who had become footman for the evening, announced the arrival of Mr. Nathanial Judge. In all the excitement, I had forgotten to ask Bartholomew who our mystery guest was to be, so I was astonished to see him, wondering if he had come all the way from London just to visit us. I stepped forward and clasped his hands in mine for a few minutes with great pleasure. I had forgotten what an attractive man he was and was pleased to see him occupy the empty seat next to Beatrice.

The meal seemed to go very quickly, with lots of lively talk and many compliments from everyone about the delicious food. As the night wore on, I couldn't help but notice a growing rapport between Beatrice and Nathanial and wondered if Bartholomew had been indulging in some secret match-making. I saw Cecilia look at them too and then turn her head towards me with a questioning smile and raised eyebrow, which of course I returned.

As the hall clock began to strike the eleventh hour, Bartholomew stood up and clinked a spoon against his glass. 'Ladies and gentlemen,' he announced, 'our dear friend Nathanial has a few words he would like to say to you.'

Nathanial pushed back his chair and rose to his feet.

'Thank you so much, Bartholomew,' he began, 'for inviting me to join you all to welcome in the new year of 1804. This last, 1803, has been a very special year with great deeds done, for sure, but much drama and danger too for some of us gathered here in this house tonight. I am happy not only that I could be here but that my companions in *Operation Capture and Recovery* - meaning, of course, the recovery of the bullion as well as the capture of all the smugglers - are able to share this occasion with Bartholomew and Esther. Now, before you tire of listening to me speechifying, I have an important announcement to make about the venture but before that, I would be grateful, Bartholomew, if Billy and his wife Cilla could join us for a few minutes.'

Barty tugged the bell pull beside the fireplace (I was surprised it worked as it was never used) and sent a request to the kitchen for them both to join us. Arrangements must have been made in advance for their presence at this hour because I'd have thought they'd be well away to Cilla's own family this late on New Year's Eve. Billy handed his wife in through the door and we offered Cilla a seat at the table as Nathanial continued.

'Firstly, I can tell you that *Operation Capture* was a complete success, thanks to some of you here, to my men, and all the soldiers who were seconded from Seaford

Barracks. Over ninety smugglers in all were apprehended and are now in the process of receiving robust judgement from the law. Just one malefactor escaped and there are only two of us in this room who know why.'

I was so relieved to hear that Sam was free but I remained still, avoiding Nathanial's eye.

'The Bank of England,' he went on, 'was gratified to get its gold back as were a number of private individuals whose valuables were with the cache of stolen goods. It is one of those individuals who has asked me to convey his personal and deepest thanks to Esther, without whom he would have been put to considerable embarrassment.'

I wondered what Nathanial was going to say next and hoped desperately that he wouldn't joke about my cavalier attempt to seek out the bullion - which he consistently appeared to believe, no matter what I said. Everyone was looking at me and I felt an unwelcome warmth creep up my face, but I needn't have worried.

'I have here,' he went on, flourishing a rolled parchment, 'a letter and deed of authority from that personage, with details of a property that has been taken on a 99-year lease for Esther, Mrs. Grieve, to create a lying-in establishment for those unfortunate mothers who cannot give birth in their own homes. This deed gives, in effect, a Royal Warrant. The letter attached is a personal testament from His Royal Highness Prince George Augustus

Frederick, Prince of Wales, who resides, on occasion, in nearby Brighthelmstone.'

I stared at Nathanial. The shock of this announcement left me entirely speechless. Everyone else gasped in amazement, turning to look at me, the surprise registering in different ways on their faces - all except Bartholomew who merely smiled. Nathanial then sat down again with an air of triumph and gave me a saucy wink. I was struggling to understand the implications of what had just happened: the words spoken, the wonder at being given such a valuable gift, not only a gift beyond my wildest dreams but also a gift from a prince, even if he was considered by so many as somewhat disreputable. Was I awake or dreaming?

Thankfully, John Elwood then rose from his chair and raised his glass, saying: 'Ladies and gentlemen, I would like to raise a toast to Esther. Please be upstanding for this young woman who came into our lives at a time of great tragedy, who has enriched our world with her kindness, her many skills and her love, from which we have all benefited. To Esther!'

I sat at the table and trembled, not knowing what to do, as our friends rose, drank a toast to me and applauded. I looked over to Barty and saw the pride on his face as he tipped his glass in my direction.

As everyone sat down again, Nathanial came round the table and proffered the parchment. It was tied with red ribbon and sealed, as he pointed out to me, with the royal crest. He placed both the document and the letter in my hands and I clutched them to my chest. Much as I longed to open them then and there, I didn't feel it right to interrupt our New Year's Eve celebrations so I put them down on the table but kept looking at them in front of me as everyone came round and kissed me and each other. I saw Nathanial raise Beatrice's hand and kiss the tips of her fingers. As she smiled back at him, he caught my eye and instantly proceeded round the table doing the same to all the ladies but not with the same intimacy. I looked at Beatrice and saw she was greatly flustered by such daring while Mrs. Makepiece and Miss Wardle were quite pink and overcome by the attentions of such a personable young man.

I went over to hug Cilla and Billy and wish them a happy new year. After offering me their congratulations, they asked to be excused as they were enjoying their own supper with Mr. and Mrs. Jenkins, Clara, Wini and Pot in the kitchen. They were tired but thrilled that the evening was going so well. Bartholomew and I followed them downstairs and said a few words thanking everyone for their hard work, inviting them to join us in the dining room just before the clock began to strike the midnight hour and the end of 1803.

We were all preparing to greet the new year, holding hands - to do things properly, as Beatrice had said we should - when at ten minutes to the hour, Barty tinkled Enid's little bell and asked everybody in the house to step outside. He handed round wraps for the ladies as we made our way to the back garden. I really had no idea why we were going outside to see in the new year but as Barty requested it, off we trooped. It was a sharp, frosty night with a fleeting and shy moon peeping between occasional ragged clouds. I breathed deeply of the crisp night air when Bartholomew called everyone to silence, and then I heard it. A single bell. Old Gabriel was tolling the midnight hour.

'Where's Billy?' I gasped, looking round to make sure he could hear this magical sound.

'He's not here, Esther,' said Cecilia, with a smile. 'Where do you think he is?'

And then it dawned on me. It was Billy up in the market tower ringing Old Gabriel, they said, for me. I was completely taken aback. It was one of the loveliest and most moving things anyone has ever done for me. I felt tears trickle down my cheeks as we all lifted our heads and hearts to welcome the new year in as Billy tolled the twelve strokes of midnight, before joining hands again and singing our welcome to 1804. Mr. Jenkins had brought out a tray with glasses of whisky for all of us to make a special toast with the strange Scottish words, 'Lang may yer lum reek'. Beatrice had to repeat them several times before we got it right and then we shouted it altogether at the tops of our voices as the rest of the town's church bells pealed joyously in a heavenly cascade of sound.

Much later, after we had said our goodbyes and everyone had departed in their various carriages or gigs to go home, Nathanial retired to Edith's old room (which Wini must have prepared when I wasn't looking) and Bartholomew and I finally found our way to our own room, at three o'clock in the morning. I opened and studied the parchment Nathanial had given me and went on to break the seal on the letter. I won't say more about that, as it is between the Prince of Wales and myself, but the deed of leasehold was signed by the prince's private secretary on his behalf. Bartholomew said: 'No one in Lewes will be able to be sniffy now about a home for new mothers with *his* name on the documents. I fear you might never have achieved this without him, Esther, and we are all so delighted by this fulfilment of your dreams.'

I flung my arms round Bartholomew, saying, 'Oh Barty, I am so happy.' My eyes filled with tears of pure joy and it was some time before I managed to dry them.

But that wasn't all. In May that year, a reward was given to those who had facilitated the capture of the smugglers and restitution of the goods. Nathanial had known that this would happen but he hadn't told anyone because the apportionment of the reward was still to be decided. In the end, it was shared between Billy-alone, the Elwoods and me. Whilst it wasn't a huge amount, it was particularly welcomed by Billy and Cilla who seemed dumbfounded to receive money that they hadn't had to work for. Cecilia and John Elwood put their share into improving their staff quarters and I was able to furnish my working house. Details of the reward were kept secret and we all signed a document to uphold that.

Nathanial passed on the news to us that the operation to bring so many smugglers to justice was the biggest in Excise history and had resulted in his own rise and subsequent preferment in the Government.

On the day we heard about the reward, there was a notice in the local paper which made my heart leap:

*News: Farmer Coad of Coad Farm, Hamsey, has been arrested for the murder of his wife following information given by his two sons Josiah and Jacob Coad.*

## CHAPTER 32

*There have always been medical men who have
gained a knowledge of botany. But the great
mass of practitioners at the present day are as
ignorant of the science of Botany as the horses
on which they ride. No medical man should
consider his education complete without a
knowledge of botany.*

Culpeper's introduction to Complete Herbal

Today, it is the first of July in the year 1804. It is a momentous day for me as I show people round the Esther Coad House for Women in Travail. I have been able to furnish the house with brightly coloured, cheerful linens, and though the rooms are undoubtedly clinical, I have sought to make them as comfortable and reassuring as possible for women who might be frightened. All around me, there are lots of praising comments and questions being asked, and I feel that people are genuinely interested in helping to make life better for poor women in the throes and agonies of giving birth.

All my family and friends are here, as well as special guests from the town. Bartholomew is at my side, not only to lend his support as my proud husband but also his professional endorsement. I am so pleased to see that many of the women (and their families) whom I have been able to help in the past have come along too; and when I cut the ribbon, a great cheer went up from them. As we enjoy a toast and some little sweetmeats prepared by Mrs. Jenkins, unhappily my mind lurches back to Becca and her final day, when she gave birth to Beth and then laid herself down in the river to die.

I walk away from my guests for a few minutes to recover myself and whisper to her: 'This is for you, Becca, my friend. Your little girl Beth is here, the happiest young creature, who brings such pleasure to all of us. I hope and pray that you can see us now and know that you were loved. And, Becca, it is because of what happened to you, that I will do everything in my power to aid women who are in difficulties, alone and suffering, as you and others I have known suffered so dreadfully. I make this pledge in your memory.'

Bartholomew has seen me walk away. He comes over to me now, putting his arm around me. I close my eyes and lean against him.

∞

1st July 1804 *The Sussex Weekly Advertiser and Lewes Journal*

*Friends, families and dignitaries from Lewes and nearby district turned out and cheered the cutting of the ceremonial ribbon by Mrs. Esther Grieve, midwife of this town, as she officially opened the Esther Coad House for Women in Travail, unveiling a plaque which states: 'Do not be afraid, you are amongst friends and those who will help you.'*

*People from the town had come to see the rooms and facilities that go to make up this unique midwifery establishment where those who are unable to give birth in their own homes can be safely delivered and cared for by locally trained midwives.*

*This reporter understands that the property received its initial funding from HRH Prince George, Prince of Wales, following which a local subscription was raised to support the brave new venture.*

*In attendance also was the founder's husband Dr. Bartholomew Grieve, senior physician as well as the town's esteemed coroner for a number of years, who has recently resumed his duties in Lewes after secondment to the Royal Navy at the request of no less a personage than Admiral Lord Horatio Nelson himself. Dr. Grieve was on board one of the ships accompanying Admiral Nelson's excursion seven years ago to seize the port of Santa Cruz in the Battle of Tenerife during which the Admiral suffered the loss of his right arm.*

*This reporter noted that other than Dr. Grieve, who has sanctioned his wife's endeavour from its beginnings, there were no other representatives of the Lewes medical establishment present.*

*The Sussex Weekly Advertiser and Lewes Journal applaud the courage and tenacity of Mrs. Esther Grieve on this auspicious day.*

# Author's Note

As this book about the adventures and troubles of Esther Grieve is the final part of the trilogy, I want to thank all those who encouraged me and bought my books. It was never my intention to write three books but in doing so I have grown with Esther and enjoyed the writing process. The books are fiction except as detailed below.

As before, I have written in some true events to bring colour to Esther's tale. The reference to Nelson and his part in the Battle of Copenhagen is factual, as is one of the local shipping tragedies depicted while the other is a composite of several events. The tragic incident in Seaford Bay actually occurred in 1809. The meteorological aspects of these events are described as befit the reports of that time.

The detail about a midwife taking a scalpel to treat a suffering mother's breast is also true, as recorded in Martha Ballard's diary, along with the subsequent use of an herbal remedy made from sorrel. Martha Ballard, an American settler of the town of Hallowell, was a courageous and hard-working midwife who left a diary which is methodical and matter-of-fact rather than anecdotal. The diary is interpreted and put in context by Laurel Thatcher Ulrich who won the Pulitzer Prize for History in 1991 for A Midwife's Tale, and to my mind deservedly so. A diary from this period of 1785-1812 is unusual, especially from a woman's perspective. It gives an insight into the hard but colourful life lived by the people who colonised the area on the banks of the Kennebec River, Hallowell, Maine, USA. Martha Ballard was so much more than a midwife and her diary gives great insight into the times, the social history and the everyday detail of her domestic life: planting, weaving, relationships and the day-to-day functions necessary to get by.

Details of the reference to Old Gabriel, the sixteenth century bell now hanging and tolling the hours in Lewes Market Tower can be found in *History of the Market Tower* by Paul Myles and *Sussex Bells and Belfries* by George P. Elphick. Whilst it is not certain that Gabriel was once one of the Lewes Priory bells, the balance of probability indicates that it was. Elphick refers to a sale of the roof material and bells for £726 at the time of the desecration.

The use of *Culpeper's Colour Herbal*, published by Foulsham, edited by David Potterton and illustrated by Michael Stringer, has been a delight; a book I never tire of looking at particularly because it has a modern usage section alongside every beautiful illustration. I felt unable to write in detail about many of the herbs detailed in this lovely book because they appear too potent for a lay person to try without expert guidance. I was pleased beyond measure however to find that Nicholas Culpeper was raised in nearby Isfield and almost certainly schooled in Lewes where Esther resides. His original *Complete Herbal* has never been out of print and I know its usage was spread far and wide because it was written in English and sold cheaply, as he intended. It is probable that the frontierswoman Martha Ballard and those who came before her had learned from his treatise. The *Complete Herbal* has some wonderful quotes and detail. His books on midwifery were also widely read.

Culpeper's early life was not without sadness. He lived with his mother and grandfather after the death of his father. He is alleged to have later engaged himself to a young woman who was an heiress and, knowing that their families would not approve, resolved to elope with her. Arrangements were in place: he was to drive by carriage to Lewes where a cleric was waiting and she was to walk with her maid over the downs. Tragedy struck in the form of a thunderstorm during which the young woman was killed. It has been suggested that Culpeper's mother never quite recovered from the shock of the proposed elopement and he was disowned by his grandfather who was the incumbent of Isfield Parish Church.

## Background reading:

*Prince of Pleasure* by Saul David (Little Brown & Co.)

*Georgiana, Duchess of Devonshire* by Amanda Foreman (Northwestern University Press)

*The Mayor of Casterbridge* by Thomas Hardy (Various Publishers)

*The Time Traveller's Guide to Regency Britain* by Ian Mortimer (Bodley Head 2020)

*Jamaica Inn* by Daphne du Maurier (Virago Modern Classics)

*The Herbalist: Nicholas Culpeper and the Fight for Medical Freedom* by Benjamin Woolley (Harper Perennial 2012)

## Bibliography:

*A Midwife's Tale: The Life of Martha Ballard based on Her Diary 1785 - 1812* by Lauren Thatcher Ulrich (First Vintage Books Ed. New York 1991)

*Culpeper's Colour Herbal* edited by David Potterton, illustrated by Michael Stringer (Foulsham & Co. Ltd. 1983)

*A Directory for Midwives: or, a guide for women, in their conception, bearing and suckling their children* by Nicholas Culpeper...

*Newly corrected from many gross errors. (ECCO Print Edition. Reproduction from British Library)*

*Culpeper's Complete Herbal (Bloomsbury Books 1992)*

*A Jane Austen Christmas: Regency Christmas Traditions* by Maria Grace (White Soup Press 2014)

*Battle of Copenhagen* www.historytoday.com and other internet sources

*A Short History of the Market Tower* by Paul Myles (Salzman L.F. [editor] 2009) Accessible on internet.

*Sussex Bells & Belfries* by George P. Elphick (Phillimore 1970)

*Beachy Head Shipwrecks of the 19th Century (Pevensey-Eastbourne-Newhaven)* by David Renno (Amherst Media 2004)

*The Street Names of Lewes:* L. S. Davey (Revised by Kim Clark) Published by Pomegranate Press

## Contributor:

Yvonne McDermott. Forest Moons. www.yvonnejmcdermott.com

Printed in Great Britain
by Amazon